Giants of the keyboard

Kempff : Gieseking : Fischer
Haskil : Backhaus : Schnabel

Discographies compiled by
John Hunt

ISBN 0 9510268 8 7
1994

Acknowledgement

This publication has been made possible by generous support from the following:

Richard Ames, New Barnet
Yoshihiro Asada, Osaka
Jonathan Brown, Paris
Roger Brown, London
Guy Burkill, London
Edward Chibas, Caracas
John Derry, Newcastle-upon-Tyne
K. Eayrs, Alderley Edge
Henry Fogel, Chicago
Peter Fulop, Toronto
J.-P. Goossens, Luxembourg
Peter Hamann, Bochum
Tadashi Hasegawa, Nagoya
Martin Hickley, Godalming
Martin Holland, Sale
John Hughes, Brisbane
Michael Jones, Birmingham
Eric Kobe, Lucerne
John Larsen, Mariager
Ernst Lumpe, Soest
John Meriton, Manchester
Gregory Page-Turner, Bridport
Tully Potter, Billericay
D. Priddon, London
Gordon Reeves, Birmingham
Robin Scott, Bradford
Clare Shepherd, Beckenham
R. Simmons, Brentford
Kazuhiko Soma, Kawasaki
Neville Sumpter, Northolt
Carl Suneson, Stockholm
Yoshihiko Suzuki, Tokyo
Malcolm Walker, Harrow
Björn Westberg, Saltsjö-Boo

Contents

Published 1994 by John Hunt

Designed by Richard Chlupaty, London

Printed by Short Run Press, Exeter

Copyright 1994   John Hunt

ISBN 0 9510268 8 7

Giants of the keyboard

I have often wondered what I would choose if suddenly confronted with a drastic reduction in the range of the music I listen to. If it were put to me that only one type or genre would be available on the proverbial "desert island", how would the choice be made ?

Many music lovers would, I know, select the human voice, either in opera, choral music or the art song. For me there is nothing more refreshing, after a heavy diet of large-scale orchestral indulgence or the complexities of Strauss and Wagner, than the sound of the solo piano and the repertoire created for it by the composers and virtuosi of the past 250 years. Things may have started with the modest fortepiano or harpsichord, but these were quickly replaced by the modern keyboard as we still know it today.

The first interpreters were composers themselves - Bach, Mozart, Beethoven, Schumann, Liszt, Brahms - but there soon emerged a 19th century breed of executant virtuoso whose dazzling technique almost outshone the music he was playing. Some 20th century pianists - Horowitz, for example - continued to remind us of the best of that virtuoso tradition, and many others can be heard on piano rolls or crackling early acoustics. Electrical recording developed, in the 1920s, just at the moment when a more serious school of performers, stemming mainly from the German tradition, was ready to put its interpretations down into the grooves of the shellac disc.

There were varying degrees of mistrust for the medium - witness Schnabel's well-known protestations - but nevertheless we possess a sound archive stretching back over 70 or more years and documenting how these keyboard giants approached the legacy bequeathed to them.

What distinguishes these representatives of a golden age of piano-playing from the more modern virtuosi of recent times ? In my view it is the same as the difference between the well-schooled young singers now making their Wigmore Hall debuts and the great personalities of a few decades ago - the Callases, the Schwarzkopfs, the Fischer-Dieskaus, the Flagstads, the Tebaldis. With artists of that calibre, as with our pianists, it was not simply a matter of an imposing technique but rather their employment of that technique, together with experience gained over many years, to express an imaginative vision of the music. It is a lack of imagination, a reluctance to take risks or to expose one's innermost feelings, which seems to characterise today's generation (of course there are exceptions), resulting in a sameness of approach and an absence of individual statement.

Figuring prominently among our pianistic giants is Edwin Fischer, who regarded his solo playing as merely part of a wider sphere of activity embracing conducting and the participation in chamber music. It is perhaps significant that two of the more imposing among recent talents have been Daniel Barenboim and Christoph Eschenbach, who similarly started out as pianists but who now regard that as merely a branch of their wider activities. Another field in which at least Kempff, Gieseking and Schnabel were engaged was that of composing, although we have only isolated examples of this on record.

The lay-out of these discographies follows my usual pattern, with original (in many cases 78rpm) catalogue numbers, important LP re-issues and all known CD versions - in other words, this is by no means a survey of all issues in all countries. A fair number of Japanese catalogue numbers are included for material which for a long time was only available in that country: the Japanese seem to possess far greater awareness and appreciation of the value of historical recordings, having in recent years alone published exemplary CD editions of recordings by Kempff and Gieseking.

All known commercial recordings are included, and all known publications on "pirate" or private labels. In addition, I have been encouraged by assistance from a number of piano specialists to include some unpublished material (such as radio broadcasts), of which more and more seems to be coming to light. The Pearl label, for example, has been including in its series of CDs devoted to Gieseking a fair number of tracks taken from unissued concert recordings.

The first column gives recording location and date (month, year), the third column the catalogue data described above. The second column is used, in the case of chamber and orchestral/concerto works, to indicate the other participating artists, orchestra and conductor. Indication will also be given in that column if the artist is performing on the record in a capacity other than his normal one, for example Fischer conducting, Kempff playing the organ and so on.

Works conceived as a group but often split up in performance (Bach's Well-Tempered Clavier, Brahms' Piano pieces or Debussy's, to name a few) are broken down into their sections for our listing - as indeed they would have been anyway if published originally in the 78rpm format. The only exception would be a group or selection (Debussy Etude, in Gieseking's version, is one) recorded for LP and always re-issued as an integral.

John Hunt

6

Wilhelm Kempff
1895-1991

with valuable assistance from
Alan Newcombe

Discography compiled by John Hunt

Introduction

In his background and training (taught in Berlin by a pupil of Liszt), Wilhelm Kempff seems to embody the best of the German humanist tradition, as does his exact musical contemporary Wilhelm Furtwängler. A deeply luminous quality in Kempff's playing is allied to a composure which knows no haste and which never resorts to exaggerated Romantic accents. Hence his playing of the solo works of both Bach and Brahms has a satisfying sense of concentration and richness.

This is not to deny an intimate identification with the spirit of Romanticism, as exemplified in Kempff's performances of both Schumann and Liszt: in my view his Liszt comes closer to the ideal than any more flamboyant approach.

Wilhelm Kempff also kept alive to the end of his long career the art of the transcription, with a comprehensive body of his own arrangements from Bach, Handel and Gluck - classical composers viewed through the eyes of the 19th century, as it were. I recall the pianist's last London recital around 1982, when he offered several of these transcriptions as encores, personally introduced in beautiful English.

But then Kempff was, like Backhaus, a truly international figure, even being the first Western pianist to have regularly visited Japan, starting in the 1930s. In the autumn of 1961 he performed the complete cycle of the Beethoven sonatas for Japanese radio (NHK), and in 1970, on the occasion of the Beethoven bi-centenary, the five piano concertos.

A misapprehension which the compiling of
this discography has helped to dispel
was the assertion that Wilhelm Kempff
had recorded the complete Beethoven
piano sonatas three times over. There
were certainly two cycles recorded in
the post-war period, mono in the 1950s
and stereo in the 1960s, and within both
of these some of the most popular works
were recorded several times over. After
some acoustic and early electric
attempts at those most popular sonatas
in the 1920s, Kempff did embark with
his colleagues in DG/Polydor on a
purposeful journey to record the
Beethoven sonatas, but certain works
were still not recorded when, presumably,
war-time conditions brought the project
to a halt around 1942. However, my
special thanks goes to Alan Newcombe of
DG in Hamburg for his guidance with the
not always firm dates for those early
78 versions.

John Hunt

Bach

Capriccio in B sopra la lontananza del suo fratello dilettissimo BWV 992

Hannover
April 1975

LP: DG 2530 723
CD: DG (Japan) POCG 9185-9204
CD: DG 438 1082/439 6722

Chorale from Cantata No 140, Wachet auf ruft uns die Stimme (Zion hört die Wächter singen), transcribed by Kempff

Berlin
1936

78: Polydor 67086/516696
78: Decca CA 8252/K 958
Originally side 10 to recording
of Beethoven Emperor Concerto

London
March 1953 — *eD PR 456 865*

78: Decca K 28224/SX 63009
45: Decca 45-71124/CEP 686
LP: Decca LXT 2820
CD: London (Japan) KICC 2198

Hannover
April 1975

LP: DG 2530 647
CD: DG (Japan) POCG 9185-9204
CD: DG 439 1082/439 6722

Chorale from Cantata No 147, Jesu bleibet meine Freude (Wohl mir, dass ich Jesum habe), transcribed by Kempff

London
March 1953 — *CD PR 456 865*

78: Decca SX 63009
45: Decca 45-71124/CEP 686
LP: Decca LXT 2820
CD: London (Japan) KICC 2198

Hannover
April 1975

LP: DG 2530 647
CD: DG (Japan) POCG 9185-9204
CD: DG 439 1082/439 6722

Chorale Prelude, Es ist gewisslich an der Zeit BWV 307/734, transcribed by Kempff

Hannover April 1975	LP: DG 2530 647 CD: DG (Japan) POCG 9185-9204 CD: DG 439 1082/439 6722

Chorale Prelude, Befiehl du deine Wege (Herzlich tut mein Verlangen) BWV 727, transcribed by Kempff

London March 1953		78: Decca K 28226 45: Decca CEP 686 LP: Decca LXT 2820 CD: London (Japan) KICC 2198
Hiroshima March 1955	Kempff plays organ of the World Peace Church	LP: DG LPE 17 069
Hannover April 1975		LP: DG 2530 647 CD: DG (Japan) POCG 9185-9204 CD: DG 439 1082/439 6722

Chorale Prelude, Ich ruf' zu dir Herr Jesu Christ BWV 639, transcribed by Kempff

Hiroshima March 1955	Kempff plays organ of the World Peace Church	LP: DG LPE 17 069
Hannover April 1975		LP: DG 2530 647 CD: DG (Japan) POCG 9185-9204 CD: DG 439 1082/439 6722

Chorale Prelude, In dulci jubilo BWV 751, transcribed by Kempff

London March 1953	45: Decca ÇEP 686 LP: Decca LXT 2820 CD: London (Japan) KICC 2198
Hannover April 1975	LP: DG 2530 647 CD: DG (Japan) POCG 9185-9204 CD: DG 439 1082/439 6722

Chorale Preludes/concluded

Chorale Prelude, Nun freut euch liebe Christen g'mein BWV 734a, transcribed by Kempff

London   LP: Decca LXT 2820
March 1953   CD: London (Japan) KICC 2198

Chorale Prelude, Nun komm' der Heiden Heiland BWV 659, transcribed by Kempff

London   _CD_   78: Decca K 28223
March 1953 — _PL 456 865_ LP: Decca LXT 2820
           CD: London (Japan) KICC 2198

Positano   LP: DG 104 486
ca. 1960

Hannover   LP: DG 2530 647
April 1975   CD: DG (Japan) POCG 9185-9204
           CD: DG 439 1082/439 6722

Chromatic Fantasia and Fugue in D minor BWV 903

London   78: Decca K 28225-28226
March 1953   LP: Decca LXT 2820/BR 3065
           CD: London (Japan) KICC 2198

English Suite No 3 in G minor BWV 808

Hannover   LP: DG 2530 723
April 1975   CD: DG (Japan) POCG 9185-9204
           CD: DG 439 1082/439 6722

French Suite No 5 in G BWV 816

Berlin   78: Polydor 67066/57000/EM 15453
1935   78: Decca CA 8217

Hannover   LP: DG 2530 723
April 1975   CD: DG (Japan) POCG 9185-9204
           CD: DG 439 6722

Goldberg Variations BWV 988

Hannover   LP: DG SLPM 139 455
July 1969   CD: DG (Japan) POCG 9185-9204
           CD: DG 435 4952

Largo (Concerto in F minor BWV 1056), transcribed by Kempff

Hannover   LP: DG 2530 647
April 1975   CD: DG (Japan) POCG 9185-9204
           CD: DG 439 1082/439 6722

Passacaglia and Fugue in C minor BWV 582

| Hiroshima
March 1955 | Kempff plays organ
of the World Peace
Church | LP: DG LPE 17 069 |

Prelude and Fugue No 1 in C BWV 846 (Well-Tempered Clavier, Book 1)

Hannover
May 1975

LP: DG 2530 807
CD: DG (Japan) POCG 9185-9204

Prelude and Fugue No 2 in C minor BWV 847 (Well-Tempered Clavier, Book 1)

Hannover
May 1975

LP: DG 2530 807
CD: DG (Japan) POCG 9185-9204

Prelude and Fugue No 3 in C sharp BWV 848 (Well-Tempered Clavier, Book 1)

Berlin
1928

78: Polydor 67166/95107
78: Decca X 210/K 958

Hannover
May 1975

LP: DG 2530 807
CD: DG (Japan) POCG 9185-9204

Prelude and Fugue No 4 in C sharp minor BWV 849 (Well-Tempered Clavier, Book 1)

Hannover
February 1980

LP: DG 2531 299
CD: DG (Japan) POCG 9185-9204
CD: DG 439 6722

Prelude and Fugue No 5 in D BWV 850 (Well-Tempered Clavier, Book 1)

Berlin
1931

78: Polydor 65699/67099/90189/
        95107
78: Decca CA 8261/DE 7010/LY 6176

Hannover
May 1975

LP: DG 2530 807
CD: DG (Japan) POCG 9185-9204

Prelude and Fugue No 6 in D minor BWV 851 (Well-Tempered Clavier, Book 1)

Hannover
May 1975

LP: DG 2530 807
CD: DG (Japan) POCG 9185-9204

Prelude and Fugue No 7 in E flat BWV 852 (Well-Tempered Clavier, Book 1)

Hannover
May 1975

LP: DG 2530 807
CD: DG (Japan) POCG 9185-9204

Prelude and Fugue No 8 in E flat minor BWV 853 (Well-Tempered Clavier, Book 1)

Hannover
May 1975

LP: DG 2530 807
CD: DG (Japan) POCG 9185-9204

Prelude and Fugue No 9 in E BWV 854 (Well-Tempered Clavier, Book 1)

Hannover
February 1980

LP: DG 2531 299
CD: DG (Japan) POCG 9185-9204
CD: DG 439 6722

Prelude and Fugue No 10 in E minor BWV 855 (Well-Tempered Clavier, Book 1)

Hannover
February 1980

LP: DG 2531 299
CD: DG (Japan) POCG 9185-9204
CD: DG 439 6722

Prelude and Fugue No 11 in F BWV 856 (Well-Tempered Clavier, Book 1)

Hannover
February 1980

LP: DG 2531 299
CD: DG (Japan) POCG 9185-9204
CD: DG 439 6722

Prelude and Fugue No 12 in F minor BWV 857 (Well-Tempered Clavier, Book 1)

Hannover
February 1980

LP: DG 2531 299
CD: DG (Japan) POCG 9185-9204
CD: DG 439 6722

Prelude and Fugue No 13 in F sharp BWV 858 (Well-Tempered Clavier, Book 1)

Hannover
February 1980

LP: DG 2531 299
CD: DG (Japan) POCG 9185-9204
CD: DG 439 6722

Prelude and Fugue No 14 in F sharp minor BWV 859 (Well-Tempered Clavier, Book 1)

Hannover
February 1980

LP: DG 2531 299
CD: DG (Japan) POCG 9185-9204
CD: DG 439 6722

Prelude and Fugue No 15 in G BWV 860 (Well-Tempered Clavier, Book 1)

Hannover   LP: DG 2530 807
May 1975   CD: DG (Japan) POCG 9185-9204

Prelude and Fugue No 16 in G minor BWV 861 (Well-Tempered Clavier, Book 1)

Hannover   LP: DG 2530 807
May 1975   CD: DG (Japan) POCG 9185-9204

Prelude and Fugue No 17 in A flat BWV 862 (Well-Tempered Clavier, Book 1)

Hannover   LP: DG 2530 807
May 1975   CD: DG (Japan) POCG 9185-9204

Prelude and Fugue No 21 in B flat BWV 866 (Well-Tempered Clavier, Book 1)

Hannover   LP: DG 2530 807
May 1975   CD: DG (Japan) POCG 9185-9204

Prelude and Fugue No 22 in B flat minor BWV 867 (Well-Tempered Clavier, Book 1)

Hannover   LP: DG 2530 807
May 1975   CD: DG (Japan) POCG 9185-9204

Prelude and Fugue No 27 in C sharp BWV 872 (Well-Tempered Clavier, Book 2)

Hannover
February 1980

LP: DG 2531 299
CD: DG (Japan) POCG 9185-9204
CD: DG 439 6722

Prelude and Fugue No 30 in D minor BWV 875 (Well-Tempered Clavier, Book 2)

Hannover
February 1980

LP: DG 2531 299
CD: DG (Japan) POCG 9185-9204
CD: DG 439 6722

Prelude and Fugue No 31 in E flat BWV 876 (Well-Tempered Clavier, Book 2)

Hannover
February 1980

LP: DG 2531 299
CD: DG (Japan) POCG 9185-9204
CD: DG 439 6722

Prelude and Fugue No 39 in G BWV 884 (Well-Tempered Clavier, Book 2)

Hannover
February 1980

LP: DG 2531 299
CD: DG (Japan) POCG 9185-9204
CD: DG 439 6722

Prelude and Fugue No 48 in B minor BWV 893 (Well-Tempered Clavier, Book 2)

Hannover
February 1980

LP: DG 2531 299
CD: DG (Japan) POCG 9185-9204
CD: DG 439 6722

Presto (Italian Concerto BWV 971)

Berlin
1931

78: Polydor 65700/25312
78: Decca DE 7010

Siciliano in G minor (Flute Sonata BWV 1031), transcribed by Kempff

Berlin
1931

78: Polydor 66045/25312
78: Decca DE 7019

London
March 1953

LP: Decca LXT 2820
CD: London (Japan) KICC 2198

Hannover
April 1975

LP: DG 2530 647
CD: DG (Japan) POCG 9185-9204
CD: DG 439 1082/439 6722

Sinfonia in D (Prelude to Cantata No 29, Wir danken dir Gott/Reichswahlkantate), transcribed by Kempff

Berlin
1931

78: Polydor 65700/90189/47016
78: Decca DE 7010

Hannover
April 1975

LP: DG 2530 647
CD: DG (Japan) POCG 9185-9204
CD: DG 439 1082/439 6722

Toccata and Fugue in D BWV 912

Hannover
April 1975

LP: DG 2530 723
CD: DG (Japan) POCG 9185-9204
CD: DG 439 6722

Beethoven

Andante favori in F

Hannover
May 1964

LP: DG LPM 18 934/SLPM 138 934
LP: DG 2720 012/2721 134/2563 765
CD: DG (Japan) POCG 9185-9204
CD: DG 429 0722

Bagatelle in A minor "Für Elise"

London
May 1955

45: Decca 45-71091
LP: Decca LW 5212/BR 3065
CD: London (Japan) KICC 2198

Hannover
May 1964

LP: DG LPM 18 934/SLPM 138 934
LP: DG 2720 012/2535 608/2535 624
LP: DG 2548 137/2563 765
CD: DG (Japan) POCG 9185-9204
CD: DG 435 4952

Bagatelle in C minor

London
May 1955

45: Decca 45-71091
LP: Decca LW 5212
CD: London (Japan) KICC 2198

Bagatelle in C op 33 no 5

Berlin
ca. 1920

78: Polydor 62400
One of Kempff's first recordings

Berlin
1931

78: Polydor 24795/47017

6 Bagatelles op 126

Hannover
May 1964

LP: DG LPM 18 934/SLPM 138 934
LP: DG 2720 012/2721 134
CD: DG (Japan) POCG 9185-9204
CD: DG 429 0722

Cello Sonata in F op 5 no 1

Bonn   Casals
1958

LP: Philips 6701 038/6747 103
CD: Philips 420 0772

Paris   Fournier
February 1965

LP: DG SLPM 138 993-138 995
LP: DG SLPM 139 305/2709 018
LP: DG 2720 018/2721 133/2733 009
CD: DG 423 2972

Cello Sonata in G minor op 5 no 2

Paris   Fournier
February 1965

LP: DG SLPM 138 993-138 995
LP: DG SLPM 139 305/2709 018
LP: DG 2720 018/2721 133/2733 009
CD: DG 423 2972

Cello Sonata in A op 69

Berlin   P.Grümmer
ca. 1936

78: Polydor 67097-67099
78: Polydor 57035-57037/516710-516712
78: Decca CA 8259-8261

Paris   Fournier
February 1965

LP: DG SLPM 138 993-138 995
LP: DG SLPM 139 306/2709 018
LP: DG 2720 018/2721 133/2733 009
CD: DG 423 2972

Cello Sonata in C op 102 no 1

Paris   Fournier
February 1965

LP: DG SLPM 138 993-138 995
LP: DG SLPM 139 306/2709 018
LP: DG 2720 018/2721 133/2733 009
CD: DG 423 2972

Cello Sonatas/concluded

Cello Sonata in D op 102 no 2

Paris   Fournier
February 1965

LP: DG SLPM 138 993-138 995
LP: DG SLPM 139 307/2709 018
LP: DG 2720 018/2721 133/2733 009
CD: DG 423 2972

Clarinet Trio in B flat op 11

Vevey   Leister, Fournier
August 1969
and April 1970

LP: DG 2530 408
LP: DG 2721 132/2735 002

Ecossaise in E flat

Berlin
ca. 1920

78: Polydor 62400
One of Kempff's first recordings

Hannover
May 1964

LP: DG LPM 18 934/SLPM 138 934
LP: DG 2720 012/2721 134/2563 898
CD: DG (Japan) POCG 9185-9204
CD: DG 429 0722/435 4952

Piano Concerto No 1

Berlin   Staatskapelle
Date uncertain   Unnamed conductor

78: Polydor 69815-69818
Considered to be the work's
first recording

Berlin   BPO
May 1953   Van Kempen

LP: DG LPM 18 129
LP: DG LPM 18 371-18 374
LP: DG 2548 130
CD: DG 435 7442

Berlin   BPO
June and July   Leitner
1961

LP: DG LPM 18 774/SLPM 138 774
LP: DG LPM 18 770-18 773/
    SLPM 138 770-138 773
LP: DG 643 608-643 613
LP: DG 2711 004/2720 008/2721 066
LP: DG 2721 128/2740 131
CD: DG 419 8562

Piano Concerto No 2

Berlin   BPO
May 1953   Van Kempen

LP: DG LP 16 071/LPE 17 083/LPM 18 310
LP: DG LPM 18 371-18 374
LP: DG 2548 190
CD: DG 435 7442

Berlin   BPO
June 1961   Leitner

LP: DG 18 775/SLPM 138 775
LP: DG LPM 18 770-138 773/
    SLPM 138 770-138 773
LP: DG 643 608-643 613
LP: DG 2711 004/2720 008/2721 066
LP: DG 2721 128/2740 131/2535 426
CD: DG 419 8562

Piano Concerto No 3

Dresden 1942	Dresden Philharmonic Van Kempen	78: Polydor 67946-67950
Berlin May 1953	BPO Van Kempen	LP: DG LPM 18 130 LP: DG LPM 18 371-18 374 LP: DG 2548 144 CD: DG 435 7442
Berlin June and July 1961	BPO Leitner	LP: DG LPM 18 776/SLPM 138 776 LP: DG LPM 18 770-18 773/ SLPM 138 770-138 773 LP: DG 643 608-643 613 LP: DG 2711 004/2720 008/2721 066 LP: DG 2721 128/2740 131 CD: DG 419 4672
Turin April 1962	RAI Turin Orchestra Kempe	CD: Curcio-Hunt CON 35
Montreal November 1966	Montreal SO Decker	CD: Music and Arts CD 768

Piano Concerto No 4

Berlin 1941	Städtische Oper Orchestra Van Kempen	78: Polydor 67674-67678
Berlin November 1941	BPO Furtwängler	Unpublished radio broadcast
Berlin May 1953	BPO Van Kempen	LP: DG LP 16 072/LPE 17 084/LPM 18 310 LP: DG LPM 18 371-18 374 LP: DG 2548 190 CD: DG 435 7442
Berlin July 1961	BPO Leitner	LP: DG LPM 18 775/SLPM 138 775 LP: DG LPM 18 770-18 773/ SLPM 138 770-138 773 LP: DG 643 608-643 613 LP: DG 2711 004/2720 008/2721 066 LP: DG 2721 128/2740 131/2721 195 LP: DG 2535 426/2543 512 CD: DG 419 4672
Munich March 1970	Bavarian RO Kubelik	Unpublished video recording

Piano Concerti/concluded

Piano Concerto No 5 "Emperor"

Berlin 1936	BPO Raabe	78: Polydor 67082-67086 78: Decca CA 8248-8252
Berlin May 1953	BPO Van Kempen	78: DG LVM 72407-72409 LP: DG LPM 18 131 LP: DG LPM 18 371-18 374 LP: DG 2548 160 CD: DG 435 7442
Berlin July 1961	BPO Leitner	LP: DG LPM 18 777/SLPM 138 777 LP: DG LPM 18 770-18 773/ SLPM 138 770-138 773 LP: DG 643 608-643 613 LP: DG 2711 004/2720 008/2721 066 LP: DG 2721 128/2740 131/410 8421 CD: DG 419 4682
Montreal November 1966	Montreal SO Ozawa	CD: Music and Arts CD 768

Piano Sonata No 1 in F minor op 2 no 1

Berlin 1940	Polydor unpublished
Hannover October and December 1951	45: DG EPA 36013-36014 LP: DG LPM 18 105 LP: Decca (USA) DL 9583 LP: DG KL 42-51/2740 228 CD: DG awaiting publication
Hannover November 1964	LP: DG 18 935/SLPM 138 935 LP: DG 2720 012/2721 060 LP: DG 2721 134/2740 130 CD: DG 429 3062

Piano Sonata No 2 in A op 2 no 2

Berlin 1940	78: Polydor 67590-67592
Hannover December 1951 _CD 456 868_ _PR._	45: DG NH 72183-72184 LP: DG LPM 18 105 LP: Decca (USA) DL 9585 LP: DG KL 42-51/2740 228 CD: DG awaiting publication _447 966_
Hannover November 1964	LP: DG 18 936/SLPM 138 936 LP: DG 2720 012/2721 060 LP: DG 2721 134/2740 130 CD: DG 429 3062

Piano Sonatas/continued

Piano Sonata No 3 in C op 2 no 3

Berlin
1940

Polydor unpublished

Hannover
October 1951

LP: DG LPM 18 079
LP: Decca (USA) DL 9583
LP: DG KL 42-51/2740 228
CD: DG awaiting publication

Hannover
November 1964

LP: DG LPM 18 936/SLPM 138 936
LP: DG 2720 012/2721 060
LP: DG 2721 134/2740 130
CD: DG 429 3062

Piano Sonata No 4 in E flat op 7

Berlin
1940

78: Polydor 67806-67809

Hannover
December 1951

45: DG NH 72 198-72 199
LP: DG LPM 18 071
LP: Decca (USA) DL 9588
LP: DG KL 42-51/2740 228
CD: DG awaiting publication

Hannover
November 1964

LP: DG LPM 18 938/SLPM 138 938
LP: DG 2720 012/2721 060
LP: DG 2721 134/2740 130
CD: DG 429 3062

Piano Sonatas/continued

Piano Sonata No 5 in C minor op 10 no 1

Berlin
1940

78: Polydor 67810-67811

Hannover
December 1951

45: DG NH 72 273-72 274
LP: DG LPM 18 106
LP: Decca (USA) DL 9587
LP: DG KL 42-51/2740 228
CD: DG awaiting publication

Hannover
November 1964

LP: DG LPM 18 937/SLPM 138 937
LP: DG 2720 012/2721 060
LP: DG 2721 134/2740 130
CD: DG 429 3062

Piano Sonata No 6 in F op 10 no 2

Berlin
1940

78: Polydor 67812-67813

Hannover
December 1951

LP: DG LPM 18 106
LP: Decca (USA) DL 9591
LP: DG KL 42-51/2740 228
CD: DG awaiting publication

Hannover
November 1964

LP: DG LPM 18 937/SLPM 138 937
LP: DG 2720 012/2721 060
LP: DG 2721 134/2740 130
CD: DG 429 3062

Piano Sonata No 7 in D op 10 no 3

Berlin
1940

78: Polydor 67814-67816

Hannover
December 1951

45: DG NH 72 275-72 276
LP: DG LPM 18 019
LP: Decca (USA) DL 9584
LP: DG KL 42-51/2740 228
CD: DG awaiting publication

Hannover
November 1964

LP: DG LPM 18 937/SLPM 138 937
LP: DG 2720 012/2721 060
LP: DG 2721 134/2740 130
CD: DG 429 3062

Piano Sonatas/continued

Piano Sonata No 8 in C minor op 13 "Pathétique"

Berlin
1927-1928

78: Polydor 66676-66677

Berlin
1931

78: Polydor 47009-47011/90184-90186
78: Decca DE 7016-7018

Berlin
December 1936

78: Polydor 67113-67114/57051-57052
78: Decca X 202-203

Berlin
1940

78: Polydor 67682-67683

Hannover
December 1950

45: DG NH 72 048
LP: DG LPM 18 019/LPE 17 026
LP: Decca (USA) DL 9578

Hannover
May 1956

LP: DG LPEM 19 087/KL 42-51
LP: DG 2535 750/2740 228
CD: DG awaiting publication

Hannover
May 1960

45: DG EPL 30 245
LP: DG LPEM 19 227/SLPEM 136 227

Hannover
November 1965

LP: DG SLPM 138 941/SLPM 139 300
LP: DG 2720 012/2721 060/2721 134
LP: DG 2740 130/2535 354
LP: DG 2726 042/415 8341
CD: DG 415 8342/423 7732/429 3062

Piano Sonata No 9 in E op 14 no 1

Berlin
1940

78: Polydor 67817-67818

Hannover
December 1951

LP: DG LPM 18 071
LP: Decca (USA) DL 9588
LP: DG KL 42-51/2740 228
CD: DG awaiting publication

Hannover
November 1964

LP: DG LPM 18 938/SLPM 138 938
LP: DG 2720 012/2721 060
LP: DG 2721 134/2740 130
CD: DG 429 3062

Piano Sonatas/continued

Piano Sonata No 10 in G op 14 no 2

Berlin
1940

78: Polydor 67819-67820

Hannover
December 1951

45: DG NH 72 262
LP: DG LPM 18 079
LP: Decca (USA) DL 9592
LP: DG KL 42-51/2740 228
CD: DG awaiting publication

Hannover
November 1964

LP: DG LPM 18 938/SLPM 138 938
LP: DG 2720 012/2721 060
LP: DG 2721 134/2740 130
CD: DG 429 3062

Piano Sonata No 11 in B flat op 22

Berlin
1941

78: Polydor 67821-67823

Hannover
December 1951 — Pl 456 868

LP: DG LPM 18 020
LP: Decca (USA) DL 9590
LP: DG KL 42-51/2740 228
CD: DG awaiting publication

Hannover
May 1956

DG unpublished 447 966

Hannover
January 1965

LP: DG LPM 18 939/SLPM 138 939
LP: DG 2720 012/2721 060
LP: DG 2721 134/2740 130
CD: DG 429 3062

Piano Sonata No 12 in A flat op 26

Berlin
1932

78: Polydor 66041-66043
78: Decca CA 8240-8242

Berlin
1940

78: Polydor 67824-67826

Hannover
December 1951

LP: DG LPM 18 076
LP: Decca (USA) DL 9589
LP: DG KL 42-51/2740 228
CD: DG awaiting publication

Hannover
November 1964

LP: DG LPM 18 935/SLPM 138 935
LP: DG 2720 012/2721 060
LP: DG 2721 134/2740 130
CD: DG 429 3062

Piano Sonatas/continued

Piano Sonata No 13 in E flat op 27 no 1

Berlin 1941	78: Polydor 67858-67859
Hannover December 1951	LP: DG LPM 18 076 LP: Decca (USA) DL 9584 LP: DG KL 42-51/2740 228 CD: DG awaiting publication
Hannover January 1965	LP: DG LPM 18 039/SLPM 138 939 LP: DG 2720 012/2721 060 LP: DG 2721 134/2740 130 CD: DG 429 3062

Piano Sonata No 14 in C sharp minor op 14 no 2 "Moonlight"

Berlin 1927-1928	78: Polydor 66172-66173 First movement only 78: Polydor 66674
Berlin 1931	78: Polydor 47012-47013
Berlin 1941	78: Polydor 67856-67857 78: Vox (USA) 462
Hannover December 1950	45: DG NH 72047/EPL 30072 LP: DG LPM 18 020/LPE 17 026 LP: Decca (USA) DL 9582 First movement only 45: DG NH 72321/EPL 30063
Hannover May 1956	LP: DG LPEM 19 087/KL 42-51 LP: DG 2535 750/2740 228 CD: DG awaiting publication
Hannover May 1960	45: DG EPL 30 574 LP: DG LPEM 19 227/SLPEM 136 227
Hannover January 1965	LP: DG SLPM 138 941/139 300 LP: DG 2720 012/2721 060/2721 134 LP: DG 2740 130/2726 042 LP: DG 2535 316/2535 639/415 8341 CD: DG 413 4352/415 8342/429 3962

Piano Sonatas/continued

Piano Sonata No 15 in D op 28 "Pastoral"

Berlin
1941

78: Polydor 67860-67862

Hannover
December 1951

LP: DG LPM 18 055/LPEM 19 118
LP: Decca (USA) DL 9585
LP: DG KL 42-51/2740 228/2535 750
CD: DG awaiting publication

Hannover
January 1965

LP: DG SLPM 138 941/139 301
LP: DG 2720 012/2721 060
LP: DG 2721 134/2740 130
LP: DG 2535 354/415 8341
CD: DG 413 4352/415 8342/429 3062

Piano Sonata No 16 in G op 31 no 3

Hannover
December 1951

LP: DG LPM 18 055
LP: Decca (USA) DL 9589
LP: DG KL 42-51/2740 228
CD: DG awaiting publication

Hannover
September 1964

LP: DG LPM 18 940/SLPM 138 940
LP: DG 2720 012/2721 060
LP: DG 2721 134/2740 130
CD: DG 429 3062

Piano Sonata No 17 in D minor op 31 no 2 "Tempest"

Hannover
December 1951

LP: DG LPM 18 056
LP: Decca (USA) DL 9586
LP: DG KL 42-51/2740 228
CD: DG awaiting publication

Hannover
September 1964

LP: DG LPM 18 942/SLPM 138 942
LP: DG 2720 012/2721 060/2721 134
LP: DG 2740 130/2535 316/2726 042
CD: DG 413 4352/419 8572/429 3062

Piano Sonatas/continued

Piano Sonata No 18 in E flat op 18 no 3

Berlin 1932	78: Polydor 57003-57005 78: Polydor 67069-67071
Berlin 1943	78: Polydor 68273-68275
Hannover December 1951	LP: DG LPM 18 056 LP: Decca (USA) DL 9586 LP: DG KL 42-51/2740 228 CD: DG awaiting publication
Hannover September 1964	LP: DG LPM 18 940/SLPM 138 940 LP: DG 2720 012/2721 060 LP: DG 2721 134/2740 130 CD: DG 429 3062

Piano Sonata No 19 in G minor op 49 no 1

Hannover September and December 1951	45: DG NH 72 185 LP: DG LPM 18 021 LP: Decca (USA) DL 9590 LP: DG KL 42-51/2740 228 CD: DG awaiting publication
Hannover November 1964	LP: DG LPM 18 935/SLPM 138 935 LP: DG 2720 012/2721 060 LP: DG 2721 134/2740 130 CD: DG 429 0722/429 3062

Piano Sonatas/continued

Piano Sonata No 20 in G op 49 no 2

Hannover
September 1951

45: DG NH 72 185/NL 32 235
LP: DG LPM 18 021
LP: Decca (USA) DL 9590
LP: DG KL 42-51/2740 228
CD: DG awaiting publication

Hannover
November 1964

LP: DG LPM 18 935/SLPM 138 935
LP: DG 2720 012/2721 060
LP: DG 2721 134/2740 130
CD: DG 429 3062

Piano Sonata No 21 in C op 53 "Waldstein"

Berlin
1926-1927

78: Polydor 27052-27056

Berlin
1932

78: Polydor 57009-57011
78: Polydor 66678-66680
78: Polydor 95474-95476
78: Decca CA 8044-8046

Berlin
1943

78: Polydor 68276-68278
78: Vox (USA) 463

Hannover
September 1951

45: DG NH 72 135-72 136
LP: DG LPM 18 089/LPEM 19 118
LP: Decca (USA) DL 9581
LP: DG KL 42-51/2740 228
CD: DG awaiting publication

Hannover
September 1964

LP: DG LPM 18 943/SLPM 138 943
LP: DG 139 301/2720 012/2721 060
LP: DG 2721 134/2740 130/2535 291
LP: DG 2726 042/419 0531
CD: DG 419 0532/429 3062

Piano Sonata No 22 in F op 54

Hannover
September 1951

LP: DG LPM 18 089
LP: Decca (USA) DL 9591
LP: DG KL 42-51/2740 228
CD: DG awaiting publication

Hannover
September 1964

LP: DG LPM 18 940/SLPM 138 940
LP: DG 2720 012/2721 060/2721 134
LP: DG 2740 130/2535 354
CD: DG 429 3062

Piano Sonatas/continued

Piano Sonata No 23 in F minor op 57 "Appassionata"

Berlin
1926-1927

78: Polydor 27046-27051

Berlin
1932

78: Polydor 57012-57014
78: Polydor 66681-66683
78: Polydor 95471-95473

Berlin
1943

78: Polydor 68270-68272

Hannover
September 1951

45: DG NH 72 123-72 124
LP: DG LPM 18 021/LPEM 19 087
LP: Decca (USA) DL 9580
LP: DG KL 42-51/2535 750/2740 228
CD: DG awaiting publication

Hannover
May 1960

LP: DG LPEM 19 227/SLPEM 136 227

Hannover
September 1964

LP: DG LPM 18 943/SLPM 138 943
LP: DG 139 300/2720 012/2721 060
LP: DG 2721 134/2740 130/2535 354
LP: DG 2627 022/2726 042/419 0531
CD: DG 413 4352/419 0532/429 3062

Piano Sonata No 24 in F sharp op 78

Berlin
1932

78: Polydor 47014/90193

Hannover
September 1951

45: DG NH 72 263
LP: DG LPM 18 135
LP: Decca (USA) DL 9578
LP: DG KL 42-51/2740 228
CD: DG awaiting publication

Hannover
January 1965

LP: DG LPM 18 941/SLPM 138 941
LP: DG 139 301/2720 012/2721 060
LP: DG 2721 134/2740 130
LP: DG 2535 291/415 8341
CD: DG 415 8342/429 3062

Piano Sonatas/continued

Piano Sonata No 25 in G op 79

Hannover
September 1951

45: DG NH 72 263
LP: DG LPM 18 135
LP: Decca (USA) DL 9578
LP: DG KL 42-51/2740 228
CD: DG awaiting publication

Hannover
September 1964

LP: DG LPM 18 943/SLPM 138 943
LP: DG 139 301/2720 012/2721 060
LP: DG 2721 134/2740 130/2535 291
CD: DG 429 3062

Piano Sonata No 26 in E flat op 81a "Les adieux"

Berlin
1926-1927

78: Polydor 66687-66688

Berlin
1932

78: Polydor 66174-66175

Hannover
September 1951

45: DG EPL 30 213
LP: DG LPM 18 135
LP: Decca (USA) DL 9582
LP: DG KL 42-51/2740 228
CD: DG awaiting publication

Hannover
September 1964

LP: DG LPM 18 942/SLPM 138 942
LP: DG 2720 012/2721 060/2721 134
LP: DG 2740 130/2535 316
LP: DG 2726 042/419 0531
CD: DG 413 4352/419 0532/429 3062

Piano Sonata No 27 in E minor op 90

Berlin
1926-1931

78: Polydor 62491 and 66039
78: Polydor 62639 and 66712

Hannover
September 1951

45: DG NH 72 243
LP: DG LPM 18 135
LP: Decca (USA) DL 9580
LP: DG KL 42-51/2740 228
CD: DG awaiting publication

Hannover
January 1965   *CD* *PL 456 865*

LP: DG LPM 18 939/SLPM 138 939
LP: DG 2720 012/2721 060
LP: DG 2721 134/2740 130
CD: DG 429 3062

b. pinar.

Greater London Council

Royal Festival Hall

Director: John Denison, C.B.E.

Pianoforte recital by

WILHELM KEMPFF

BEETHOVEN

Sonata in C, Op. 2 No. 3
Sonata in E minor, Op. 90

INTERVAL

Sonata in D minor, Op. 31 No. 2
Sonata in A flat, Op. 110

Sunday 9th November 1975
3.15 pm

Management: IBBS & TILLETT

Piano sonata No 28 in A op 101

Berlin
1926-1927

78: Polydor 66178-66179

Hannover
September 1951

LP: DG LPM 18 145
LP: Decca (USA) DL 9581
LP: DG KL 42-51/2740 228
CD: DG awaiting publication

Hannover
September 1964

LP: DG LPM 18 942/SLPM 138 942
LP: DG 2720 012/2721 060
LP: DG 2721 134/2740 130
CD: DG 429 3062

Piano Sonata No 29 in B flat op 106 "Hammerklavier"

Berlin
1932-1936

78: Polydor 67077-67081
78: Polydor 516697-516701
78: Decca CA 8254-8258

Hannover
September 1951

LP: DG LPM 18 146
LP: Decca (USA) DL 9579
LP: DG KL 42-51/2740 228
CD: DG awaiting publication

Hannover
January 1964

LP: DG LPM 18 944/SLPM 138 944
LP: DG 2720 012/2721 060/2721 134
LP: DG 2740 130/2535 329/2726 033
CD: DG 419 8572/429 3062
Excerpts
LP: DG 104 486

Piano Sonatas/concluded

Piano Sonata No 30 in E op 109

Berlin
1932-1936

78: Polydor 67091-67092
78: Polydor 57056-57057
78: Polydor 516756-7/566305-7
78: Decca CA·8266-8267

Hannover
September 1951

45: DG NH 72 210
LP: DG LPM 18 145
LP: Decca (USA) DL 9591
LP: DG KL 42-51/2740 228
CD: DG awaiting publication

Hannover
January 1964

LP: DG LPM 18 944/SLPM 138 944
LP: DG 2720 012/2721 060/2721 134
LP: DG 2740 130/2535 329/2726 033
CD: DG 429 3062
Excerpts
LP: DG 104 486

Piano Sonata No 31 in A flat op 110

Berlin
1932-1936

78: Polydor 67088-67090
78: Polydor 57053-57055
78: Decca X 151-153

Hannover
September 1951

45: DG NH 72 244-72 245
LP: DG LPM 18 045
LP: Decca (USA) DL 9592
LP: DG KL 42-51/2740 228
CD: DG awaiting publication

Hannover
January 1964

LP: DG LPM 18 945/SLPM 138 945
LP: DG 2720 012/2721 060/2721 134
LP: DG 2740 130/2726 033
CD: DG 429 3062

Piano Sonata No 32 in C minor op 111

Berlin
1932-1936

78: Polydor 67093-67095
78: Polydor 57058-57060/516743-5
78: Decca X 177-179

Hannover
September 1951

LP: DG LPM 18 045
LP: Decca (USA) DL 9587
LP: DG KL 42-51/2740 228
CD: DG awaiting publication

Hannover
January 1964

LP: DG LPM 18 945/SLPM 138 945
LP: DG 2720 012/2721 060/2721 134
LP: DG 2740 130/2726 033
CD: DG 419 4682/429 3062
Excerpts
LP: DG 104 486

Piano Trio in E flat op 1 no 1

Vevey   Szeryng, Fournier LP: DG 2720 016/2721 132/2734 003
April 1970   CD: DG 415 8792

Piano Trio in G op 1 no 2

Vevey   Szeryng, Fournier LP: DG 2720 016/2721 132
April 1970   LP: DG 2530 408/2734 003
               CD: DG 415 8792

Piano Trio in C minor op 1 no 3

Vevey   Szeryng, Fournier LP: DG 2720 016/2721 132/2734 003
April 1970   CD: DG 415 8792

Piano Trio in D op 70 no 1 "Ghost"

Vevey   Szeryng, Fournier LP: DG 2720 016/2721 132
April 1970   LP: DG 2734 003/2535 389
               CD: DG 415 8792/429 7122

Piano Trio in E flat op 70 no 2

Vevey   Szeryng, Fournier LP: DG 2720 016/2721 132
April 1970   LP: DG 2530 207/2734 003
               CD: DG 415 8792

Piano Trio in B flat op 97 "Archduke"

Vevey   Szeryng, Fournier LP: DG 2720 016/2721 132/2734 003
April 1970   LP: DG 2530 147/2535 355
               CD: DG 415 8792/429 7122

Piano Trio in E flat (1787/1790)

Vevey   Szeryng, Fournier LP: DG 2720 016/2721 132/2734 003
April 1970

Piano Trio in B flat (1812)

Vevey   Szeryng, Fournier LP: DG 2720 016/2721 132/2734 003
April 1970

Rondo in C op 51 no 1

Hannover
January 1953 *(handwritten) 456 868*

45: DG EPL 30 121
CD: DG 435 7442

London
May 1955

LP: Decca LW 5212

Hannover
January-
November 1968

LP: DG SLPM 138 934/2535 639
LP: DG 2720 012/2721 134
CD: DG 429 0722
CD: DG (Japan) POCG 9185-9204

Rondo in G op 51 no 2

Berlin
1931

78: Polydor 66040

Hannover
January 1953

45: DG EPL 30 121
CD: DG 435 7442

London
May 1955

LP: Decca LW 5212

Hannover
January-
November 1968

LP: DG SLPM 138 934
LP: DG 2720 012/2721 134
CD: DG 429 0722
CD: DG (Japan) POCG 9185-9204

Rondo a capriccio in G op 129 "Wut über den verlorenen Groschen"

Berlin
1936

78: Polydor 62802/47201
78: Decca PO 5129

Hannover
January-
November 1968

LP: DG SLPM 138 934/2720 012
LP: DG 2721 134/2535 657
LP: DG 2548 137/2563 765
CD: DG 429 0722
CD: DG (Japan) POCG 9185-9204

Rondo in G for violin and piano

London   Menuhin
June 1970

LP: DG 2720 018/2721 133
LP: DG 2530 205/2735 001
CD: DG 415 8742

12 Variations in F on Mozart's "Se vuol ballare" for violin and piano

London   Menuhin
June 1970

LP: DG 2720 018/2721 133
LP: DG 2530 205/2735 001
CD: DG 415 8742

Variations/continued

6 Variations on Paisiello's "Nel cor più"

Berlin 1932-1936	78: Polydor 67090/57055
	78: Decca X 153
	Coupled with Piano Sonata No 31

Berlin
1932-1936

78: Polydor 67090/57055
78: Decca X 153
Coupled with Piano Sonata No 31

Hannover
January-
November 1968

LP: DG SLPM 138 934
LP: DG 2720 012/2721 134
CD: DG 429 0722
CD: DG (Japan) POCG 9185-9204

32 Variations in C minor (1806)

Hannover
January-
November 1968

LP: DG 2530 249
CD: DG (Japan) POCG 9185-9204

7 Variations on Mozart's "Bei Männern, welche Liebe fühlen" for cello and piano

Paris   Fournier
February 1965

LP: DG SLPM 138 993-138 995/
    SLPM 139 306
LP: DG 2709 018/2720 018
LP: DG 2721 133/2733 009
CD: DG 423 2972

12 Variations on Handel's "See the conquering hero" for cello and piano

Paris   Fournier
February 1965

LP: DG SLPM 138 993-138 995/
    SLPM 139 307
LP: DG 2709 018/2720 018
LP: DG 2721 133/2733 009
CD: DG 423 2972

12 Variations on Mozart's "Ein Mädchen oder Weibchen"

Paris   Fournier
February 1965

LP: DG SLPM 138 993-138 995/
    SLPM 139 307
LP: DG 2709 018/2720 018
LP: DG 2721 133/2733 009

Variations/concluded

6 Variations in F op 34

Hannover
January-
November 1968

LP: DG 2530 249
CD: DG (Japan) POCG 9185-9204

Eroica Variations op 35

Hannover
January-
November 1968

LP: DG 2530 249
CD: DG (Japan) POCG 9185-9204

6 Variations on a Turkish march op 76

Berlin
1936

78: Polydor 62762
78: Fonit 81009
Coupled with Schumann Träumerei

Violin Sonata No 1 op 12 no 1

Hannover   Schneiderhan
1952

LP: DG LPM 18 083

London   Menuhin
June 1970

LP: DG 2720 018/2721 133/2735 001
CD: DG 415 8742

Violin Sonata No 2 op 12 no 2

Hannover   Schneiderhan
1952

LP: DG LPM 18 083

London   Menuhin
June 1970

LP: DG 2720 018/2721 133/2735 001
CD: DG 415 8742

Violin Sonata No 3 op 12 no 3

Hannover   Schneiderhan
1952

LP: DG LPM 18 138

London   Menuhin
June 1970

LP: DG 2720 018/2721 133/2735 001
CD: DG 415 8742

Violin Sonata No 4 op 23

Hannover   Schneiderhan
1952

LP: DG LPM 18 138

London   Menuhin
June 1970

LP: DG 2720 018/2721 133
LP: DG 2530 458/2735 001
CD: DG 415 8742

Violin Sonata No 5 op 24 "Spring"

Hannover 1952	Schneiderhan	LP: DG LPM 18 082
London June 1970	Menuhin	LP: DG 2720 018/2721 133 LP: DG 2530 205/2735 001 CD: DG 415 8742/427 2512

Violin Sonata No 6 op 30 no 1

Hannover 1952	Schneiderhan	LP: DG LPM 18 082
London June 1970	Menuhin	LP: DG 2720 018/2721 133 LP: DG 2530 458/2735 001 CD: DG 415 8742

Violin Sonata No 7 op 30 no 2

Hannover 1952	Schneiderhan	LP: DG LPM 18 209
London June 1970	Menuhin	LP: DG 2720 018/2721 133 LP: DG 2530 346/2735 001 CD: DG 415 8742

Violin Sonatas/concluded

Violin Sonata No 8 op 30 no 3

| Hannover
1952 | Schneiderhan | LP: DG LPM 18 144 |

| London
June 1970 | Menuhin | LP: DG 2720 018/2721 133/2530 135
LP: DG 2735 001/410 9841
CD: DG 415 8742 |

Violin Sonata No 9 op 47 "Kreutzer"

| Berlin
May 1935 | Kulenkampff | 78: Polydor 67062-67065
78: Polydor 35017-20/516621-4
78: Decca CA 2807-2810
LP: DG 2548 712 |

| Hannover
1952 | Schneiderhan | LP: DG LPM 18 092/LPE 17 153
LPE 17 153 may contain the
performance with Kulenkampff |

| London
June 1970 | Menuhin | LP: DG 2720 018/2721 133/2530 135
LP: DG 2531 300/2735 001/410 9841
CD: DG 415 8742/427 2512/439 4532 |

Violin Sonata No 10 op 96

| Hannover
1952 | Schneiderhan | LP: DG LPM 18 209 |

| London
June 1970 | Menuhin | LP: DG 2720 018/2721 133
LP: DG 2530 346/2735 001
CD: DG 415 8742 |

Brahms

Piano Concerto No 1

Dresden   Dresden   LP: DG LPM 18 376/2548 100
1957   Staatskapelle   CD: DG 437 3742
               Konwitschny

Piano Sonata No 3 in F minor op 5

Hannover   LP: DG LPM 18 510/SLPM 138 010
March 1958   LP: DG 135 154
                        CD: DG (Japan) POCG 9185-9204
                        CD: DG 437 3742

Ballade in D minor op 10 no 1 "Edward"

London   CD   LP: Decca LXT 2914
November 1953 PL 456 862

Hannover   LP: DG 2530 321
1972   CD: DG (Japan) POCG 9185-9204
                        CD: DG 437 3742

Ballade in D op 10 no 2

London   CD   LP: Decca LXT 2914
November 1953 PL 456 862

Hannover   LP: DG 2530 321
1972   CD: DG (Japan) POCG 9185-9204
                        CD: DG 437 3742

Ballade in B minor op 10 no 3

London   CD   LP: Decca LXT 2914
November 1953 PL456 862

Hannover   LP: DG 2530 321
1972   CD: DG (Japan) POCG 9185-9204
                        CD: DG 437 3742

Ballade in B op 10 no 4

London   CD   LP: Decca LXT 2914
November 1953 PL 456 862

Hannover   LP: DG 2530 321
1972   CD: DG (Japan) POCG 9185-9204
                        CD: DG 437 3742

Capriccio in F sharp minor op 76 no 1

London
November 1953   *CD* 456 862

LP: Decca LXT 2914

Hannover
December 1963

LP: DG LPM 18 902/SLPM 138 902
LP: DG 2627 022
CD: DG (Japan) POCG 9185-9204
CD: DG 437 3742

Capriccio in B minor op 76 no 2

London
November 1953   *CD* 456 862

LP: Decca LXT 2914

Hannover
December 1963

LP: DG LPM 18 902/SLPM 138 902
CD: DG (Japan) POCG 9185-9204
CD: DG 437 3742

Intermezzo in A flat op 76 no 3

London
November 1953   *CD* 456 862

LP: Decca LXT 2914

Intermezzo in B flat op 76 no 4

London
November 1953   *CD* 456 862

LP: Decca LXT 2914

Hannover
December 1963

LP: DG LPM 18 902/SLPM 138 902
CD: DG (Japan) POCG 9185-9204
CD: DG 437 3742

Capriccio in C sharp minor op 76 no 5

London
November 1953   *CD* 456 862

LP: Decca LXT 2914

Intermezzo in A op 76 no 6

London
November 1953   *CD* 456 862

LP: Decca LXT 2914

Intermezzo in A minor op 76 no 7

London
November 1953   *CD* 456 862

LP: Decca LXT 2914

Capriccio in C op 76 no 8

London
November 1953   *CD* 456 862

LP: Decca LXT 2914

Rhapsody in B minor op 79 no 1

London
? March 1950   ~~SD~~ 456 868   Decca
  11 53
Hannover
December 1963

LP: Decca LX 3033/LX 3134/LW 5211
LP: Turnabout (USA) TVS 34386

LP: DG LPM 18 902/SLPM 138 902
LP: DG 2627 022
CD: DG (Japan) POCG 9185-9204
CD: DG 435 4952/437 3742

Rhapsody in G minor op 79 no 2

? London
  March 1950   CD 456 868   Decca
  11 53
Hannover
December 1963

45: Decca CEP 689
LP: Decca LX 3033/LX 3134/LW 5211
LP: Turnabout (USA) TVS 34386

LP: DG LPM 18 902/SLPM 138 902
LP: DG 2627 022
CD: DG (Japan) POCG 9185-9204
CD: DG 435 4952/437 3742

Capriccio in D minor op 116 no 1

London   CD PL
? November 1953   456
         Oct 50   862
Hannover
December 1963

LP: Decca LXT 2935

LP: DG LPM 18 902/SLPM 138 902
LP: DG 135 160
CD: DG (Japan) POCG 9185-9204
CD: DG 435 4952/437 2492

Intermezzo in A minor op 116 no 2

London
? November 1953   Oct 50 CD
                    PL 456 862
Hannover
December 1963

LP: Decca LXT 2935

LP: DG LPM 18 902/SLPM 138 902
CD: DG (Japan) POCG 9185-9204
CD: DG 435 4952/437 2492

Capriccio in G minor op 116 no 3

London   CD
? November 1953   Oct 50
         PL 456 862
Hannover
December 1963

LP: Decca LXT 2935

LP: DG LPM 18 902/SLPM 138 902
LP: DG 135 160
CD: DG (Japan) POCG 9185-9204
CD: DG 435 4952/437 2492

Piano pieces op 116/concluded

Intermezzo in E op 116 no 4

London
November 1953

LP: Decca LXT 2935

Hannover
December 1963

LP: DG LPM 18 902/SLPM 138 902
LP: DG 135 160
CD: DG (Japan) POCG 9185-9204
CD: DG 435 4952/437 2492

Intermezzo in E minor op 116 no 5

London
November 1953

LP: Decca LXT 2935

Hannover
December 1963

LP: DG LPM 18 902/SLPM 138 902
CD: DG (Japan) POCG 9185-9204
CD: DG 435 4952/437 2492

Intermezzo in E op 116 no 6

London
November 1953

LP: Decca LXT 2935

Hannover
December 1963

LP: DG LPM 18 902/SLPM 138 902
CD: DG (Japan) POCG 9185-9204
CD: DG 435 4952/437 2492

Capriccio in D minor op 116 no 7

London
November 1953

LP: Decca LXT 2935

Hannover
December 1963

LP: DL LPM 18 902/SLPM 138 902
CD: DG (Japan) POCG 9185-9204
CD: DG 435 4952/437 2492

Intermezzo in E flat op 117 no 1

London
November 1953

45: Decca 45-71132/CEP 689
LP: Decca LX 3033/LX 3134
LP: Turnabout (USA) TVS 34386

Hannover
December 1963

LP: DG LPM 18 903/SLPM 138 903
LP: DG 135 140/2535 608/2548 137
CD: DG 423 7732/435 4952/437 2492
CD: DG (Japan) POCG 9185-9204

Piano pieces op 117/concluded

Intermezzo in B flat minor op 117 no 2

London
November 1953 _CD PL 456 862_
Oct 50

45: Decca 45-71132
LP: Decca LX 3033/LX 3134
LP: Turnabout (USA) TVS 34386

Hannover
December 1963

LP: DG LPM 18 903/SLPM 138 903
LP: DG 135 140/2535 608/2548 137
CD: DG (Japan) POCG 9185-9204
CD: DG 435 4952/437 2492

Intermezzo in C sharp minor op 117 no 3

London
November 1953 _CD_
Oct 50 PL 456 862
Hannover
December 1963

LP: Decca LX 3033/LX 3134
LP: Turnabout (USA) TVS 34386

LP: DG LPM 18 903/SLPM 138 903
LP: DG 135 140/2535 608/2548 137
CD: DG (Japan) POCG 9185-9204
CD: DG 435 4952/437 2492

Intermezzo in A minor op 118 no 1

London _CD PL 456 862_
March 1950
_11 53_
Hannover
December 1963

LP: Decca LX 3032

LP: DG LPM 18 903/SLPM 138 903
CD: DG (Japan) POCG 9185-9204
CD: DG 437 2492/431 1622

Intermezzo in A op 118 no 2

London _CD_
March 1950 _PL 456 862_
_11 53_
Hannover
December 1963

78: Decca X 363
LP: Decca LX 3032

LP: DG LPM 18 903/SLPM 138 903
CD: DG (Japan) POCG 9185-9204
CD: DG 437 2492/431 1622

Piano pieces op 118/concluded

Ballade in G minor op 118 no 3

London
March 1950

[handwritten: CD, PL 456 862, 11 53]

78: Decca X 363
45: Decca 45-71064
LP: Decca LX 3032

Hannover
December 1963

LP: DG LPM 18 903/SLPM 138 903
CD: DG (Japan) POCG 9185-9204
CD: DG 437 2492/431 1622

Intermezzo in F minor op 118 no 4

London
March 1950

[handwritten: CD, PL 456 862, 11.53]

LP: Decca LX 3032

Hannover
December 1963

LP: DG LPM 18 903/SLPM 138 903
CD: DG (Japan) POCG 9185-9204
CD: DG 437 2492/431 1622

Romanze in F op 118 no 5

London
March 1950

[handwritten: CD, PL 456 862, 11.53]

LP: Decca LX 3032

Hannover
December 1963

LP: DG LPM 18 903/SLPM 138 903
CD: DG (Japan) POCG 9185-9204
CD: DG 437 2492/431 1622

Intermezzo in E flat minor op 118 no 6

London
March 1950

[handwritten: CD, PL 456 862, 11.53]

45: Decca 45-71064
LP: Decca LX 3032

Hannover
December 1963

LP: DG LPM 18 903/SLPM 138 903
CD: DG (Japan) POCG 9185-9204
CD: DG 437 2492/431 1622

Intermezzo in B minor op 119 no 1

London
November 1953

LP: Decca LXT 2935

Hannover
December 1963

LP: DG LPM 18 903/SLPM 138 903
CD: DG (Japan) POCG 9185-9204
CD: DG 435 4952/437 2492

Intermezzo in E minor op 119 no 2

London
November 1953

45: Decca 45-71119
LP: Decca LXT 2935

Hannover
December 1963

LP: DG LPM 18 903/SLPM 138 903
CD: DG (Japan) POCG 9185-9204
CD: DG 435 4952/437 2492

Intermezzo in C op 119 no 3

London
November 1953

45: Decca CEP 689
LP: Decca LXT 2935

Hannover
December 1963

LP: DG LPM 18 903/SLPM 138 903
CD: DG (Japan) POCG 9185-9204
CD: DG 435 4952/437 2492

Piano pieces op 119/concluded

Rhapsody in E flat op 119 no 4

Berlin
1927-1928

78: Polydor 66180

London
November 1953   ~~CD~~ PE 456 802

45: Decca 45-71119
LP: Decca LXT 2935

Hannover
December 1963

LP: DG LPM 18 903/SLPM 138 903
CD: DG (Japan) POCG 9185-9204
CD: DG 435 4952/437 2492

Scherzo in E minor op 4

Hannover
March 1958

LP: DG LPM 18 510/SLPM 138 010
LP: DG 135 154
CD: DG (Japan) POCG 9185-9204
CD: DG 437 3742

Variations and Fugue on a theme of Handel op 24

Hannover
January 1957

LP: DG LPM 18 461

Certain Brahms piano works played by Kempff may also have been recorded by
Decca in 1950-1953 but not published

Chopin

Andante Spianato and Grande Polonaise op 22

London
February 1958

LP: Decca LXT 5445/SXL 2081
LP: Decca ADD 140/SDD 140/ECS 768

Ballade No 3 in A flat op 47

London
February 1958

LP: Decca LXT 5445/SXL 2081
LP: Decca ADD 140/SDD 140

Barcarolle in F sharp op 60

London
February 1958

LP: Decca LXT 5451/SXL 2024
LP: Decca BR 3032/SWL 8023

Berceuse in D flat op 57

London
February 1958

LP: Decca LXT 5451/SXL 2024
LP: Decca BR 3032/SWL 8023
LP: Decca 414 4981

Fantasie in F minor op 49

London
February 1958

LP: Decca LXT 5445/SXL 2081
LP: Decca ADD 140/SDD 140

Fantasie Impromptu in C sharp minor op 66

London
February 1958

LP: Decca LXT 5451/SXL 2024

Impromptu No 1 in A flat op 29

London
February 1958

LP: Decca LXT 5451/SXL 1024
LP: Decca BR 3032/BR 3065/SWL 2024

Impromptu No 2 in F sharp op 36

London
February 1958

LP: Decca LXT 5451/SXL 2024
45: Decca SEC 5005

Impromptu No 3 in G sharp op 51

London
February 1958

LP: Decca LXT 5451/SXL 2024

Piano Concerto No 2

Prague   Czech PO
1959   Ancerl

CD: Praga PR 254 000-254 001

Piano Sonata No 2 in B flat minor op 35

London
February 1958

LP: Decca LXT 5452/SXL 2025

Piano Sonata No 3 in B minor op 58

London
February 1958

LP: Decca LXT 5452/SXL 2025

Polonaise-Fantaisie in A flat op 61

London
February 1958

LP: Decca LXT 5445/SXL 2081
LP: Decca ADD 140/SDD 140

Nocturne No 3 in B op 9

London
February 1958

LP: Decca LXT 5451/SXL 2024
LP: Decca BR 3032/SWL 8023

Scherzo No 3 in C sharp minor op 39

London
February 1958

45: Decca SEC 5005
LP: Decca LXT 5451/SXL 2024
LP: Decca BR 3032/SWL 8023

Couperin

Le carillon de Cithère

London
May 1955

45: Decca 45-71083

Gluck

Orfeo's Lament and Dance of the blessed spirits (Orfeo ed Euridice), transcribed
by Kempff

Hannover
April 1975

LP: DG 2530 647
CD: DG (Japan) POCG 9185-9204
CD: DG 439 1082/439 9662

Gavotte, arranged by Brahms

Berlin
ca. 1920

78: Polydor 66045
One of Kempff's first recordings

Handel

<u>Minuet in G minor (Suite de pièces), transcribed by Kempff</u>

London
May 1955

45: Decca 45-71113
LP: Decca LW 5212
CD: London (Japan) KICC 2198

Hannover
April 1975

LP: DG 2530 647
CD: DG (Japan) POCG 9185-9204
CD: DG 439 1082

<u>Air and Variations (Harmonious Blacksmith)</u>

London
May 1955

45: Decca 45-71113
LP: Decca LW 5212/BR 3065
CD: London (Japan) KICC 2198

Kempff

<u>4 Lieder to poems by C.F. Meyer: Lied der Seele; Es sprach der Geist; Gesang
des Meeres; In einer Sturmnacht</u>

Berlin   Fischer-Dieskau   LP: DG LPM 18 946/SLPM 138 946
May 1964

Liszt

Piano Concerto No 1

London   LSO   LP: Decca LXT 5025/LW 5339/ACL 58
June 1954   Fistoulari

Piano Concerto No 2

London   LSO   LP: Decca LXT 5025/ACL 58
June 1954   Fistoulari

Au lac de Wallenstadt (Années de pèlerinage: Suisse)

London   *C D*   LP: Decca LXT 2572
November 1950 *PL 456 865*   LP: Turnabout (USA) TVS 34385

Au bord d'une source (Années de pèlerinage: Suisse)

London   *C D*   LP: Decca LXT 2572
November 1950 *PL 456 865*   LP: Turnabout (USA) TVS 34385

Eglogue (Années de pèlerinage: Suisse)

London   *C D*   LP: Decca LXT 2572
November 1950 *PL 456 865*   LP: Turnabout (USA) TVS 34385

Sposalizio (Années de pèlerinage: Italie)

Hannover   LP: DG 2530 560
September 1974   CD: DG 435 4952

Il penseroso (Années de pèlerinage: Italie)

London
November 1950

LP: Decca LXT 2572
LP: Turnabout (USA) TVS 34385

Hannover
September 1974

LP: DG 2530 560
CD: DG 435 4952

Canzonetta del Salvator Rosa (Années de pèlerinage: Italie)

London
November 1950

LP: Decca LXT 2572
LP: Turnabout (USA) TVS 34385

Hannover
September 1974

LP: DG 2530 560
CD: DG 435 4952

Petrarch Sonnet No 47 (Années de pèlerinage: Italie)

London
November 1951

LP: Decca LXT 2670
LP: Turnabout (USA) TVS 34385
CD: Decca 433 4042

Hannover
September 1974

LP: DG 2530 560
CD: DG 435 4952

Années de pèlerinage/concluded

Petrarch Sonnet No 104 (Années de pèlerinage: Italie)

London
November 1951

LP: Decca LXT 2670
LP: Turnabout (USA) TVS 34385
CD: Decca 433 4042

Hannover
September 1974

LP: DG 2530 560

Petrarch Sonnet No 123 (Années de pèlerinage: Italie)

London
November 1951

45: Decca CEP 684
LP: Decca LXT 2670
LP: Turnabout (USA) TVS 34385
CD: Decca 433 4042

Hannover
September 1974

LP: DG 2530 560
CD: DG 435 4952

Gondoliera (Années de pèlerinage: Italie)

London
November 1950

LP: Decca LXT 2572
LP: Turnabout (USA) TVS 34385

Hannover
September 1974

LP: DG 2530 560/2545 031
CD: DG 423 7732

Saint François d'Assise prêchant aux oiseaux (2 Légendes)

London
November 1950

78: Decca SK 63017/X 515
LP: Decca LXT 2572
LP: Decca LW 5073/BR 3065
LP: Turnabout (USA) TVS 34385

Hannover
September 1974

LP: DG 2530 560
CD: DG 435 4952

Saint François de Paule marchant sur les flots (2 Légendes)

London
November 1950

LP: Decca LXT 2572/LW 5073
LP: Turnabout (USA) TVS 34385

Hannover
September 1974

LP: DG 2530 560
CD: DG 435 4952

Mendelssohn

Capriccio in E minor op 16

Berlin
ca. 1926

78: Polydor 66044

Lied ohne Worte op 62 no 6 "Frühlingslied"

Berlin
ca. 1926

78: Polydor 66044

Lied ohne Worte op 102 no 5 "Kinderstück"

Berlin
ca. 1926

78: Polydor 66044

Mozart

Fantasia in D minor K397

Berlin
January 1962

LP: DG LPM 18 707/SLPM 138 707
LP: DG 135 140/135 160/2535 168
LP: DG 2548 137/ 2726 022
CD: DG (Japan) POCG 9185-9204
CD: DG 423 7732/435 4952

Fantasia in C minor K475

Berlin
January 1962

LP: DG LPM 18 707/SLPM 138 707
LP: DG 135 160/2535 168
CD: DG (Japan) POCG 9185-9204
CD: DG 435 4952

Piano Concerto No 8 K246

Berlin   BPO
January 1962   Leitner

CD ph 456 868

LP: DG LPM 18 812/SLPM 138 812
LP: DG 2535 183/2726 024
CD: DG (Japan) POCG 9185-9204
CD: DG 439 6992

Piano Concerto No 9 K271 "Jeunehomme"

Geneva   Members of
September 1953   Suisse Romande
                and Stuttgart
                Chamber Orchestras
                Münchinger

LP: Decca LXT 2861

Piano Concerti/continued

Piano Concerto No 15 K450

Geneva
September 1953

Members of
Suisse Romande
and Stuttgart
Chamber Orchestras
Münchinger

LP: Decca LXT 2861/BR 3069

Piano Concerto No 20 K466

Dresden
1941

Dresden
Philharmonic
Van Kempen

78: Polydor 67706-67709
78: Fonit 91144-7/96083-6

Berlin
January 1956

BPO
Karajan

LP: Cetra LO 531
LP: Foyer FO 1034
LP: Longanesi CGL 14
CD: Natise HVK 105
CD: Joker 44122
CD: Hunt CDKAR 231
CD: Artemis 710.005

Piano Concerto No 21 K467

Munich
May 1977

Bavarian RO
Klee

LP: DG 2531 372
Cadenzas by Kempff

Piano Concerto No 22 K482

Munich
May 1977

Bavarian RO
Klee

LP: DG 2531 372
Cadenzas by Kempff

Piano Concerto No 23 K488

Bamberg
April 1960

Bamberg SO
Leitner

LP: DG LPM 18 645/SLPM 138 645
LP: DG 2535 204/2721 195/2726 024
CD: DG (Japan) POCG 9185-9204
CD: DG 423 8852/439 6992

CDPR 456 865

Piano Concerti/concluded

Piano Concerto No 24 K491

Bamberg
April 1960

Bamberg SO
Leitner

LP: DG LPM 18 645/SLPM 138 645
LP: DG 2535 204/2726 024
CD: DG (Japan) POCG 9185-9204
CD: DG 423 8852/439 6992
Cadenzas by Kempff

Piano Concerto No 27 K595

Berlin
January 1962

BPO
Leitner

LP: DG LPM 18 812/SLPM 138 812
LP: DG 135 137/2535 183/2726 024
CD: DG (Japan) POCG 9185-9204
CD: DG 439 6992

Piano Sonata No 8 in A minor K310

Berlin
January 1962

LP: DG LPM 18 707/SLPM 138 707
LP: DG 2535 168
CD: DG (Japan) POCG 9185-9204
CD: DG 435 4952

Piano Sonata No 11 in A K331

Berlin
1935

78: Polydor 67067-67068
78: Polydor 57001-57002

Berlin
January 1962

LP: DG LPM 18 707/SLPM 138 707
LP: DG 2535 168/2538 079/2627 022
CD: DG (Japan) POCG 9185-9204
CD: DG 435 4952

Rondo in D K382 for piano and orchestra

Dresden
1941

Dresden
Philharmonic
Van Kempen

78: Polydor 67710

Rameau

Le rappel des oiseaux, arranged by Kempff

London
May 1955

45: Decca 45-71083

Schubert

Allegretto in C minor D900

Hannover
August 1967

LP: DG 139 322/2530 090/2545 036
CD: DG (Japan) POCG 9185-9204

Horch' horch' die Lerch' (Morgenständchen), transcribed by Liszt

Berlin
1935

78: Polydor 62746/47007

Impromptu in C minor D899 no 1

Hannover
March 1965

LP: DG LPEM 19 149/SLPEM 139 149
LP: DG 2726 022/2740 188
CD: DG (Japan) POCG 9185-9204
CD: DG 435 4952

Impromptu in E flat D899 no 2

Hannover
March 1965

LP: DG LPEM 19 149/SLPEM 139 149
LP: DG 2726 022/2740 188
CD: DG (Japan) POCG 9185-9204
CD: DG 435 4952

Impromptu in G D899 no 3

Hannover
March 1965

LP: DG LPEM 19 149/SLPEM 139 149
LP: DG 2726 022/2740 188
CD: DG (Japan) POCG 9185-9204
CD: DG 435 4952

Impromptus/concluded

Impromptu in A flat D899 no 4

Hannover
March 1965

LP: DG LPEM 19 149/SLPEM 139 149
LP: DG 2726 022/2740 188
CD: DG (Japan) POCG 9185-9204
CD: DG 435 4952

Impromptu in F minor D935 no 1

Hannover
March 1965

LP: DG LPEM 19 149/SLPEM 139 149
LP: DG 2740 188
CD: DG (Japan) POCG 9185-9204
CD: DG 435 4952

Impromptu in A flat D935 no 2

Hannover
March 1965

LP: DG LPEM 19 149/SLPEM 139 149
LP: DG 2740 188
CD: DG (Japan) POCG 9185-9204
CD: DG 435 4952

Impromptu in B flat D935 no 3

Berlin
1935

78: Polydor 47004/62745

Hannover
March 1965

LP: DG LPEM 19 149/SLPEM 139 149
LP: DG 2740 188
CD: DG (Japan) POCG 9185-9204
CD: DG 435 4952

Impromptu in F minor D935 no 4

Hannover
March 1965

LP: DG LPEM 19 149/SLPEM 139 149
LP: DG 2740 188
CD: DG (Japan) POCG 9185-9204
CD: DG 435 4952

Klavierstück in A D604

Hannover
August 1967

LP: DG 2530 090
CD: DG (Japan) POCG 9185-9204

Klavierstück in E flat minor D946 no 1

Hannover
August 1967

LP: DG 2530 090/2545 036
CD: DG (Japan) POCG 9185-9204

Klavierstück in E flat D946 no 2

Hannover
August 1967

LP: DG 2530 090/2545 036
CD: DG (Japan) POCG 9185-9204

Klavierstück in C D946 no 3

Hannover
August 1967

LP: DG 2530 090
CD: DG (Japan) POCG 9185-9204

Piano Sonata in E D157, incomplete

Hannover
August 1968

LP: DG 2740 132
CD: DG 423 4962

Piano Sonata in C D279, incomplete

Hannover
November 1968

LP: DG 2530 327/2740 132/2535 240
CD: DG 423 4962

Piano Sonata in E (5 Klavierstücke) D459

Hannover
January 1969

LP: DG 2740 132
CD: DG 423 4962

Piano Sonata in A minor D537

Hannover
August 1968

LP: DG 2740 132
CD: DG 423 4962

Piano Sonata in A flat D557

Hannover
November 1968

LP: DG 2740 132
CD: DG 423 4962

Piano Sonatas/continued

Piano Sonata in E minor D566, incomplete

Hannover
November 1968

LP: DG 2530 354/2740 132
CD: DG 423 4962

Piano Sonata in E flat D568

Hannover
August 1968

LP: DG 2740 132
CD: DG 423 4962

Piano Sonata in B D575

Hannover
November 1968

LP: DG 2530 148/2740 132
CD: DG 423 4962

Piano Sonata in F minor D625

Hannover
January 1969

LP: DG 2530 354/2740 132
CD: DG 423 4962

Piano Sonata No 13 in A D664

Hannover
January 1967

LP: DG 139 322/2740 132
CD: DG 423 4962

Piano Sonata No 14 in A minor D784

Hannover
January 1968

LP: DG 2740 132
CD: DG 423 4962

Piano Sonatas/concluded

Piano Sonata No 15 in C D840, incomplete

Hannover
January 1967 *CD PL 456 868*

LP: DG 139 322/2740 132
CD: DG 423 4962

Piano Sonata No 16 in A minor D845

London
March 1953 *CD PL 456 865*

LP: Decca LXT 2834

Hannover
February 1965

LP: DG LPEM 19 104/SLPEM 139 104
LP: DG 2740 132
CD: DG 423 4962

Piano Sonata No 17 in D D850

Hannover
August 1968

LP: DG 2740 132
CD: DG 423 4962

Piano Sonata No 18 in G D894

Hannover
February 1965

LP: DG LPEM 19 104/SLPEM 139 104
LP: DG 2740 132
CD: DG 423 4962

Piano Sonata No 19 in C minor D958

Hannover
November 1968

LP: DG 2530 148/2740 132
CD: DG 423 4962

Piano Sonata No 20 in A D959

Hannover
January 1969

LP: DG 2530 327/2740 132
CD: DG 423 4962

Piano Sonata No 21 in B flat D960

London
November 1950

LP: Decca LXT 2577

Hannover
January 1967

LP: DG 139 323/2740 132
LP: DG 2740 188/2535 240
CD: DG 423 4962

Moment musical in C D780 no 1

Hannover
August 1967

LP: DG 139 372/2535 271
LP: DG 2548 137/2740 188
CD: DG (Japan) POCG 9185-9204

Moment musical in A flat D780 no 2

Hannover
August 1967

LP: DG 139 372/2535 271
LP: DG 2548 137/2740 188
CD: DG (Japan) POCG 9185-9204

Moment musical in F minor D780 no 3

Berlin
1935

78: Polydor 47008
78: Decca DE 7040

Hannover
August 1967

LP: DG 139 372/2535 271
LP: DG 2548 137/2740 188
CD: DG (Japan) POCG 9185-9204

Moments musicaux/concluded

Moment musical in C sharp minor D780 no 4

Berlin
1935

78: Polydor 47008
78: Decca DE 7040

Hannover
August 1967

LP: DG 139 372/2535 271
LP: DG 2548 137/2740 188
CD: DG (Japan) POCG 9185-9204

Moment musical in F minor D780 no 5

Hannover
August 1967

LP: DG 139 372/2535 271
LP: DG 2548 137/2740 188
CD: DG (Japan) POCG 9185-9204

Moment musical in A flat D780 no 6

Hannover
August 1967

LP: DG 139 372/2535 271
LP: DG 2548 137/2740 188
CD: DG (Japan) POCG 9185-9204

Scherzo in B flat D593

Hannover
January 1967

LP: DG 139 323/2545 036

13 Variations on a theme of Hüttenbrenner D576

Hannover
August 1967

LP: DG 2530 090
CD: DG (Japan) POCG 9185-9204

Wanderer Fantasy D760

Hannover
August 1967

LP: DG 139 372/135 160
LP: DG 2535 271/2740 188
CD: DG (Japan) POCG 9185-9204
CD: DG 435 4952

Schumann

Arabeske op 18

London
November 1951

CD PL 456862

45: Decca CEP 684
LP: Decca LXT 2670
LP: Turnabout (USA) TVS 34386
CD: Decca 433 4042

Hannover
January 1967

LP: DG 2530 321/2531 297/2740 133
CD: DG (Japan) POCG 9185-9204
CD: DG 435 0452/445 0252

Aufschwung (Fantasiestücke op 12)

Berlin
1935

78: Polydor 62746/47007

Carnaval op 9

Hannover
February 1971

LP: DG 2530 185/2740 133
CD: DG (Japan) POCG 9185-9204
CD: DG 435 0452

Davidsbündlertänze op 6

Hannover
January 1967

LP: DG 139 316/2740 133
CD: DG (Japan) POCG 9185-9204
CD: DG 435 0452

Fantasie in C op 17

Hannover
January 1957

LP: DG LPM 18 461/2535 740

Hannover
March 1971

LP: DG 2530 185/2740 133
CD: DG (Japan) POCG 9185-9204
CD: DG 435 0452/445 0252

Humoreske op 20

Hannover
February 1973

LP: DG 2530 410/2740 133
CD: DG (Japan) POCG 9185-9204
CD: DG 435 0452

Kinderszenen op 15

Hannover
February 1973

LP: DG 2530 348/2531 297/2740 133
CD: DG (Japan) POCG 9185-9204
CD: DG 435 0452

Träumerei (Kinderszenen)

Berlin
1936

78: Polydor 62762
78: Fonit 81009

Konzertstück in G op 92 for piano and orchestra

Munich
1975

Bavarian RO
Kubelik

LP: DG 2530 494
CD: DG (Japan) POCG 9185-9204

Kreisleriana op 16

Hannover
May 1956

LP: DG LPEM 19 077/2535 740

Hannover
February 1972

LP: DG 2530 317/2740 133
CD: DG (Jaoan) POCG 9185-9204
CD: DG 435 0452

Nachtstücke op 23

Hannover
February 1973

LP: DG 2740 133
CD: DG (Japan) POCG 9185-9204
CD: DG 435 0452

Novelette No 9 (Bunte Blätter op 99)

Hannover
February 1972

LP: DG 2530 321/2531 297
CD: DG (Japan) POCG 9185-9204
CD: DG 435 0452

Papillons op 2

London
November 1951

LP: Decca LXT 2670
LP: Turnabout (USA) TVS 34386
CD: Decca 433 4042

Hannover
January 1967

LP: DG 139 316/2740 133/2548 137
CD: DG (Japan) POCG 9185-9204
CD: DG 435 0452

Piano Concerto

London   LSO
March 1953   Krips

LP: Decca LXT 2806/LW 5337/ECS 802
CD: Decca 433 4042

Munich   Bavarian RO
1975   Kubelik

LP: DG 2530 484/2543 512
CD: DG (Japan) POCG 9185-9204

Piano Sonata No 2 op 22

Hannover
February 1973

LP: DG 2530 348/2740 133
CD: DG (Japan) POCG 9185-9204
CD: DG 435 0452

3 Romanzen op 28

Hannover
February 1972

(handwritten: CD PL 456 868)

LP: DG 2530 321/2531 297/2740 133
CD: DG (Japan) POCG 9185-9204
CD: DG 435 0452

Symphonic Studies op 13

Hannover
January 1956

LP: DG LPEM 19 077

Hannover
February 1972

LP: DG 2530 317/2740 133
CD: DG (Japan) POCG 9185-9204
CD: DG 435 0452

Toccata op 7

Berlin
ca. 1932

78: Polydor 66180

Waldszenen op 82

Hannover
February 1973

LP: DG 2530 410/2740 133
CD: DG (Japan) POCG 9185-9204
CD: DG 435 0452
Vogel als Prophet
LP: DG 2530 321

Miscellaneous

Wilhelm Kempff in Hiroshima

Hiroshima March 1955	Kempff plays organ of the World Peace Church	LP: DG LPE 17 069 In addition to playing the Bach works BWV 582, 639 and 727 listed in the main discography, Kempff also gives a spoken introduction

Wilhelm Kempff in Positano

Positano ca. 1960	LP: DG 104 486 Kempff speaks about his Beethoven interpretations and his master classes in Positano, with illustrations taken from his later (stereo) recordings of the Sonatas; additional Bach work BWV 659a (see main discography) appears to have been recorded especially for this LP

Wilhelm Kempff in Positano

EINE AUFNAHME AUS DEM BEETHOVEN-INTERPRETATIONSKURS

A-SEITE:

LUDWIG VAN BEETHOVEN
(1770-1827)

Klaviersonate Nr. 29 B-dur
op. 106
(Sonate für das Hammerklavier)

1. Satz: Allegro
4. Satz: Allegro risoluto (Fuge, 2. Teil)

Klaviersonate Nr. 30 E-dur
op. 109

1. Satz: Vivace, ma non troppo – Adagio espressivo

B-SEITE:

3. Satz: Gesangvoll, mit innigster Empfindung
(Andante, molto cantabile ed espressivo)

Klaviersonate Nr. 32 c-moll
op. 111

1. Satz: Maestoso: Allegro con brio ed appassionato

JOHANN SEBASTIAN BACH
(1685-1750)

Choralvorspiel
»Nun komm', der Heiden Heiland«
BWV 659a

aus »18 Choräle von verschiedener Art« BWV 651-668

Aufnahme: Heinz Wildhagen
Porträt Wilhelm Kempff: Lothar Oppermann, Hamburg
Photo Wilhelm Kempff: Rudolf Betz, München
Abdruck des Autographs von Beethoven
mit freundlicher Genehmigung der Deutschen Staatsbibliothek, Berlin

Printed in Germany by Gebrüder Jänecke, Hannover · Manufactured by Deutsche Grammophon, Hamburg 10/66

STEREO 104 486

Kempff in duo with Wilhelm Furtwängler

Walter Gieseking
1895-1956

Discography compiled by John Hunt

Introduction

IN THE WINTER of 1947 I spent a few weeks in Wiesbaden where I stayed with some publisher friends of mine. Next to their home stood a large but unpretentious house with a beautifully-kept garden. In this garden, digging at a flower-bed, stood a man I took to be the gardener in heavy boots and muddy corduroy trousers. ' There goes our next door neighbour ' said my host, looking out of the window. The gardener was Walter Gieseking. ' Let's go and see him today ' added my friend, and proceeded to ring him up to find out whether we could come. ' Certainly ' was his reply, ' come for tea and bring some food '. That same afternoon we baked a strudel and went to visit him.

He received us unceremoniously in his slippers. His wife was there, a small elderly woman with a lot of white tight curls, and also his two grown-up daughters, who looked exactly like him and bore the unexpected names of Freya and Jutta.

I noticed at once that he looked even bigger and taller than on the stage, where I had already seen him innumerable times. What struck me immediately were his hands which I had always seen only from a distance. They were rather small for such a massive frame. They were also the most beautiful hands I had ever seen, finely shaped, delicate and almost feminine with long tapering fingers.

His house, seen from the inside, was even less attractive than from the outside. I had expected it to be full of Renoirs (most of my musician friends, including Fischer, Casella and Petrassi were keen and discriminative collectors) but the only adornment in Gieseking's drawing-room was a large, ugly, nondescript painting hanging from one of the walls. He must have followed my gaze and read some disapproval in it because he shrugged his shoulders and said ' It was given to me '. The room was almost entirely taken up by two grand pianos (Grotrian-Steinwegs) and by an unbelievable quantity of sheet music strewn all over the place. There was music on the shelves and under the shelves, on the pianos and under the pianos. I was surprised that such a refined and tidy player as Gieseking could look so perfectly at ease in such unrefined and untidy surroundings.

My surprises were, however, not yet over. When I sat at one of the pianos I discovered that it was shockingly bad. The other, I soon found out, was no better. In fact I suspected that they too, like the painting, had been given to him. I remembered how particular Fischer was on the matter of pianos. ' A piano ' he always said ' is the tool of your trade. Keep it well, spend as much money as you can afford on it, never practise on an instrument which is uneven or out of tune.' I could not help asking Gieseking how he managed to achieve such wonderful effects on such an unsuitable tool of his trade. ' It is not the instrument on which you play that counts ' he coldly replied ' but how you play it.' This reminded me how Casella once said to me that a really good pianist should be able to achieve some sort of effect even playing on the kitchen table.

At the time Gieseking was, so to speak, out of work. He had been accused of pro-Nazi feelings and was kept in cold storage for a couple of years. He seemed totally unconcerned about this. In fact, he rather welcomed the opportunity of staying at home with his family, tending his garden and cataloguing his butterflies. He was an expert lepidopterist, always took his butterfly net with him on tours to distant countries, and often brought back rare and highly valuable specimens. He already had over 10,000 specimens when I was there.

Although I was told that he had many pupils he did not seem to be running any organised courses when I was there. These, I believe, were held later at the Musik Hochschule of Saarbrücken. As I never studied with him I could not really say what he was like as a teacher. On the other hand, that first visit was followed by several more and on all occasions we played and discussed all kinds of music.

Although he did not believe in practising (at least not for himself) he was always ready to play and seemed to have an infinite capacity both for playing and for listening. Of practising he used to say : ' Wer badet hat's nötig, wer übt auch ' (meaning ' the one who has to take a bath or to practise must obviously need it '). He could not recollect having ever practised more than three hours in a day, although he was ready to admit that some hands may need more practising than others. If someone had some physical defects practising would make them less noticeable, even if it could not obliterate them altogether. He had never done special studies or exercises of any kind and therefore could

not have recommended any, but he did recommend complete relaxation in all muscles of fingers, forearm and shoulder. ' Make yourself comfortable ' he always used to say before one started to play. He could hardly make himself comfortable when playing. His gigantic frame did not fit any instrument. Perhaps he should have played the double-bass.

I never heard him say ' Let's play this ' but ' Let's try this '. He usually disappeared for a few minutes under one of the various heaps of music and emerged from it with the newest or the dustiest score he could find, put it on the piano and said : ' Turn my pages and count my wrong notes '.

He was the most fantastic sight-reader I have ever encountered—taking into account people like Casella and Fernando Previtali. Music seemed to hold no secrets and no difficulties for him. One of the pieces he thus tried whilst I was there was Scriabin's immensely difficult Fifth Sonata which he read as if he had played nothing else all his life. As I looked impressed by this work he had it photocopied and sent to me as soon as I left Wiesbaden without my even mentioning to him that I would have liked to have it. In fact he said that I should ' try it '.

Of all the great pianists I have heard Gieseking was one of the most versatile, if not the most versatile. He could not strictly be called a virtuoso although he had an uncanny virtuosity. He played modern music incredibly well, and extremely often, but never specialised in it. He surely must have given more first performances than any other pianist of similar calibre, and his programmes always contained something new or at least unusual. He played Debussy and Ravel like no one else, but his performances of Beethoven's opus 101, 109 and 111 were equally memorable. His Schumann was among the best I have known but his Scarlatti was just perfect. After hearing so many performances of Scarlatti which are either too noisy or too delicate, too dull or too fanciful, one surely realises how difficult it is to play a composer whose music is specifically meant for display on a particular instrument and which has very little besides a good surface.

The surface of Gieseking's playing was so remarkable that it alone could justify a performance. I have here the last movement of Bach's Partita No. 5 where the listener is immediately struck by the sheer beauty of pure, unadulterated, untrimmed finger technique. All is possible and absolutely sufficient with a finger technique of such a kind.

We discussed together modern music at great length. It never appeared to me that Gieseking either passionately believed in it or thought that to play it was everyone's duty. I felt rather that he played it because of his insatiable appetite and curiosity for music and because to play always the same things bored him to distraction.

It would be difficult to describe Gieseking's repertoire. He had no real repertoire because a repertoire means a selected and therefore limited choice of works and of composers one always plays, whilst Gieseking played almost everything. When I asked Mr. Saul for some records, I was showered with a deluge of them, and we had the greatest difficulty in selecting not those which would best represent him but simply those which would give a pale idea of the limitless range of his playing.

Not all the works he played were masterpieces ; they were just performed in a masterly way. When I tackled him about his rather undiscriminating taste in music, he replied that masterpieces were few and far between and that if only masterpieces were to be played half the concert halls would be shut and the others would be working short time.

He held the view that music was bad when it was useless, when it was too ambitious, or too pretentious, when it was boring, when it had no purpose whatsoever. On the other hand, music could be put to a great number of purposes and fit many needs. He was a great admirer of jazz and could play it wonderfully well (had in fact, I believe, played jazz in the army during the first world war ; he had also played in the regimental band, I do not know which instrument, I only know that he played the violin remarkably well). He played jazz entirely like a professional with all the improvisations and variations which are now the prerogative of outstanding jazz players alone. I remember him once turning into jazz variations the second movement of Beethoven's Sonata, op. 31, No. 3, and I only wish I had a tape of it. Viennese waltzes fitted him like a glove and he often played the *Blue Danube* or the *Tales from the Vienna Woods* as an encore in his recitals. I never heard him play Schoenberg or Webern but at the time I knew him these composers were rarely played for a variety of reasons, not all musical ones.

His lack of enthusiastic statements about music could be deceptive as he was a master of understatement. The highest praise I have heard from him was ' not bad '.

He was the darling of all living composers I knew and often visited them to ask whether they had anything new worth playing. He once visited Castelnuovo-Tedesco, a rather undistinguished Italian composer now living in America, and saw there the manuscript of a Suite Castelnuovo-Tedesco had just completed. Gieseking tried it out on the piano and then asked the composer whether he could borrow it to have another look at it. He took it back to his hotel where he literally looked at it once more. He never, as far as I know, travelled with a piano and I am sure never felt the need of having one in his hotel room. The next morning he faithfully returned the Suite to Castelnuovo-Tedesco and three days later played it at his Milan recital. He gave the first performance of Casella's Sinfonia, Arioso e Toccata, a long and difficult work written rather on the pattern of Busoni's Toccata, after having had the score for barely a fortnight, and he learned Petrassi's Piano Concerto, of which he also gave the first performance in Rome whilst on tour, in less than 10 days. Admittedly both performances could have been better but they were, in Gieseking's own words, ' not bad at all '.

Every moment I spent with him I was aware of the immense facility and versatility with which he was blessed. He spoke at least four languages perfectly. His favourite language was French, as he was born in Lyons and had retained many characteristics of his native country, among these a sharp but never malicious sense of humour, a quick-witted adaptability to all situations, and a real gift for conversation. He seemed to have an almost encyclopaedic knowledge of a great number of subjects and the ability to shift from one to the other with the casual ease of a magician pulling rabbits out of a hat. He nevertheless affirmed that he never went to school (he had led a rather nomadic life in his youth until he returned to Germany with his parents). ' At the age of five ' he used to recall ' I discovered that I could read and write. I never needed to learn anything else after that '.

Facility, to such a high degree, can be a great blessing and a great burden. It has ruined many fine players and even more composers by giving them the impression that the Gods were always on their side. I feel that Gieseking's greatest merit was his capacity to prevent this incredible facility from taking the upper hand.

Although much of our time was spent in trying out something new including several piano duets, an experience which to a shockingly bad sight-reader as I am could have been shattering had not Gieseking always been so charmingly casual about it (whenever I became flustered or confused he used to turn round and say : ' Don't mind me, I shall wait for you at the bottom of the page '). I also tried to use these golden opportunities to play for him or ask him to play for me many works I already knew and had studied with others. Naturally, among these were Debussy's 24 Preludes.

Going through each one of them with him made me fully realise how many things I did wrong which on the surface sounded right. Debussy's scores are full of musical notations, every effect is carefully noted down and specified. It is also complemented by literary and pictorial implications, and is in fact the reflection of a figurative image on the abstract mirror of the music. The border-line between poetic fantasy and technical reality is but a narrow strip and the player has to cross it continuously holding within his fingers the threads of this image which, however evocatively expressed,

must never be approximate. Gieseking's playing of Debussy had both the weightless elasticity of poetic fantasy and the chiselled precision of musical discipline. I think he achieved this measure of perfection because he had solved all problems of technical effects and no longer needed to think about them at all.

He used his pedal very judiciously and in a very personal way. Some of the Preludes (notably No. 3 and the beginning of No. 24) sounded as if there were none at all. In fact, he only kept it down very slightly and changed it very frequently, letting his ear guide his foot, so that the effect was not woolly or blurred but each note was clearly perceptible and featherlight. In fact, his playing of Debussy was so marvellously transparent because he carefully avoided wrapping it up in too many layers of vibrations. He always kept an even though elastic tempo, something which is far from easy in pieces which are forever floating between ' Cédez ' and ' Retournez au Mouvement '.

This question of pedalling, which I have already mentioned, was a special feature of Gieseking's playing and I shall have to refer to it again. Both pedals were a technical asset of the instrument and were always used as such, not as something which one has to use because it happens to be there.

I remember discussing with him the matter of Beethoven's pedalling in several of his Sonatas, a detail which has bothered many pianists at all times. Schnabel faithfully marked them in his editions and equally faithfully obeyed them. Fischer compromised by letting his foot up from time to time to reshuffle the harmonies when they became too blurred. Gieseking, on the other hand, behaved here more or less in the same way as in Debussy. He kept his pedal only half-way down as required, so that although the general effect was one of continuity (and this is obviously what Beethoven had in mind, as he was clearly conscious of the fact that several harmonies together do not mix) yet the vibrations caused by the sustaining pedal were less tenacious and less resounding, in brief, they only half held. I must say that, of all three, this appeared to me as the most sensible way of solving the problem of whether to conform or not to the composer's indications.

He used the soft pedal very generously. In Scarlatti he often kept it on, even in the forte, in order to achieve that brittle sound and to reduce the full-blooded scale of the modern piano. In the Mozart Sonatas we discussed together, as well as in the Partita you have just heard, he used no pedal at all. 'What do you need it for?' was the simple question he asked, a question many pianists could ask themselves and not only in Mozart's Sonatas. Although I did not always like his Mozart as much as Fischer's the slow movement of the Sonata in D Major, K.576 is a very good example of the sheer beauty and purity of tone which was Gieseking's and which was achieved with the greatest economy of means.

I heard him play comparatively few Beethoven Sonatas but those I heard were played superbly. Despite the inner concentration and immense relaxation of his playing he seemed to have little inclination for very slow tempi and sometime showed a tendency to hurry fast ones. The Second Movement of Beethoven's Opus 31, No. 2, however proves me wrong. He takes it at an almost static tempo and the effect is one of absolute peace and perfect stillness. It is not so much played as thought.

On the other hand, the last variation of Op. 109 is rolled out like a magic carpet. It has lyricism, classical beauty, a gracefully moving line, and it also has a lot of pedal, culminating in four whole bars before the return of the theme. It is as you will notice, nevertheless crystal clear, and not a single note is lost.

The only thing Gieseking possibly lacked was that certain heroic quality which has saved many pianists who had precious little else. Perhaps he lacked only the lion's roar. Although his playing was never really emotional, it was extremely sensitive and sincere. This extremely civilized intellectual sensitivity was undoubtedly the best feature he showed in the great romantic works. Mind you, there were many others; for example Schubert's Impromptu in G major,

D.899, No. 3, which is played with a transparent three-dimensional quality. The piece is firmly anchored by the bass, the melody flows freely over the top and the accompaniment ripples away in the middle, almost staccato but with a lot of featherlight pedal. If you have ever thought that this Impromptu is easy try to play it this way. And his performance of Brahms' Intermezzo, Op. 117 No. 2 seems to me to be one of the most wonderful interpretations of Brahms that I have ever heard.

Although Gieseking played a good deal of Chopin, he only played a handful of the Studies. His wife once complained because Walter never played Chopin Studies and she liked them so much. Gieseking shrugged his shoulders and replied: 'I haven't the technique for them'. Absurd though this may seem, it was really true in respect of Studies such as, for example, numbers 12, 22, 23 and 24. All players are entitled to and indeed have technical limitations. It is musical limitations that they should not have. Although Gieseking's technique was marvellous in texture and so abundant in quantity, some of the more turbulent, passionate Studies could be considered unsuited even to his almost limitless means.

It is curious how a man who appeared so casual in many ways could be so scrupulous as to consult, with the utmost care, all early editions and possibly the manuscripts of most of the works he played, studying and comparing them in a deeply serious search for truth. He insisted that the only way to learn a piece was to study the score, reading it in detail, and without a piano, until one knew all there was in it, and had worked out in one's mind how all problems of technique and of interpretation should be solved. Then, and only then could one proceed to try the work out on the piano to see whether the actual effects faithfully reproduced what one's mind had wanted to do. If they didn't, one must see what had gone wrong and start again. There was nothing more pernicious, in his opinion, than to rely upon one faculty alone at the time, be it your hands, your ear or your mind. The order of these factors should, in fact, be reversed: a musician should work out in his mind what he wanted to do and let his ear advise him. As for his hands, they should be sufficiently trained to translate his thoughts and should not be required to make a particular effort every time one had to learn a new piece, although some composers, like Debussy and Schoenberg, for instance, presented for their particular type of writting some special technical problems which, in this case, would be dealt with separately.

I think that Gieseking will long be remembered as the incarnation of supreme craftsmanship. Perhaps one could find a few pianists more inspired, more powerful in their conception, but none who could manage as well as Gieseking to turn absolute craftsmanship into art with a capital A. Although he was a master of effects (he conjured them rather than played them) he never produced effects for their own sake. All his performances had true nobility and great distinction. He wore all his splendid gifts in the same way as Royalties wear their diamonds. Some people did not like Schnabel because they said that he did not play to his audience ; he educated it. I suppose some people did not like Gieseking because he made us all feel somewhat inadequate. At least, this is the way I feel when I listen to his record of Schumann's *Davidbündlertänze*.

Gieseking had, or at least gave the impression of having limitless resources of energy, of health, of mental and physical strength, all carefully maintained on a spiritless, smokeless, strictly vegetarian diet. Except during the short period of his denazification, he gave an enormous number of concerts and travelled thousands of miles each year. He always remained fresh and unperturbed at the end of each day. After Wiesbaden, we met in London quite often when he came to England for concerts or to make recordings, and he always looked as rested and relaxed as he did at home. He was a devoted family man, and often travelled with his wife or one of his two daughters, or with all three. As he always said that the best opportunities for studying were to be found in railway journeys, had it not been for his garden he would have had little need to go home at all.

It was during one of these journeys, about six years ago, that the airport coach in which he was travelling with his wife skidded on the wet road and crashed. Gieseking was injured, his wife was killed. She had never liked travelling but always followed him out of love and devotion. I did not see him again after that accident, but our common friend, his neighbour in Wiesbaden, used to write to me : ' Walter looks unwell and so sad since Gisy died '. He came to London for the last time in October 1956, and whilst recording suddenly collapsed, was rushed to hospital and died. Sudden deaths such as his always have a highly dramatic impact, but they are really the easiest and the best. This gentle giant, who like all giants was felled by a single blow, died whilst still at the height of his career, practically at his work, without fuss or time for tears. Even the difficult task of dying he despatched as easily as he had done everything else. If it is true that when people are about to die they see their whole life flashing before their eyes, I am sure that Gieseking, taking one final look at what he had possessed and achieved in life, must have said : ' It was not bad '.

Text of a lecture delivered at the British Institute of Recorded in 1961 by Marcella Barzetti; reproduced with kind permission of the National Sound Archive

Bach

Brandenburg Concerto No 5 in D BWV 1050

London
Early 1920s

Almgill, Kutcher
London Chamber
Orchestra
Bernard

78: Brunswick 30140-30144

Capriccio in B sopra la lontanezza del suo fratello dilettissimo BWV 992

Saarbrücken
June 1950

LP: DG 2535 823

Chorale "Wohl mir, dass ich Jesum habe" (Cantata BWV 147)

London
1937

78: Columbia (Australia) LO 47
78: Columbia (USA) 17150D
LP: EMI 3C 153 52700-52705M

Chromatic Fantasy and Fugue in D minor BWV 903

Saarbrücken
June 1950

LP: DG 2535 823
CD: Music and Arts CD 612

English Suite No 1 in A BWV 806

Saarbrücken
April and June
1950

Unpublished radio broadcast

English Suite No 2 in A minor BWV 807

Saarbrücken
June 1950

CD: Music and Arts CD 743

English Suite No 3 in G minor BWV 808

Saarbrücken
June 1950

CD: Music and Arts CD 743

English Suite No 4 in F BWV 809

Saarbrücken
June 1950

CD: Music and Arts CD 743

English Suite No 5 in E minor BWV 810

Saarbrücken
April and June
1950

Unpublished radio broadcast

English Suite No 6 in D minor BWV 811

Berlin
January 1945

LP: Discocorp IGI 380

Frankfurt
November 1949

Unpublished radio broadcast

Saarbrücken
April and June
1950

CD: Music and Arts CD 743

Fantasy and Fugue in A minor BWV 944

Saarbrücken
June 1950

LP: DG 2535 823

Fantasy in C minor BWV 906

Saarbrücken
June 1950

LP: DG 2535 823

French Suite No 1 in D minor BWV 812

Saarbrücken
June 1950

Unpublished radio broadcast

French Suite No 2 in C minor BWV 813

Saarbrücken
June 1950

LP: DG 2700 706
CD: Music and Arts CD 743

French Suite No 3 in B minor BWV 814

Saarbrücken
June 1950

Unpublished radio broadcast

French Suite No 4 in E flat BWV 815

Saarbrücken
June 1950

Unpublished radio broadcast

French Suite No 5 in G BWV 816

Saarbrücken
June 1950

CD: Music and Arts CD 743

Gigue (French Suite No 5)

London
1937

78: Columbia (Australia) LO 47
78: Columbia (USA) 17150D
LP: EMI 3C 153 52700-52705M

French Suite No 6 in E BWV 817

Saarbrücken
June 1950

Unpublished radio broadcast

15 Two-part Inventions BWV 772-786

Saarbrücken
March 1950

LP: DG 2535 834/2548 732
CD: Music and Arts CD 743
Music and Arts incorrectly
dated May 1950

15 Three-part Inventions BWV 787-801

Saarbrücken
June 1950

LP: DG 2535 834/2548 732
CD: Music and Arts CD 743
Recording omits No 6 BWV 792

Italian Concerto in F BWV 971

Berlin
1939

78: Columbia (Germany) LW 33-34
LP: Discocorp MLG 70
LP: EMI 3C 153 52700-52705M
CD: Pearl GEMMCD 9011

Frankfurt
March 1947

Unpublished radio broadcast

Saarbrücken
January 1950

LP: DG 2535 823

Berlin
1955

CD: Melodram MEL 18023

Kleine Präludien: C BWV 924; D BWV 925; F BWV 927; F BWV 928; C BWV 933; D minor BWV 935; D BWV 936; E flat BWV 937; E minor BWV 938; C minor BWV 999

Saarbrücken
June 1950

LP: DG 2535 823

Partita No 1 in B flat BWV 825

Vienna
September 1934
(2 Minuets and Gigue)
and Berlin 1939
(Prelude & Sarabande)

78: Columbia (Germany) LWX 336
CD: Pearl GEMMCD 9930
2 Minuets and Gigue only
78: Columbia LX 346
78: Columbia (USA) 68399D/71273D
LP: Rococo 2019
LP: EMI 3C 153 52700-52705M
2 Minuets & Gigue originally
published as fill-up to Beethoven
Piano Concerto No 5 cond. Walter

Frankfurt
November 1949

Unpublished radio broadcast

Saarbrücken
January 1950

LP: DG 2700 706

Munich
December 1950

CD: Hunt CDGI 907

Partita No 2 in C minor BWB 826

Saarbrücken
January 1950

LP: DG 2700 706

Partita No 3 in A minor BWV 827

Saarbrücken
January 1950

LP: DG 2700 706

Partita No 4 in D BWV 828

Saarbrücken
January 1950

LP: DG 2700 706

Partita No 5 in G BWV 829

Saarbrücken
January 1950

LP: DG 2700 706

Partita No 6 in E minor BWV 830

Saarbrücken
January 1950

LP: DG 2700 706

London
September 1951

78: Columbia (USA) X 153
LP: Columbia (USA) ML 4646
LP: EMI 3C 153 52434-52441M

Toccata in C minor BWV 911

Saarbrücken   LP: DG 2700 706
June 1950

Das wohltemperierte Klavier, Books 1 and 2 (complete performance of the 48
Preludes and Fugues BWV 846-BWV 893)

Saarbrücken   LP: DG 2702 701
March and April 1950   CD: DG 429 9292

Beethoven

<u>Bagatelle in E flat op 33 no 1</u>

Berlin
August 1938

78: Columbia LX 783
78: Columbia (Germany) LWX 265
78: Columbia (USA) M 358
78: International Columbia LCX 144
LP: EMI 3C 153 52700-52705M
CD: Pearl GEMMCD 9930
<u>Original 78 issue coupled with</u>
<u>Waldstein Sonata</u>

<u>Bagatelle in A minor "Für Elise"</u>

London
October 1948

78: Columbia LX 1232/LX 8698
78: Columbia (France) LFX 947
78: Columbia (USA) M 959
78: International Columbia LCX 144
LP: EMI 3C 153 52700-52705M
<u>Original 78 issue coupled with</u>
<u>Piano Sonata No 12</u>

Piano Concerto No 1

Berlin April 1937	Staatskapelle Rosbaud	78: Columbia LX 631-634 78: Columbia (Germany) LWX 229-232 78: Columbia (France) LFX 494-497 78: Columbia (USA) M 308 78: Columbia (Italy) GQX 10879-10882 LP: Discocorp RR 411 LP: EMI 3C 153 52700-52704M CD: Classical Collector FDC 2008
London October 1948	Philharmonia Kubelik	78: Columbia LX 1312-1315/ LX 8732-8735 auto 78: Columbia (Germany) LWX 394-397 78: Columbia (France) LFX 983-986 LP: Columbia (USA) ML 4307 LP: Columbia (France) FCX 109 LP: Columbia (Germany) C 91244 LP: EMI 3C 153 52425-52431M <u>As the conductor was an HMV artist, his name did not appear on any of these issues; it was at one stage erroneously thought that the conductor had been Herbert von Karajan</u>
Frankfurt December 1950	Orchestra of Hessischer Rundfunk Zillig	Unpublished radio broadcast

Piano Concerto No 4

Dresden 1939	Dresden Staatskapelle Böhm	78: Columbia LX 847-850/ LX 8462-8465 auto 78: Columbia (Germany) LWX 288-291 78: Columbia (France) LFX 709-712 78: Columbia (USA) M 411 LP: Discocorp RR 415 LP: EMI 3C 153 52700-52705M LP: EMI 1C 137 53500-53504M
London June 1951	Philharmonia Karajan	78: Columbia LX 1443-1446/ LX 8831-8834 auto LP: Columbia 33C 1007 LP: Columbia (USA) ML 4535 LP: Columbia (Germany) C 91244 LP: Odyssey 3216 0371 LP: EMI 3C 153 52425-52431M LP: Toshiba EAC 37001-37019
Cologne September 1953	WDR Orchestra Keilberth	LP: Discocorp IGI 363
London September 1955	Philharmonia Galliera	LP: Columbia (Germany) SMC 91481 Cassette: EMI TCC2-POR 154 5949 CD: EMI CDZ 762 6072 Publication of this version delayed at the request of the pianist's heirs

Piano Concerto No 5 "Emperor"

Vienna September 1934	VPO Walter	78: Columbia LX 342-346 78: Columbia (Germany) LWX 83-87 78: Columbia (France) LFX 359-363 78: Columbia (USA) M 243 LP: Rococo 2019 LP: EMI 3C 153 52700-52705M CD: Toshiba TOCE 8051-8064
Berlin September 1944	Berlin RO Rother	CD: Melodram MEL 18023 CD: Hunt CDHP 588 CD: Music and Arts CD 637 Reichsrundfunk stereo recording Also published by Varèse- Sarabande and other LP editions
London June 1951	Philharmonia Karajan	78: International Columbia LCX 5008-5012 LP: Columbia 33CX 1010 LP: Columbia (France) FCX 135 LP: Columbia (Germany) C 90295 LP: Columbia (USA) ML 4623 LP: Odyssey 3216 0029 LP: EMI 3C 153 52425-52431M LP: EMI 3C 053 01022 LP: Toshiba EAC 37001-37019
London September 1955	Philharmonia Galliera	Cassette: EMI TCC2-POR 154 5949 CD: EMI CDZ 762 6072/CDM 767 796 Publication of this version delayed at the request of the pianist's heirs
New York March 1956	NYPO Cantelli	LP: Cetra LO 521/DOC 54/ SLF 5013 CD: Stradivarius STR 13594

Piano Quintet in E flat op 16

London June 1955	Sutcliffe, Walton, Brain, James	LP: Columbia 33CX 1322 LP: EMI 3C 153 52700-52705M

Piano Sonata No 1 in F minor op 2 no 1

Saarbrücken
1949-1950

Unpublished radio broadcast

London
September 1956

LP: Columbia 33CX 1488
LP: EMI 3C 153 52384-52393

Piano Sonata No 2 in A op 2 no 2

Saarbrücken
1949-1950

Unpublished radio broadcast

London
September 1956

LP: Columbia 33CX 1537
LP: Angel 35654
LP: EMI 3C 153 52384-52393

Piano Sonata No 3 in C op 2 no 3

Saarbrücken
1949-1950

Unpublished radio broadcast

London
September 1956

LP: Columbia 33CX 1537
LP: Angel 35654
LP: EMI 3C 153 52384-52393

Piano Sonata No 4 in E flat op 7

Saarbrücken
1949-1950

Unpublished radio broadcast

London
September 1956

LP: Columbia 33CX 1564
LP: Angel 35655
LP: EMI 3C 153 52384-52393

Piano Sonata No 5 in C minor op 10 no 1

Saarbrücken
1949-1950

Unpublished radio broadcast

London
September 1956

LP: Columbia 33CX 1564
LP: Angel 35655
LP: EMI 3C 153 52384-52393

Piano Sonata No 6 in F op 10 no 3

Saarbrücken
1949-1950

Unpublished radio broadcast

London
September 1956

LP: Columbia 33CX 1564
LP: Angel 35655
LP: EMI 3C 153 52384-52393

Piano Sonata No 7 in D op 10 no 3

Saarbrücken
1949-1950

Unpublished radio broadcast

London
September 1956

LP: Columbia 33CX 1498
LP: Angel 35653
LP: EMI 3C 153 52384-52393

Piano Sonata No 8 in C minor op 13 "Pathétique"

Saarbrücken
1949-1950

Unpublished radio broadcast

Zürich
June 1951

LP: Columbia 33CX 1073
LP: Angel 35025
LP: EMI 3C 053 00823

London
October 1956

LP: Columbia 33CX 1488
LP: EMI SXLP 30129
LP: EMI 3C 153 52384-52393
CD: EMI CDZ 762 8572/CDZ 767 8342
CD: EMI CDU 650 502

Piano Sonata No 9 in E op 14 no 1

Saarbrücken
1949-1950

Unpublished radio broadcast

London
October 1956

LP: Columbia 33CX 1519/SAX 2259
LP: Angel 35652
LP: EMI 3C 153 52384-52393
CD: EMI CDZ 762 8572

Piano Sonata No 10 in G op 14 no 2

Saarbrücken
1949-1950

Unpublished radio broadcast

London
October 1956

LP: Columbia 33CX 1519/SAX 2259
LP: Angel 35652
LP: EMI 3C 153 52384-52393
CD: EMI CDZ 762 8572

Piano Sonata No 11 in B flat op 22

Saarbrücken
1949-1950

Unpublished radio broadcast

London
October 1956

LP: Columbia 33CX 1498
LP: Angel 35653
LP: EMI 3C 153 52384-52393

Piano Sonata No 12 in A flat op 26

London
October 1948

78: Columbia LX 1230-1232/
    LX 8696-8698 auto
78: Columbia (France) LFX 945-947
78: Columbia (USA) M 959
LP: Columbia (USA) ML 4334

Saarbrücken
1949-1950

Unpublished radio broadcast

London
October 1956

LP: Columbia 33CX 1603
LP: EMI 3C 153 52384-52393

Piano Sonata No 13 in E flat op 27 no 1

Saarbrücken
1949-1950

Unpublished radio broadcast

London
October 1956

LP: Columbia 33CX 1519/SAX 2259
LP: Angel 35652
LP: EMI 3C 153 52384-52393

Piano Sonata No 14 in C sharp minor op 27 no 2 "Moonlight"

Saarbrücken
1949-1950

Unpublished radio broadcast

Zürich
June 1951

LP: Columbia 33CX 1073
LP: Angel 35025
LP: EMI 3C 053 00823

London
October 1956

45: Columbia SEL 1583/ESL 6253
LP: Columbia 33CX 1519/SAX 2259
LP: EMI SXLP 30129
LP: EMI 3C 153 52384-52393
CD: EMI CDZ 762 8572/CDZ 767 8342
CD: EMI CDU 650 502

Piano Sonata No 15 in D op 28 "Pastoral"

Saarbrücken
June 1949

LP: Discocorp IGI 380

Zürich
June 1951

Columbia unpublished

London
October 1956

LP: Columbia 33CX 1603
LP: EMI 3C 153 52384-52393
First three movements only
recorded: Gieseking's last
official recording

Piano Sonata No 16 in G op 31 no 1

Saarbrücken
June 1949

LP: Discocorp RR 493
CD: Music and Arts CD 743
Discocorp incorrectly dated

Piano Sonata No 17 in D minor op 31 no 2 "Tempest"

London
March 1931

78: Columbia DX 277-278
78: Columbia (Germany)
DWX 5027-5028
78: Columbia (France) DFX 132-133
78: Columbia (USA) X 39
CD: Pearl GEMMCD 9011

Saarbrücken
1949-1950

Unpublished radio broadcast

London
August 1955

LP: Columbia 33CX 1417
LP: Angel 35352
LP: EMI 3C 153 52384-52393

Berlin
September 1955

CD: Melodram MEL 18023
CD: Hunt CDGI 907

Piano Sonata No 18 in E flat op 18 no 3

Saarbrücken
1949-1950

Unpublished radio broadcast

London
August 1955

LP: Columbia 33CX 1417
LP: Angel 35352
LP: EMI 3C 153 52384-52393

Piano Sonata No 19 in G minor op 49 no 1

Saarbrücken
1949-1950

Unpublished radio broadcast

London
October 1956

LP: Columbia 33CX 1488
LP: Angel 35652
LP: EMI 3C 153 52384-52393

Piano Sonata No 20 in G op 49 no 2

Berlin
1939

78: Columbia (Germany) LW 39
CD: Pearl GEMMCD 9930

Saarbrücken
1949-1950

Unpublished radio broadcast

London
October 1956

LP: Columbia 33CX 1488
LP: Angel 35652
LP: EMI 3C 153 52384-52393

Piano Sonata No 21 in C op 53 "Waldstein"

Berlin
August 1938

78: Columbia LX 781-783/
    LX 8421-8423 auto
78: Columbia (Germany) LWX 263- 265
78: Columbia (USA) M 358

Frankfurt
March 1949

Unpublished radio broadcast

Saarbrücken
1949-1950

Unpublished radio broadcast

Zürich
June 1951

LP: Columbia 33CX 1055
LP: Odyssey 3216 0314
LP: Angel 35024
LP: EMI 3C 153 52384-52393

Piano Sonata No 22 in F op 54

Saarbrücken
1949-1950

Unpublished radio broadcast

Piano Sonata No 23 in F minor op 57 "Appassionata"

New York   78: Columbia (USA) M 365
1939-1940   Also published on Columbia
                                      78s in Argentina

Frankfurt   Unpublished radio broadcast
April 1947

Saarbrücken   Unpublished radio broadcast
1949-1950

Zürich   LP: Columbia 33CX 1055
June 1951   LP: Odyssey 3216 0314
                                      LP: Angel 35024
                                      LP: EMI 3C 053 00823
                                      LP: EMI 3C 153 52384-52393

Piano Sonata No 24 in F sharp op 78

Saarbrücken   LP: Discocorp RR 493
1949   CD: Music and Arts CD 743

Piano Sonata No 25 in G op 79

Saarbrücken   LP: Discocorp RR 493
1949   CD: Music and Arts CD 743

Piano Sonata No 26 in E flat op 81a "Les adieux"

Saarbrücken   LP: Discocorp RR 493
1949   CD: Music and Arts CD 743

Piano Sonata No 27 in E minor op 90

Saarbrücken   CD: Music and Arts CD 743
November 1949

Piano Sonata No 28 in A op 101

London
1937

78: Columbia (USA) X 172
78: Columbia (Australia)
    LOX 527-528
Also published on Columbia 78s
in Argentina and Canada

Saarbrücken
November 1949

CD: Music and Arts CD 743

Piano Sonata No 29 in B flat op 106 "Hammerklavier"

Saarbrücken
1949

LP: Discocorp RR 493
CD: Music and Arts CD 743

Piano Sonata No 30 in E op 109

Berlin
1939

78: Columbia (Germany)
    LWX 347-348
CD: Pearl GEMMCD 9930

Frankfurt
April 1947

Unpublished radio broadcast

Saarbrücken
1949-1950

Unpublished radio broadcast

London
August 1955

LP: Columbia 33CX 1374
LP: Angel 35363
LP: EMI 3C 153 52384-52393

Piano Sonata No 31 in A flat op 110

Saarbrücken
1949-1950

CD: Music and Arts CD 612

London
August 1955

LP: Columbia 33CX 1374
LP: Angel 35363
LP: EMI 3C 153 52384-52393

Piano Sonata No 32 in C minor op 111

Frankfurt
April 1947

LP: Discocorp IGI 272/RR 493
CD: Music and Arts CD 743
Various incorrect dates given

Saarbrücken
1949-1950

Unpublished radio broadcast

Variations for cello and piano on a theme from Handel's Judas Maccabaeus

Frankfurt   Hoelscher, cello   Unpublished radio broadcast
September 1948

Brahms

Piano Concerto No 1

Baden-Baden 1951	Südwestfunk- orchester Rosbaud	LP: Paragon LB 153003 Also published on LP by International Piano Archive

Piano Sonata No 3 in F minor op 5

Frankfurt
September 1948

LP: Melodiya M10 43395-43398

Piano Trio in C minor op 101

Frankfurt   Taschner, Hoelscher   Unpublished radio broadcast
November 1947

Capriccio in F sharp minor op 76 no 1

Zürich
June 1951

LP: Columbia 33CX 1255
LP: EMI 1C 147 01575-01576M
LP: EMI 3C 153 52434-52441M
CD: Toshiba TOCE 8131-8136

Berlin
September 1955

Unpublished radio broadcast

Location uncertain
April 1956

CD: Pearl GEMMCD 9930

Capriccio in B minor op 76 no 2

Zürich
June 1951

LP: Columbia 33CX 1255
LP: EMI 1C 147 01575-01576M
LP: EMI 3C 153 52434-52441M
CD: Toshiba TOCE 8131-8136

Berlin
September 1955

Unpublished radio broadcast

Piano pieces op 76/continued

Intermezzo in A flat op 76 no 3

London
1937

78: Columbia (Australia) LOX 556
78: Columbia (USA) X 201

Frankfurt
March 1949

Unpublished radio broadcast

Zürich
June 1951

LP: Columbia ˉ33CX 1255
LP: EMI 1C 147 01575-01576M
LP: EMI 3C 153 52434-52441M
CD: Toshiba TOCE 8131-8136

Berlin
September 1955

Unpublished radio broadcast

Intermezzo in B flat op 76 no 4

London
1937

78: Columbia (Australia) LOX 556
78: Columbia (USA) X 201

Frankfurt
March 1949

Unpublished radio broadcast

Zürich
June 1951

LP: Columbia 33CX 1255
LP: EMI 1C 147 01575-01576M
LP: EMI 3C 153 52434-52441M
CD: Toshiba TOCE 8131-8136

Berlin
September 1955

Unpublished radio broadcast

Capriccio in C sharp minor op 76 no 5

Zürich
June 1951

LP: Columbia 33CX 1255
LP: EMI 1C 147 01575-01576M
LP: EMI 3C 153 52434-52441M
CD: Toshiba TOCE 8131-8136

Berlin
September 1955

Unpublished radio broadcast

Intermezzo in A op 76 no 6

Zürich
June 1951

LP: Columbia 33CX 1255
LP: EMI 1C 147 01575-01576M
LP: EMI 3C 153 52434-52441M
CD: Toshiba TOCE 8131-8136

Berlin
September 1955

Unpublished radio broadcast

Piano pieces op 76/concluded

Intermezzo in A minor op 76 no 7

Zürich
June 1951

LP: Columbia 33CX 1255
LP: EMI 1C 147 01575-01576M
LP: EMI 3C 153 52434-52441M
CD: Toshiba TOCE 8131-8136

Berlin
September 1955

Unpublished radio broadcast

Capriccio in C op 76 no 8

Frankfurt
March 1949

Unpublished radio broadcast

Zürich
June 1951

LP: Columbia 33CX 1255
LP: EMI 1C 147 01575-01576M
LP: EMI 3C 153 52434-52441M
CD: Toshiba TOCE 8131-8136

Berlin
September 1955

Unpublished radio broadcast

Rhapsody in B minor op 79 no 1

Zürich
June 1951

78: Columbia LX 1561
LP: Columbia 33CX 1256
LP: EMI 1C 147 01575-01576M
LP: EMI 3C 153 52434-52441M
CD: Toshiba TOCE 8131-8136

Rhapsody in C minor op 79 no 2

March
1924

78: Homochord 1-8503
CD: Pearl GEMMCD 9038

Zürich
June 1951

78: Columbia LX 1586
LP: Columbia 33CX 1256
LP: EMI 1C 147 01575-01576M
LP: EMI 3C 153 52434-52441M
CD: Toshiba TOCE 8131-8136

Capriccio in D minor op 116 no 1

Zürich
June 1951

LP: Columbia 33CX 1255
LP: Angel 35028
LP: EMI 1C 147 01575-01576M
LP: EMI 3C 153 52434-52441M
CD: Toshiba TOCE 8131-8136

Intermezzo in A minor op 116 no 2

Zürich
June 1951

LP: Columbia 33CX 1255
LP: Angel 35028
LP: EMI 1C 147 01575-01576M
LP: EMI 3C 153 52434-52441M
CD: Toshiba TOCE 8131-8136

Capriccio in G minor op 116 no 3

Zürich
June 1951

LP: Columbia 33CX 1255
LP: Angel 35028
LP: EMI 1C 147 01575-01576M
LP: EMI 3C 153 52434-52441M
CD: Toshiba TOCE 8131-8136

Intermezzo in E op 116 no 4

London
1937

78: Columbia (Australia) LOX 557
78: Columbia (USA) X 201

Zürich
June 1951

78: Columbia LX 1586
45: Columbia SED 2163
LP: Columbia 33CX 1255
LP: Angel 35028
LP: EMI 1C 147 01575-01576M
LP: EMI 3C 153 52434-52441M
CD: Toshiba TOCE 8131-8136

Intermezzo in E minor op 116 no 5

Zürich
June 1951

LP: Columbia 33CX 1255
LP: Angel 35028
LP: EMI 1C 147 01575-01576M
LP: EMI 3C 153 52434-52441M
CD: Toshiba TOCE 8131-8136

Piano pieces op 116/concluded

Intermezzo in E op 116 no 6

Frankfurt   Unpublished radio broadcast
March 1949

Zürich   LP: Columbia 33CX 1255
June 1951   LP: Angel 35028
                                               LP: EMI 1C 147 01575-01576M
                                               LP: EMI 3C 153 52434-52441M
                                               CD: Toshiba TOCE 8131-8136

Capriccio in D minor op 116 no 7

Zürich   LP: Columbia 33CX 1255
June 1951   LP: Angel 35028
                                               LP: EMI 1C 147 01575-01576M
                                               LP: EMI 3C 153 52434-52441M
                                               CD: Toshiba TOCE 8131-8136

Intermezzo in E flat op 117 no 1

Zürich   Columbia unpublished
June 1951

Intermezzo in B flat minor op 117 no 2

Berlin   78: Columbia (Germany) LWX 337
1939   78: Columbia (France) LFX 899
                                               LP: Melodiya M10 43395-43398
                                               CD: Pearl GEMMCD 9930

Zürich   Columbia unpublished
June 1951

Intermezzo in C sharp minor op 117 no 3

Zürich   Columbia unpublished
June 1951

Intermezzo in A minor op 118 no 1

Zürich
June 1951

LP: Columbia 33CX 1256
LP: Angel 35027
LP: EMI 1C 147 01575-01576M
LP: EMI 3C 153 52434-52441M
CD: Toshiba TOCE 8131-8136

Intermezzo in A op 118 no 2

Zürich
June 1951

LP: Columbia 33CX 1256
LP: Angel 35027
LP: EMI 1C 147 01575-01576M
LP: EMI 3C 153 52434-52441M
CD: Toshiba TOCE 8131-8136

Ballade in G minor op 118 no 3

Zürich
June 1951

LP: Columbia 33CX 1256
LP: Angel 35027
LP: EMI 1C 147 01575-01576M
LP: EMI 3C 153 52434-52441M
CD: Toshiba TOCE 8131-8136

Intermezzo in F minor op 118 no 4

Zürich
June 1951

LP: Columbia 33CX 1256
LP: Angel 35027
LP: EMI 1C 147 01575-01576M
LP: EMI 3C 153 52434-52441M
CD: Toshiba TOCE 8131-8136

Romanze in F op 118 no 5

Berlin
1939

78: Columbia (Germany) LWX 337
78: Columbia (France) LFX 899
LP: Melodiya M10 43395-43398
CD: Pearl GEMMCD 9038

Frankfurt
March 1949

Unpublished radio broadcast

Zürich
June 1951

LP: Columbia 33CX 1256
LP: Angel 35027
LP: EMI 1C 147 01575-01576M
LP: EMI 3C 153 52434-52441M
CD: Toshiba TOCE 8131-8136

Piano pieces op 118/concluded

Intermezzo in E flat minor op 118 no 6

London
1937

78: Columbia (Australia) LOX 556
78: Columbia (USA) X 201

Zürich
June 1951

LP: Columbia 33CX 1256
LP: Angel 35027
LP: EMI 1C 147 01575-01576M
LP: EMI 3C 153 52434-52441M
CD: Toshiba TOCE 8131-8136

Intermezzo in B minor op 119 no 1

Zürich
June 1951

78: Columbia LB 135
LP: Columbia 33CX 1256
LP: Angel 35027
LP: EMI 1C 147 01575-01576M
LP: EMI 3C 153 52434-52441M
CD: Toshiba TOCE 8131-8136

Intermezzo in E minor op 119 no 2

London
1937

78: Columbia (Australia) LOX 557
78: Columbia (USA) X 201

Zürich
June 1951

78: Columbia LX 1581
LP: Columbia 33CX 1256
LP: Angel 35027
LP: EMI 1C 147 01575-01576M
LP: EMI 3C 153 52434-52441M
CD: Toshiba TOCE 8131-8136

Intermezzo in C op 119 no 3

London
1934

78: Columbia LB 31
78: Columbia (Germany) LW 18
78: Columbia (USA) 17079D
78: Columbia (Australia) LO 19

Zürich
June 1951

78: Columbia LB 135
LP: Columbia 33CX 1256
LP: Angel 35027
LP: EMI 1C 147 01575-01576M
LP: EMI 3C 153 52434-52441M
CD: Toshiba TOCE 8131-8136

Rhapsody in E flat op 119 no 4

Zürich
June 1951

78: Columbia LX 1581
LP: Columbia 33CX 1256
LP: Angel 35027
LP: EMI 1C 147 01575-01576M
LP: EMI 3C 153 52434-52441M
CD: Toshiba TOCE 8131-8136

Casella

Partita for piano and orchestra

Frankfurt
June 1950

Orchestra of
Hessischer Rundfunk
Schröder

Unpublished radio broadcast

Sonatina

Frankfurt
October 1947

CD: Pearl GEMMCD 9038

Chopin

Ballade in A flat op 47

Frankfurt
November 1947

CD: Pearl GEMMCD 9038

Barcarolle in F sharp minor op 60

Berlin
August 1938

78: Columbia LX 859
78: Columbia (Germany) LWX 299
78: Columbia (USA) 71026D
CD: Pearl GEMMCD 9930
CD: Classical Collector FDC 2008

London
October 1956

LP: Columbia 33CX 1526
LP: Angel 35501
LP: EMI 3C 153 52434-52441M

Berceuse in D flat op 57

Berlin
August 1938

78: Columbia (Germany) LWX 304
78: Columbia (Italy) GQX 11049
CD: Pearl GEMMCD 9011

London
October 1956

LP: Columbia 33CX 1761
LP: Angel 35488
LP: EMI 3C 153 52434-52441M

Etude in A flat op 25 no 1

March
1925

78: Homochord 1-8614
CD: Pearl GEMMCD 9038

Etude in F minor op 25 no 2

March
1925

78: Homochord 1-8614
CD: Pearl GEMMCD 9038

Mazurka in A minor op 17 no 4

Berlin
August 1938

78: Columbia (Germany) LWX 304
LP: EMI 3C 153 52700-52705M
CD: Pearl GEMMCD 9011

Nocturne in B op 9 no 3

March
1925

78: Homochord 1-8614
CD: Pearl GEMMCD 9038

Nocturne in F sharp op 15 no 2

March
1924

78: Homochord 1-8503
CD: Pearl GEMMCD 9038

Polonaise in A flat op 53

March
1925

78: Homochord 1-8704
CD: Pearl GEMMCD 9038

Prélude in F op 28 no 23

London
1934

78: Columbia LB 31
78: Columbia (Germany) LW 18
78: Columbia (Australia) LO 19
78: Columbia (USA) 17079D
LP: EMI 3C 153 52700-52705M

Valse in D flat op 64 no 1

London
1934

78: Columbia LB 31
78: Columbia (Germany) LW 18
78: Columbia (Australia) LO 19
78: Columbia (USA) 17979D
LP: EMI 3C 153 52700-52705M

Debussy

Arabesque No 1 in E

November
1928

78: Homochord 4-8936
78: Parlophone E 11109
78: Columbia (USA) 17145D
CD: Pearl GEMMCD 9930

London
September 1951

78: Columbia LX 1556
45: Columbia SEL 1548
LP: Columbia 33CX 1149
LP: EMI HQM 1225
LP: EMI 2C 061 01546/3C 053 01024
LP: EMI 3C 153 52331-52440M
LP: EMI F 667.473-667.478M
CD: Toshiba TOCE 6147-6150

Arabesque No 2 in G

November
1928

78: Homochord 4-8936
78: Parlophone E 11109
78: Columbia (USA) 17145D
CD: Pearl GEMMCD 9930

London
September 1951

78: Columbia LX 1556
45: Columbia SEL 1548
LP: Columbia 33CX 1149
LP: EMI HQM 1225
LP: EMI 2C 061 01546/3C 053 01024
LP: EMI 3C 153 52331-52440M
LP: EMI F 667.473-667.478M
CD: Toshiba TOCE 6147-6150

Ballade

London
October 1948

78: Columbia LB 97
45: Columbia SEL 1552
LP: Columbia 33CX 1149
LP: EMI 2C 061 01546/3C 053 01024
LP: EMI 3C 153 52331-52440M
LP: EMI F667.473-667.478M
CD: Toshiba TOCE 6147-6150

Berceuse héroïque

London
August 1953

LP: Columbia 33CX 1149
LP: EMI 2C 061 01546/3C 053 01024
LP: EMI 3C 153 52331-52440M
LP: EMI F667.473-667.478M
CD: Toshiba TOCE 6147-6150

Doctor gradus ad parnassum (Children's Corner)

London
1937

78: Columbia LX 597
78: Columbia (France) LFX 473
78: Columbia (USA) 68962D
78: Columbia (Australia) LOX 333

Frankfurt
March 1949

Unpublished radio broadcast

London
September 1951

78: International Columbia LC 4000
45: Columbia SEL 1540
LP: Columbia 33C 1014
LP: Columbia (USA) ML 4539
LP: Angel 35067
LP: Odyssey 3236 0021
LP: EMI 2C 061 01029/3C 053 01029
LP: EMI 3C 153 52331-52440M
LP: EMI F 667.473-667.478M
LP: EMI RLS 143 6203
CD: Toshiba TOCE 6147-6150

Jimbo's lullaby (Children's Corner)

London
1937

78: Columbia LB 33
78: Columbia (France) LF 155
78: Columbia (USA) 17088D
78: Columbia (Australia) LO 21

Frankfurt
March 1949

Unpublished radio broadcast

London
September 1951

78: International Columbia LC 4001
LP: Columbia 33C 1014
LP: Columbia (USA) ML 4539
LP: Angel 35067
LP: Odyssey 3236 0021
LP: EMI 2C 061 01029/3C 053 01029
LP: EMI 3C 153 52331-52440M
LP: EMI F 667.473-667.478M
LP: EMI RLS 143 6203
CD: Toshiba TOCE 6147-6150

Serenade for the doll (Children's Corner)

London 1937	78: Columbia LB 33 78: Columbia (France) LF 155 78: Columbia (USA) 17088D 78: Columbia (Australia) LO 21
Frankfurt October 1947	Unpublished radio broadcast
London September 1951	78: International Columbia LC 4002 45: Columbia SEL 1540 LP: Columbia 33C 1014 LP: Columbia (USA) ML 4539 LP: Angel 35067 LP: Odyssey 3236 0021 LP: EMI 2C 061 01029/3C 053 01029 LP: EMI 3C 153 52331-52440M LP: EMI F 667.473-667.478M LP: EMI RLS 143 6203 CD: Toshiba TOCE 6147-6150

The snow is dancing (Children's Corner)

London 1937	78: Columbia LX 597 78: Columbia (France) LFX 473 78: Columbia (USA) 68962D 78: Columbia (Australia) LOX 333
Frankfurt March 1949	Unpublished radio broadcast
London September 1951	78: International Columbia LC 4002 LP: Columbia 33C 1014 LP: Columbia (USA) ML 4539 LP: Angel 35067 LP: Odyssey 3236 0021 LP: EMI 2C 061 01029/3C 053 01029 LP: EMI 3C 153 52331-52440M LP: EMI F 667.473-667.478M LP: EMI RLS 143 6203 CD: Toshiba TOCE 6147-6150

The little shepherd (Children's Corner)

, London
1937

78: Columbia LX 597
78: Columbia (France) LFX 473
78: Columbia (USA) 68962D
78: Columbia (Australia) LOX 333

Frankfurt
March 1949

Unpublished radio broadcast

London
September 1951

78: International Columbia LC 4001
LP: Columbia 33C 1014
LP: Columbia (USA) ML 4539
LP: Odyssey 3236 0021
LP: Angel 35067
LP: EMI 2C 061 01029/3C 053 01029
LP: EMI 3C 153 52331-52440M
LP: EMI F 667.473-667.478M
LP: EMI RLS 143 6203
CD: Toshiba TOCE 6147-6150

Golliwog's cake-walk (Children's Corner)

London
1937

78: Columbia LX 597
78: Columbia (France) LFX 473
78: Columbia (USA) 68962D
78: Columbia (Australia) LOX 333

Frankfurt
November 1947

Unpublished radio broadcast

London
September 1951

78: International Columbia LC 4000
45: Columbia SEL 1540
LP: Columbia 33C 1014/33CX 1761
LP: Columbia (USA) ML 4539
LP: Odyssey 3236 0021
LP: Angel 35067/35488
LP: EMI 2C 061 01029/3C 053 01029
LP: EMI 3C 153 52331-52440M
LP: EMI F 667.473-667.478M
LP: EMI RLS 143 6203
CD: Toshiba TOCE 6147-6150

Danse (Tarantelle styrienne)

Frankfurt
November 1947

Unpublished radio broadcast

London
October 1948

78: Columbia LX 1146
78: Columbia (France) LFX 869
45: Columbia SCB 105
LP: Columbia 33CX 1149
LP: EMI 2C 061 01546/3C 053 01024
LP: EMI 3C 153 52331-52440M
LP: EMI F 667.473-667.478M
LP: EMI RLS 143 6203
CD: Toshiba TOCE 6147-6150

Danse bohémienne

London
August 1953

LP: Columbia 33CX 1149
LP: EMI 2C 061 01546/3C 053 01024
LP: EMI 3C 153 52331-52440M
LP: EMI F 667.473-667.478M
CD: Toshiba TOCE 6147-6150

Pagodes (Estampes)

Berlin
August 1938

78: Columbia LX 830
78: Columbia (USA) 69841D
78: Columbia (Australia) LOX 451

London
August 1953

LP: Columbia 33CX 1137
LP: EMI 2C 061 00413/3C 053 01025
LP: EMI 3C 153 52331-52440M
LP: EMI F 667.473-667.478M
LP: EMI RLS 752
CD: Toshiba TOCE 6147-6150

Soirée dans Grenade (Estampes)

London
1934

78: Columbia LX 480
78: Columbia (France) LFX 423
78: Columbia (USA) M 314
78: Columbia (Australia) LOX 280

Munich
December 1950

CD: Hunt CDGI 907

London
August 1953

LP: Columbia 33CX 1137
LP: EMI 2C 061 00413/3C 053 01025
LP: EMI 3C 153 52331-52440M
LP: EMI F 667.473-667.478M
LP: EMI RLS 752
CD: Toshiba TOCE 6147-6150

Jardins sous la pluie (Estampes)

Berlin
1939

78: Columbia LB 52
78: Columbia (France) LF 163
78: Columbia (USA) M 352
78: International Columbia LC 29

London
August 1953

LP: Columbia 33CX 1137/33CX 1761
LP: Angel 35488
LP: EMI 2C 061 00413/3C 053 01025
LP: EMI 3C 153 52331-52440M
LP: EMI F 667/473-667.478M
LP: EMI RLS 752
CD: Toshiba TOCE 6147-6150

12 Etudes, Books 1 and 2

London
December 1954

LP: Columbia 33CX 1261
LP: Columbia (Germany) C 90431
LP: Angel 35250
LP: EMI 2C 061 01028/3C 053 01028
LP: EMI 3C 153 52331-52440M
LP: EMI F 667.473-667.478M
CD: Toshiba TOCE 6147-6150

Fantaisie pour piano et orchestre

Amsterdam
October 1938

Concertgebouw
Orchestra
Mengelberg

CD: Music and Arts CD 780

Frankfurt
October 1951

Orchestra of
Hessischer Rundfunk
Schröder

Unpublished radio broadcast

Paris
July 1955

Orchestre National
Cluytens

LP: International Piano Archive
IPA 505

Hommage à Haydn

London
August 1953

LP: Columbia 33CX 1149
LP: EMI 2C 061 01546/3C 053 01024
LP: EMI 3C 153 52331-52440M
LP: EMI F 667.473-667.478M
CD: Toshiba TOCE 6147-6150

Reflets dans l'eau (Images, Book 1)

London
1934

78: Columbia LX 480
78: Columbia (France) LFX 423
78: Columbia (USA) M 314
78: Columbia (Australia) LOX 280

Zürich
August 1944

CD: Music and Arts CD 612

London
October 1948

78: Columbia LX 1395/LX 8797
45: Columbia SEL 1527
LP: Columbia 33CX 1137
LP: Columbia (USA) ML 2188
LP: EMI 2C 061 00413/3C 053 01025
LP: EMI 3C 153 52331-52440M
LP: EMI F 667.473-667.478M
LP: EMI RLS 752
CD: Toshiba TOCE 6147-6150

Images, Book 1/concluded

Hommage à Rameau (Images, Book 1)

London
October 1948

78: Columbia LX 1395-1396/
    LX 8798-8799 auto
LP: Columbia 33CX 1137
LP: Columbia (USA) ML 2188
LP: EMI 2C 061 00413/3C 053 01025
LP: EMI 3C 153 52331-52440M
LP: EMI F 667.473-667.478M
LP: EMI RLS 752
CD: Toshiba TOCE 6147-6150

Mouvement (Images, Book 1)

Berlin
1939

78: Columbia LB 56
78: Columbia (USA) 17218D
78: Columbia (Australia) LO 41

London
October 1948

78: Columbia LX 1396/LX 8799
LP: Columbia 33CX 1137
LP: Columbia (USA) ML 2188
LP: EMI 2C 061 00413/3C 053 01025
LP: EMI 3C 153 52331-52440M
LP: EMI F 667.473-667.478M
LP: EMI RLS 752
CD: Toshiba TOCE 6147-6150

Cloches à travers les feuilles (Images, Book 2)

Berlin
1939

78: Columbia LB 56
78: Columbia (USA) 17218D
78: Columbia (Australia) LO 41

London
October 1948

78: Columbia 1396/LX 8799
LP: Columbia 33CX 1137
LP: Columbia (USA) ML 2188
LP: EMI 2C 061 00413/3C 053 0102
LP: EMI 3C 153 52331-52440M
LP: EMI F 667.473-667.478M
LP: EMI RLS 752
CD: Toshiba TOCE 6147-6150

Et la lune descend sur la temple qui fut (Images, Book 2)

London
October 1948

78: Columbia LX 1397/LX 8798
LP: Columbia 33CX 1137
LP: Columbia (USA) ML 2188
LP: EMI 2C 061 00413/3C 053 01025
LP: EMI 3C 153 52331-52440M
LP: EMI F 667/473-667/478M
LP: EMI RLS 752
CD: Toshiba TOCE 6147-6150

Poissons d'or (Images, Book 2)

London
1937

78: Columbia LX 623
78: Columbia (USA) 69020D
78: Columbia (Australia) LOX 354

London
October 1948

78: Columbia LX 1397/LX 8797
LP: Columbia 33CX 1137
LP: Columbia (USA) ML 2188
LP: EMI 2C 061 00413/3C 053 01025
LP: EMI 3C 153 52331-52440M
LP: EMI F 667.473-667.478M
LP: EMI RLS 752
CD: Toshiba TOCE 6147-6150

L'isle joyeuse

Berlin
August 1938

78: Columbia LX 830
78: Columbia (USA) 69841D
78: Columbia (Australia) LOX 451

London
August 1953

78: Columbia LX 1618
LP: Columbia 33CX 1149
LP: EMI HQM 1225
LP: EMI 2C 061 01546/3C 053 01024
LP: EMI 3C 153 52331-52440M
LP: EMI F 667.473-667.478M
LP: EMI RLS 143 6203
CD: Toshiba TOCE 6147-6150

Masques

London
August 1953

78: Columbia LX 1618
LP: Columbia 33CX 1149
LP: EMI HQM 1225
LP: EMI 2C 061 01546/3C 053 01024
LP: EMI 3C 153 52331-52440M
LP: EMI F 667.473-667.478M
CD: Toshiba TOCE 6147-6150

Mazurka

London
August 1953

45: Columbia SEL 1552
LP: Columbia 33CX 1149
LP: EMI 2C 061 01546/3C 053 01024
LP: EMI 3C 153 52331-52440M
LP: EMI F 667.473-667.478M
CD: Toshiba TOCE 6147-6150

Nocturne in D flat

London
October 1948

78: Columbia LB 105
78: Columbia (France) LF 277
LP: Columbia 33CX 1149
LP: EMI 2C 061 01546/3C 053 01024
LP: EMI 3C 153 52331-52440M
LP: EMI F 667/473-667.478M
CD: Toshiba TOCE 6147-6150

Le petit nègre

London
August 1953

45: Columbia SEL 1548
LP: Columbia 33CX 1149
LP: EMI 2C 061 01546/3C 053 01024
LP: EMI 3C 153 52331-52440M
LP: EMI F 667.473-667.478M
LP: EMI RLS 143 6203
CD: Toshiba TOCE 6147-6150

La plus que lente

London
October 1948

78: Columbia LX 1146
78: Columbia (France) LFX 869
45: Columbia SEL 1552/SCB 105
LP: Columbia 33CX 1149
LP: EMI 2C 061 01546/3C 053 01024
LP: EMI 3C 153 52331-52440M
LP: EMI F 667.473-667.478M
LP: EMI RLS 143 6203
CD: Toshiba TOCE 6147-6150

Frankfurt
March 1949

Unpublished radio broadcast

Pour le piano (Prélude; Sarabande; Toccata)

Saarbrücken
November 1949

Unpublished radio broadcast

London
September 1951

Columbia unpublished

London
August 1953

LP: Columbia 33CX 1137
LP: Angel 35065
LP: EMI 2C 061 00413/3C 053 01025
LP: EMI 3C 153 52331-52440M
LP: EMI F 667.473-667.478M
CD: Toshiba TOCE 6147-6150

Danseuses de Delphe (Préludes, Book 1)

Berlin
August 1938

78: Columbia LB 47
78: Columbia (Germany) LW 25
78: Columbia (France) LF 158
78: International Columbia LC 24
78: Columbia (USA) M 352

Berlin
May 1950

CD: Hunt CDGI 907

London
September 1951

LP: Columbia (USA) ML 4537
LP: Odyssey 3236 0021

London
August 1953

LP: Columbia 33CX 1098
LP: EMI 2C 061 00412/3C 053 01026
LP: EMI 3C 153 52331-52440M
LP: EMI F 667.473-667.478M
LP: EMI RLS 752
CD: EMI CDH 761 0042
CD: Toshiba TOCE 6147-6150

Voiles (Préludes, Book 1)

Berlin
August 1938

78: Columbia LB 47
78: Columbia (Germany) LW 25
78: Columbia (France) LF 158
78: International Columbia LC 24
78: Columbia (USA) M 352

Berlin
May 1950

CD: Hunt CDGI 907

London
September 1951

LP: Columbia (USA) ML 4537
LP: Odyssey 3236 0021

London
August 1953

LP: Columbia 33CX 1098
LP: EMI 2C 061 00412/3C 053 01026
LP: EMI 3C 153 52331-52440M
LP: EMI F 667.473-667.478M
LP: EMI RLS 752
CD: EMI CDH 761 0042
CD: Toshiba TOCE 6147-6150

Le vent dans la plaine (Préludes, Book 1)

Berlin
August 1938

78: Columbia LB 48
78: Columbia (Germany) LW 26
78: Columbia (France) LF 159
78: International Columbia LC 25
78: Columbia (USA) M 352

London
September 1951

LP: Columbia (USA) ML 4537
LP: Odyssey 3236 0021

London
August 1953

LP: Columbia 33CX 1098
LP: EMI 2C 061 00412/3C 053 01026
LP: EMI 3C 153 52331-52440M
LP: EMI F 667.473-667.478M
LP: EMI RLS 752
CD: EMI CDH 761 0042
CD: Toshiba TOCE 6147-6150

Les sons et les parfums (Préludes, Book 1)

Berlin
August 1938

78: Columbia LB 48
78: Columbia (Germany) LW 26
78: Columbia (France) LF 159
78: International Columbia LC 25
78: Columbia (USA) M 352

London
September 1951

LP: Columbia (USA) ML 4537
LP: Odyssey 3236 0021

London
August 1953

LP: Columbia 33CX 1098
LP: EMI 2C 061 00412/3C 053 01026
LP: EMI 3C 153 52331-52440M
LP: EMI F 667.473-667.478M
LP: EMI RLS 752
CD: EMI CDH 761 0042
CD: Toshiba TOCE 6147-6150

Les collines d'Anacapri (Préludes, Book 1)

Berlin
August 1938

78: Columbia LB 49
78: Columbia (Germany) LW 27
78: Columbia (France) LF 160
78: International Columbia LC 26
78: Columbia (USA) M 352

Berlin
May 1950

CD: Hunt CDGI 907

London
September 1951

LP: Columbia (USA) ML 4537
LP: Odyssey 3236 0021

London
August 1953

LP: Columbia 33CX 1098
LP: EMI 2C 061 00412/3C 053 01026
LP: EMI 3C 153 52331-52440M
LP: EMI F 667.473-667.478M
LP: EMI RLS 752
CD: EMI CDH 761 0042
CD: Toshiba TOCE 6147-6150

Des pas sur la neige (Préludes, Book 1)

Berlin
August 1938

78: Columbia LB 49
78: Columbia (Germany) LW 27
78: Columbia (France) LF 160
78: International Columbia LC 26
78: Columbia (USA) M 352

Berlin
May 1950

CD: Hunt CDGI 907

London
September 1951

LP: Columbia 33CX 1098
LP: Columbia (USA) ML 4537
LP: Odyssey 3236 0021

London
August 1953

LP: Columbia 33CX 1098
LP: EMI 2C 061 00412/3C 053 01026
LP: EMI 3C 153 52331-52440M
LP: EMI F 667.473-667.478M
LP: EMI RLS 752
CD: EMI CDH 761 0042
CD: Toshiba TOCE 6147-6150

Préludes, Book 1/continued

Ce qu'a vu le vent d'ouest (Préludes, Book 1)

Berlin August 1938	78: Columbia LB 50 78: Columbia (Germany) LW 28 78: Columbia (France) LF 161 78: International Columbia LC 27 78: Columbia (USA) M 352
London September 1951	LP: Columbia (USA) ML 4537 LP: Odyssey 3236 0021
London August 1953	LP: Columbia 33CX 1098 LP: EMI 2C 061 00412/3C 053 01026 LP: EMI 3C 153 52331-52440M LP: EMI F 667.473-667.478M LP: EMI RLS 752 CD: EMI CDH 761 0042 CD: Toshiba TOCE 6147-6150

La fille aux cheveux de lin (Préludes, Book 1)

Berlin August 1938	78: Columbia LB 50 78: Columbia (Germany) LW 28 78: Columbia (France) LF 161 78: Columbia (USA) M 352 78: International Columbia LC 27
Frankfurt November 1947	Unpublished radio broadcast
Berlin May 1950	CD: Hunt CDGI 907
London September 1951	LP: Columbia (USA) ML 4537 LP: Odyssey 3236 0021
London August 1953	45: Columbia SEL 1527 LP: Columbia 33CX 1098/33CX 1761 LP: Angel 35488 LP: EMI 2C 061 00412/3C 053 01026 LP: EMI 3C 153 52331-52440M LP: EMI F 667.473-667.478M LP: EMI RLS 752 CD: EMI CDH 761 0042 CD: Toshiba TOCE 6147-6150

Préludes, Book 1/continued

La sérénade interrompue (Préludes, Book 1)

Berlin
August 1938

78: Columbia LB 51
78: Columbia (Germany) LW 29
78: Columbia (France) LF 162
78: Columbia (USA) M 352
78: International Columbia LC 28

London
September 1951

LP: Columbia (USA) ML 4537
LP: Odyssey 3236 0021

London
August 1953

LP: Columbia 33CX 1098
LP: EMI 2C 061 00412/3C 053 01026
LP: EMI 3C 153 52331-52440M
LP: EMI F 667.473-667.478M
LP: EMI RLS 752
CD: EMI CDH 761 0042
CD: Toshiba TOCE 6147-6150

La cathédrale engloutie (Préludes, Book 1)

London
1934

78: Columbia LB 30
78: Columbia (Germany) LW 30
78: Columbia (USA) M 352
Note that this Prélude was
recorded out of sequence and in
a different location from the
remainder of the Book 1 set for
this pre-war edition

Frankfurt
March 1949

Unpublished radio broadcast

Berlin
May 1950

CD: Hunt CDGI 907

London
September 1951

LP: Columbia (USA) ML 4537
LP: Odyssey 3236 0021

London
August 1953

45: Columbia SEL 1527
LP: Columbia 33CX 1098
LP: EMI 2C 061 00412/3C 053 01026
LP: EMI 3C 153 52331-52440M
LP: EMI F 667.473-667.478M
LP: EMI RLS 752
CD: EMI CDH 761 0042
CD: Toshiba TOCE 6147-6150

Préludes, Book 1/continued

La danse de Puck (Préludes, Book 1)

Berlin
August 1938

78: Columbia LB 51
78: Columbia (Germany) LW 29
78: Columbia (France) LF 162
78: Columbia (USA) M 352
78: International Columbia LC 28

Berlin
May 1950

CD: Hunt CDGI 907

London
September 1951

LP: Columbia (USA) ML 4537
LP: Odyssey 3236 0021

London
August 1953

LP: Columbia 33CX 1098
LP: EMI 2C 061 00412/3C 053 01026
LP: EMI 3C 153 52331-52440M
LP: EMI F 667.473-667.478M
LP: EMI RLS 752
CD: EMI CDH 761 0042
CD: Toshiba TOCE 6147-6150

Minstrels (Préludes, Book 1)

Berlin
August 1938

78: Columbia LB 52
78: Columbia (Germany) LW 31
78: Columbia (France) LF 163
78: Columbia (USA) M 352
78: International Columbia LC 29

Saarbrücken
November 1949

Unpublished radio broadcast

Berlin
May 1950

CD: Hunt CDGI 907

London
September 1951

LP: Columbia (USA) ML 4537
LP: Odyssey 3236 0021

London
August 1953

LP: Columbia 33CX 1098
LP: EMI 2C 061 00412/3C 065 01026
LP: EMI 3C 153 52331-52440M
LP: EMI F 667.473-667.478M
LP: EMI RLS 752
CD: EMI CDH 761 0042
CD: Toshiba TOCE 6147-6150

Brouillards (Préludes, Book 2)

New York
1939-1940

78: Columbia (Switzerland) LZ 3
78: Columbia (USA) M 382

Berlin
May 1950

CD: Hunt CDGI 907

London
September 1951

78: International Columbia LC 4011

London
December 1954

LP: Columbia 33CX 1304
LP: Columbia (USA) ML 4538
LP: Angel 35249
LP: Columbia (Germany) C 90467
LP: Odyssey 3236 0021
LP: EMI 2C 061 00815/3C 053 01027
LP: EMI 3C 153 52331-52440M
LP: EMI F 667.473-667.478M
LP: EMI RLS 752
CD: EMI CDH 761 0042
CD: Toshiba TOCE 6147-6150

Feuilles mortes (Préludes, Book 2)

New York
1939-1940

78: Columbia (Switzerland) LZ 3
78: Columbia (USA) M 382

Frankfurt
March 1947

Unpublished radio broadcast

Berlin
May 1950

CD: Hunt CDGI 907

London
September 1951

78: International Columbia LC 4011

London
December 1954

LP: Columbia 33CX 1304
LP: Columbia (USA) ML 4538
LP: Angel 35249
LP: Columbia (Germany) C 90467
LP: Odyssey 3236 0021
LP: EMI 2C 061 00815/3C 053 01027
LP: EMI 3C 153 52331-52440M
LP: EMI F 667.473-667.478M
LP: EMI RLS 752
CD: EMI CDH 761 0042
CD: Toshiba TOCE 6147-6150

Préludes, Book 2/continued

La puerta del vino (Préludes, Book 2)

New York   78: Columbia (Switzerland) LZ 4
1939-1940   78: Columbia (USA) M 382

Frankfurt   Unpublished radio broadcast
March 1947

Berlin   CD: Hunt CDGI 907
May 1950

London   78: International Columbia LC 4012
September 1951

London   LP: Columbia 33CX 1304
December 1954   LP: Columbia (USA) ML 4538
            LP: Columbia (Germany) C 90467
            LP: Angel 35249
            LP: Odyssey 3236 0021
            LP: EMI 2C 061 00815/3C 053 01027
            LP: EMI 3C 153 52331-52440M
            LP: EMI F 667.473-667.478M
            LP: EMI RLS 752
            CD: EMI CDH 761 0042
            CD: Toshiba TOCE 6147-6150

Les fées sont d'exquises danseuses (Préludes, Book 2)

New York   78: Columbia (Switzerland) LZ 4
1939-1940   78: Columbia (USA) M 382

London   78: International Columbia LC 4012
September 1951

London   LP: Columbia 33CX 1304
December 1954   LP: Columbia (USA) ML 4538
            LP: Columbia (Germany) C 90467
            LP: Angel 35249
            LP: Odyssey 3236 0021
            LP: EMI 2C 061 00815/3C 053 01027
            LP: EMI 3C 153 52331-52440M
            LP: EMI F 667.473-667.478M
            LP: EMI RLS 752
            CD: EMI CDH 761 0042
            CD: Toshiba TOCE 6147-6150

Bruyères (Préludes, Book 2)

New York
1939-1940

78: Columbia (Switzerland) LZ 5
78: Columbia (USA) M 382

Frankfurt
March 1949

Unpublished radio broadcast

Berlin
May 1950

CD: Hunt CDGI 907

London
September 1951

78: International Columbia LC 4013

London
December 1954

LP: Columbia 33CX 1304
LP: Columbia (USA) ML 4538
LP: Columbia (Germany) C 90467
LP: Angel 35249
LP: Odyssey 3236 0021
LP: EMI 2C 061 00815/3C 053 01027
LP: EMI 3C 153 52331-52440M
LP: EMI F 667.473-667.478M
LP: EMI RLS 752
CD: EMI CDH 761 0042
CD: Toshiba TOCE 6147-6150

Général Lavine eccentric (Préludes, Book 2)

New York
1939-1940

78: Columbia (Switzerland) LZ 5
78: Columbia (USA) M 382

Frankfurt
March 1949

Unpublished radio broadcast

Berlin
May 1950

CD: Hunt CDGI 907

London
September 1951

78: International Columbia LC 4013

London
December 1954

LP: Columbia 33CX 1304
LP: Columbia (USA) ML 4538
LP: Columbia (Germany) C 90467
LP: Angel 35249
LP: Odyssey 3236 0021
LP: EMI 2C 061 00815/3C 053 01027
LP: EMI 3C 153 52331-52440M
LP: EMI F 667.473-667.478M
LP: EMI RLS 752
CD: EMI CDH 761 0042
CD: Toshiba TOCE 6147-6150

Préludes, Book 2/continued

La terrasse des audiences (Préludes, Book 2)

New York
1939-1940

78: Columbia (Switzerland) LZ 6
78: Columbia (USA) M 382

Frankfurt
March 1947

Unpublished radio broadcast

London
September 1951

78: International Columbia LC 4014

London
December 1954

LP: Columbia 33CX 1304
LP: Columbia (USA) ML 4538
LP: Columbia (Germany) C 90467
LP: Angel 35249
LP: Odyssey 3236 0021
LP: EMI 2C 061 00815/3C 053 01027
LP: EMI 3C 153 52331-52440M
LP: EMI F 667.473-667.478M
LP: EMI RLS 752
CD: EMI CDH 761 0042
CD: Toshiba TOCE 6147-6150

Ondine (Préludes, Book 2)

New York
1939-1940

78: Columbia (Switzerland) LZ 6
78: Columbia (USA) M 382

Berlin
May 1950

CD: Hunt CDGI 907

London
September 1951

78: International Columbia LC 4014

London
December 1954

LP: Columbia 33CX 1304
LP: Columbia (USA) ML 4538
LP: Columbia (Germany) C 90467
LP: Angel 35249
LP: Odyssey 3236 0021
LP: EMI 2C 061 00815/3C 053 01027
LP: EMI 3C 153 52331-52440M
LP: EMI F 667.473-667.478M
LP: EMI RLS 752
CD: EMI CDH 761 0042
CD: Toshiba TOCE 6147-6150

Préludes, Book 2/continued

Hommage à S. Pickwick Esq. (Préludes, Book 2)

New York
1939-1940

78: Columbia (Switzerland) LZ 7
78: Columbia (USA) M 382

London
September 1951

78: International Columbia LC 4015

London
December 1954

LP: Columbia 33CX 1304
LP: Columbia (USA) ML 4538
LP: Columbia (Germany) C 90467
LP: Angel 35249
LP: Odyssey 3236 0021
LP: EMI 2C 061 00815/3C 053 01027
LP: EMI 3C 153 52331-52440M
LP: EMI F 667.473-667.478M
LP: EMI RLS 752
CD: EMI CDH 761 0042
CD: Toshiba TOCE 6147-6150

Canope (Préludes, Book 2)

New York
1939-1940

78: Columbia (Switzerland) LZ 7
78: Columbia (USA) M 382

London
September 1951

78: International Columbia LC 4015

London
December 1954

LP: Columbia 33CX 1304
LP: Columbia (USA) ML 4538
LP: Columbia (Germany) C 90467
LP: Angel 35249
LP: Odyssey 3236 0021
LP: EMI 2C 061 00815/3C 053 01027
LP: EMI 3C 153 52331-52440M
LP: EMI F 667.473-667.478M
LP: EMI RLS 752
CD: EMI CDH 761 0042
CD: Toshiba TOCE 6147-6150

Les tierres alternées (Préludes, Book 2)

New York
1939-1940

78: Columbia (Switzerland) LZ 8
78: Columbia (USA) M 382

London
September 1951

78: International Columbia LC 4016

London
December 1954

LP: Columbia 33CX 1304
LP: Columbia (USA) ML 4538
LP: Columbia (Germany) C 90467
LP: Angel 35249
LP: Odyssey 3236 0021
LP: EMI 2C 061 00815/3C 053 01027
LP: EMI 3C 153 52331-52440M
LP: EMI F 667.473-667.478M
LP: EMI RLS 752
CD: EMI CDH 761 0042
CD: Toshiba TOCE 6147-6150

Préludes, Book 2/concluded

Feux d'artifice (Préludes, Book 2)

New York
1939-1940

78: Columbia (Switzerland) LZ 8
78: Columbia (USA) M 382

Frankfurt
March 1947

Unpublished radio broadcast

Berlin
May 1950

CD: Hunt CDGI 907

London
September 1951

78: International Columbia LC 4016

London
December 1954

LP: Columbia 33CX 1304
LP: Columbia (USA) ML 4538
LP: Columbia (Germany) C 90467
LP: Angel 35249
LP: Odyssey 3236 0021
LP: EMI 2C 061 00815/3C 053 01027
LP: EMI 3C 153 52331-52440M
LP: EMI F 667.473-667.478M
LP: EMI RLS 752
CD: EMI CDH 761 0042
CD: Toshiba TOCE 6147-6150

4 Préludes, unspecified

Frankfurt
March 1949

Unpublished radio broadcast

Rêverie

London
October 1948

78: Columbia LB 60
78: Columbia (USA) 17138D

London
August 1953

78: Columbia LX 1598
45: Columbia SCB 114
LP: Columbia 33CX 1149
LP: EMI 2C 061 01546/3C 053 01024
LP: EMI 3C 153 52331-52440M
LP: EMI F 667.473-667.478M
CD: Toshiba TOCE 6147-6150

Prélude (Suite bergamasque)

London
September 1951

78: Columbia LX 8898
78: Columbia (France) LFX 1025
78: International Columbia LCX 5002
LP: Columbia (USA) ML 4539
LP: Odyssey 3236 0021
LP: Angel 35067/60210
LP: EMI HQM 1225
LP: EMI 2C 061 01029/3C 053 01029
LP: EMI 3C 153 52331-52440M
LP: EMI F 667.473-667.478M
CD: Toshiba TOCE 6147-6150

Menuet (Suite bergamasque)

London
September 1951

78: Columbia LX 8899
78: Columbia (France) LFX 1025
78: International Columbia LCX 5002
LP: Columbia (USA) ML 4539
LP: Odyssey 3236 0021
LP: Angel 35067/60210
LP: EMI HQM 1225
LP: EMI 2C 061 01029/3C 053 01029
LP: EMI 3C 153 52331-52440M
LP: EMI F 667.473-667.478M
CD: Toshiba TOCE 6147-6150

Clair de lune (Suite bergamasque)

London
September 1951

78: Columbia LX 8899
78: Columbia (France) LFX 1026
78: Columbia (Denmark) LDX 13
78: International Columbia LCX 5002
45: Columbia SEL 1540
LP: Columbia 33CX 1761
LP: Columbia (USA) ML 4539
LP: Odyssey 3236 0021
LP: Angel 35067/35488/60210
LP: EMI HQM 1225
LP: EMI 2C 061 01029/3C 053 01029
LP: EMI 3C 153 52331-52440M
LP: EMI F 667.473-667.478M
CD: Toshiba TOCE 6147-6150

Suite bergamasque/concluded

Passepied (Suite bergamasque)

London
September 1951

78: Columbia LX 8898
78: Columbia (France) LFX 1026
78: International Columbia LCX 5002
LP: Columbia (USA) ML 4539
LP: Odyssey 3236 0021
LP: Angel 35067/60210
LP: EMI HQM 1225
LP: EMI 2C 061 01029/3C 053 01029
LP: EMI 3C 153 52331-52440M
LP: EMI F 667.473-667.478M
CD: Toshiba TOCE 6147-6150

Valse romantique

London
August 1953

78: Columbia LX 1598
45: Columbia SCB 114
LP: Columbia 33CX 1149
LP: EMI 2C 061 01546/3C 053 01024
LP: EMI 3C 153 52331-52440M
LP: F 667.473-667.478M
CD: Toshiba TOCE 6147-6150

Falla

Noches en los jardines de Espana

Frankfurt December 1951	Orchestra of Hessischer Rundfunk Schröder	CD: Pearl GEMMCD 9011

Fauré

Barcarolle No 4 in A flat

London September 1951	Columbia unpublished

Nocturne No 4 in E flat

Frankfurt March 1949	CD: Pearl GEMMCD 9930

Fortner

Cello Sonata

Frankfurt September 1948	Hoelscher	Unpublished radio broadcast

Franck

Variations symphoniques

London March and November 1931	LPO Wood	78: Columbia LX 192-193 78: Columbia (France) LFX 311-312 78: Columbia (USA) X 210 LP: EMI 3C 053 01609 LP: EMI 3C 153 52700-52705M LP: Melodiya M10 43701-43702 CD: Classical Collector FDC 2008
Amsterdam October 1940	Concertgebouw Orchestra Mengelberg	LP: Discocorp MLG 70 CD: Seven Seas (Japan) KICC 2061
Frankfurt June 1950	Orchestra of Hessischer Rundfunk Schröder	Unpublished radio broadcast
London June 1951	Philharmonia Karajan	78: Columbia LX 8937-8938 78: International Columbia LCX 5000-5001 LP: Columbia (USA) ML 4536 LP: EMI 1C 047 01363 LP: Toshiba EAC 37001-37019
Paris July 1955	Orchestre National Cluytens	CD: Hunt CDHP 588

Gieseking

Kinderlieder

London April 1955	Schwarzkopf	CD: EMI CDM 763 6553/ CHS 763 7902

Sonatina for cello and piano

Frankfurt September 1948	Hoelscher	Unpublished radio broadcast

Sonatina for flute and piano

Berlin 1937	Scheck	Columbia unpublished

Grieg

Piano Concerto

Berlin April 1937	Staatskapelle Rosbaud	78: Columbia LX 647-650 78: Columbia (Germany) LWX 210-213 78: Columbia (France) LFX 498-500 78: Columbia (USA) M 313
Berlin ca. 1944	BPO Conductor unknown	LP: Melodiya 36605-36606 LP: Everest SDBR 8434 LP: Discocorp IGI 348 CD: Melodiya (Japan) MEL 711 <u>Conductor incorrectly named</u> <u>on all issues as Wilhelm</u> <u>Furtwängler</u>
London June 1951	Philharmonia Karajan	78: Columbia LX 1503-1506/ LX 8888-8891 auto LP: Columbia 33C 1003 LP: Columbia (USA) ML 4431 LP: EMI 1C 047 01363M LP: EMI 3C 153 52425-52431M LP: Toshiba EAC 37001-37019
Frankfurt October 1951	Orchestra of Hessischer Rundfunk Schröder	Unpublished radio broadcast

Norwegian Bridal Procession (Sketches of Norwegian Life)

London October 1948		78: Columbia LB 75 78: Columbia (France) LF 268

Waltz op 12 no 2 (Lyric Pieces)

London
September 1956

LP: Columbia 33CX 1467
LP: Angel 35450
LP: EMI 3C 053 01309
LP: EMI 3C 153 52331-52440M
CD: Toshiba TOCE 8131-8136

Albumblatt op 12 no 7 (Lyric Pieces)

London
September 1956

LP: Columbia 33CX 1467
LP: Angel 35450
LP: EMI 3C 053 01309
LP: EMI 3C 153 52331-52440M
CD: Toshiba TOCE 8131-8136

Cradle Song op 38 no 1 (Lyric Pieces)

London
September 1956

LP: Columbia 33CX 1467
LP: Angel 35450
LP: EMI 3C 053 01309
LP: EMI 3C 153 52331-52440M
CD: Toshiba TOCE 8131-8136

Melody op 38 no 3 (Lyric Pieces)

London
September 1956

LP: Columbia 33CX 1467
LP: Angel 35450
LP: EMI 3C 053 01309
LP: EMI 3C 153 52331-52440M
CD: Toshiba TOCE 8131-8136

Butterfly op 43 no 1 (Lyric Pieces)

1924

78: Homochord H 8937
78: Parlophone E 11136
78: Decca (USA) 25283

London
October 1948

78: Columbia LB 75
78: Columbia (France) LF 268
LP: Columbia (USA) ML 4334

London
September 1956

45: Columbia SEL 1693
LP: Columbia 33CX 1467/33CX 1761
LP: Angel 35450/35488
LP: EMI HQM 1225
LP: EMI 3C 053 01309
LP: EMI 3C 153 52331-52440M
LP: EMI RLS 143 6203
CD: Toshiba TOCE 8131-8136

Lyric Pieces/continued

Solitary traveller op 43 no 2 (Lyric Pieces)

London
October 1948

78: Columbia LX 1194
78: Columbia (France) LFX 1016
78: Columbia (USA) A 1452
45: Columbia SCB 108
LP: Columbia (USA) ML 4334

London
September 1956

LP: Columbia 33CX 1467
LP: Angel 35450
LP: EMI 3C 053 01309
LP: EMI 3C 153 52331-52440M
LP: EMI RLS 143 6203
CD: Toshiba TOCE 8131-8136

In my native land op 43 no 3 (Lyric Pieces)

London
September 1956

LP: Columbia 33CX 1467
LP: Angel 35450
LP: EMI 3C 053 01309
LP: EMI 3C 153 52331-52440M
CD: Toshiba TOCE 8131-8136

Little bird op 43 no 4 (Lyric Pieces)

London
October 1948

78: Columbia LB 75
78: Columbia (France) LF 268
LP: Columbia (USA) ML 4334

London
September 1956

LP: Columbia 33CX 1467
LP: Angel 35450
LP: EMI HQM 1225
LP: EMI 3C 053 01309
LP: EMI 3C 153 52331-52440M
LP: EMI RLS 143 6203
CD: Toshiba TOCE 8131-8136

Love song op 43 no 5 (Lyric Pieces)

London
September 1956

45: Columbia SEL 1693
LP: Columbia 33CX 1467
LP: Angel 35450
LP: EMI 3C 053 01309
LP: EMI 3C 153 52331-52440M
CD: Toshiba TOCE 8131-8136

Lyric Pieces/continued

To the spring op 43 no 6 (Lyric Pieces)

1924   78: Homochord H 8937
                                        78: Parlophone E 11136
                                        78: Decca (USA) 25283

London   78: Columbia LX 1194
October 1948   78: Columbia (France) LFX 1016
                                        78: Columbia (USA) A 1452
                                        45: Columbia SCB 108
                                        LP: Columbia (USA) ML 4334

London   45: Columbia SEL 1693
September 1956   LP: Columbia 33CX 1467/33CX 1761
                                        LP: Angel 35450/35488
                                        LP: EMI 3C 053 01309
                                        LP: EMI 3C 153 52331-52440M
                                        LP: EMI RLS 143 6203
                                        CD: Toshiba TOCE ·8131-8136

Albumblatt op 47 no 2 (Lyric Pieces)

London   LP: Columbia 33CX 1467
September 1956   LP: Angel 35450
                                        LP: EMI HQM 1225
                                        LP: EMI 3C 053 01309
                                        LP: EMI 3C 153 52331-52440M
                                        LP: EMI RLS 143 6203
                                        CD: Toshiba TOCE 8131-8136

Melody op 47 no 3 (Lyric Pieces)

London   LP: Columbia 33CX 1467
September 1956   LP: Angel 35450
                                        LP: EMI HQM 1225
                                        LP: EMI 3C 053 01309
                                        LP: EMI 3C 153 52331-52440M
                                        CD: Toshiba TOCE 8131-8136

Halling op 47 no 4 (Lyric Pieces)

London   LP: Columbia 33CX 1467
September 1956   LP: Angel 35450
                                        LP: EMI HQM 1225
                                        LP: EMI 3C 053 01309
                                        LP: EMI 3C 153 52331-52440M
                                        LP: EMI RLS 143 6203
                                        CD: Toshiba TOCE 8131-8136

Shepherd boy op 54 no 1 (Lyric Pieces)

London
September 1956

LP: Columbia 33CX 1467
LP: Angel 35450
LP: EMI 3C 053 01309
LP: EMI 3C 153 52331-52440M
LP: EMI RLS 143 6203
CD: Toshiba TOCE 8131-8136

March of the trolls op 54 no 3 (Lyric Pieces)

London
September 1956

LP: Columbia 33CX 1467
LP: Angel 35450
LP: EMI 3C 053 01309
LP: EMI 3C 153 52331-52440M
LP: EMI RLS 143 6203
CD: Toshiba TOCE 8131-8136

Notturno op 54 no 4 (Lyric Pieces)

London
September 1956

LP: Columbia 33CX 1467
LP: Angel 35450
LP: EMI 3C 053 01309
LP: EMI 3C 153 52331-52440M
LP: EMI RLS 143 6203
CD: Toshiba TOCE 8131-8136

Bell-ringing op 54 no 6 (Lyric Pieces)

London
September 1956

LP: Columbia 33CX 1467
LP: Angel 35450
LP: EMI HQM 1225
LP: EMI 3C 053 01309
LP: EMI 3C 153 52331-52440M
CD: Toshiba TOCE 8131-8136

Home-sickness op 57 no 6 (Lyric Pieces)

London
September 1956

LP: Columbia 33CX 1468
LP: Angel 35451
LP: EMI 3C 053 01310
LP: EMI 3C 153 52331-52440M
CD: Toshiba TOCE 8131-8136

French Serenade op 62 no 3 (Lyric Pieces)

Berlin
April 1937

78: Columbia LX 650
78: Columbia (Germany) LWX 213
78: Columbia (France) LFX 501
78: Columbia (USA) M 313

London
September 1956

LP: Columbia 33CX 1468/33CX 1761
LP: Angel 35451/35488
LP: EMI 3C 053 01310
LP: EMI 3C 153 52331-52440M
CD: Toshiba TOCE 8131-8136

Lyric Pieces/continued

Phantom op 62 no 5 (Lyric Pieces)

London
September 1956

LP: Columbia 33CX 1468
LP: Angel 35451
LP: EMI 3C 053 01310
LP: EMI 3C 153 52331-52440M
CD: Toshiba TOCE 8131-8136

Homeward op 62 no 6 (Lyric Pieces)

London
September 1956

LP: Columbia 33CX 1468
LP: Angel 35451
LP: EMI 3C 053 01310
LP: EMI 3C 153 52331-52440M
CD: Toshiba TOCE 8131-8136

From days of youth op 65 no 1 (Lyric Pieces)

London
September 1956

LP: Columbia 33CX 1468
LP: Angel 35451
LP: EMI 3C 053 01310
LP: EMI 3C 153 52331-52440M
CD: Toshiba TOCE 8131-8136

Peasants' song op 65 no 2 (Lyric Pieces)

London
September 1956

LP: Columbia 33CX 1468
LP: Angel 35451
LP: EMI 3C 053 01310
LP: EMI 3C 153 52331-52440M
CD: Toshiba TOCE 8131-8136

Wedding day at Troldhaugen op 65 no 6 (Lyric Pieces)

London
October 1948

78: Columbia LX 1194
78: Columbia (France) LFX 1016
78: Columbia (USA) A 1452
45: Columbia SCB 108
LP: Columbia (USA) ML 4334

London
September 1956

45: Columbia SEL 1693
LP: Columbia 33CX 1468
LP: Angel 35451
LP: EMI 3C 053 01310
LP: EMI 3C 153 52331-52440M
LP: EMI RLS 143 6203
CD: Toshiba TOCE 8131-8136

Grandmother's Minuet op 68 no 2 (Lyric Pieces)

London
September 1956

LP: Columbia 33CX 1468
LP: Angel 35451
LP: EMI 3C 053 01310
LP: EMI 3C 153 52331-52440M
CD: Toshiba TOCE 8131-8136

At your feet op 68 no 3 (Lyric Pieces)

London
September 1956

LP: Columbia 33CX 1468
LP: Angel 35451
LP: EMI 3C 053 01310
LP: EMI 3C 153 52331-52440M
CD: Toshiba TOCE 8131-8136

At the cradle op 68 no 5 (Lyric Pieces)

Berlin
April 1937

78: Columbia LX 650
78: Columbia (Germany) LWX 213
78: Columbia (France) LFX 501
78: Columbia (USA) M 313

London
September 1956

LP: Columbia 33CX 1468
LP: Angel 35451
LP: EMI 3C 053 01310
LP: EMI 3C 153 52331-52440M
CD: Toshiba TOCE 8131-8136

Summer evening op 71 no 2 (Lyric Pieces)

London
September 1956

LP: Columbia 33CX 1468
LP: Angel 35451
LP: EMI 3C 053 01310
LP: EMI 3C 153 52331-52440M
CD: Toshiba TOCE 8131-8136

Puck op 71 no 3 (Lyric Pieces)

London
September 1956

LP: Columbia 33CX 1468
LP: Angel 35451
LP: EMI 3C 053 01310
LP: EMI 3C 153 52331-52440M
LP: EMI RLS 143 6203
CD: Toshiba TOCE 8131-8136

Quiet of the woods op 71 no 4 (Lyric Pieces)

London
September 1956

LP: Columbia 33CX 1468
LP: Angel 35451
LP: EMI 3C 053 01310
LP: EMI 3C 153 52331-52440M
CD: Toshiba TOCE 8131-8136

Recollection op 71 no 7 (Lyric Pieces)

London
September 1956

LP: Columbia 33CX 1468
LP: Angel 35451
LP: EMI 3C 053 01310
LP: EMI 3C 153 52331-52440M
LP: EMI RLS 143 6203
CD: Toshiba TOCE 8131-8136

Handel

Suite No 5 in E

London
September 1951

78: Columbia LX 1532
LP: Columbia (USA) ML 4646
LP: EMI 3C 153 52434-52441M

Harmonious Blacksmith (Air and Variations from Suite No 5)

London
1934

78: Columbia LX 514
78: Columbia (France) LWX 117
78: Columbia (USA) 68595D
78: Columbia (Australia) LOX 307
LP: EMI 3C 153 52700-52705M

Hindemith

Theme and Variations for piano and strings (Die 4 Temperamente)

Frankfurt
October 1952

Orchestra of
Hessischer Rundfunk
Zillig

Unpublished radio broadcast

Liszt

Piano Concerto No 1

London	LPO	78: Columbia LX 181-182
March 1931	Wood	LP: EMI 3C 053 01609
		LP: EMI 3C 153 52425-52431M
		CD: Classical Collection FDC 2008

Hungarian Rhapsody No 12 in C sharp minor

March	78: Homochord B 8488
1924	CD: Pearl GEMMCD 9011

Mendelssohn

Andante and Rondo capriccioso

April
1956

CD: Pearl GEMMCD 9930

Lied ohne Worte No 1 in E op 19 no 1

London
September 1956

LP: Columbia 33CX 1479
LP: Angel 35428
LP: EMI 1C 047 00451/3C 053 00451
LP: EMI 3C 153 52434-52441M
LP: EMI RLS 143 6203
CD: Toshiba TOCE 8131-8136

Lied ohne Worte No 3 op 19 no 3

Berlin
October 1955

Unpublished radio broadcast

Lied ohne Worte No 6 in G minor op 19 no 6

London
September 1956

LP: Columbia 33CX 1479/33CX 1761
LP: Angel 35428/35488
LP: EMI 1C 047 00451/3C 053 00451
LP: EMI 3C 153 52434-52441M
LP: EMI RLS 143 6203
CD: Toshiba TOCE 8131-8136

Lied ohne Worte No 12 in F sharp minor op 30 no 6

London
September 1956

LP: Columbia 33CX 1479
LP: Angel 35428
LP: EMI 1C 047 00451/3C 053 00451
LP: EMI 3C 153 52434-52441M
LP: EMI RLS 143 6203
CD: Toshiba TOCE 8131-8136

Lied ohne Worte No 16 in A op 38 no 4

London
September 1956

LP: Columbia 33CX 1479
LP: Angel 35428
LP: EMI 1C 047 00451/3C 053 00451
LP: EMI 3C 153 52434-52441M
CD: Toshiba TOCE 8131-8136

Lied ohne Worte No 18 in A flat op 38 no 6 "Duetto"

London
September 1956

LP: Columbia 33CX 1479
LP: Angel 35428
LP: EMI 1C 047 00451/3C 053 00451
LP: EMI 3C 153 52434-52441M
LP: EMI RLS 143 6203
CD: Toshiba TOCE 8131-8136

Lied ohne Worte No 20 in E flat op 53 no 2

London
September 1956

LP: Columbia 33CX 1479
LP: Angel 35428
LP: EMI 1C 047 00451/3C 053 00451
LP: EMI 3C 153 52434-52441M
LP: EMI RLS 143 6203
CD: Toshiba TOCE 8131-8136

Lied ohne Worte No 21 in G minor op 53 no 3

London
September 1956

LP: Columbia 33CX 1479
LP: Angel 35428
LP: EMI 1C 047 00451/3C 053 00451
LP: EMI 3C 153 52434-52441M
CD: Toshiba TOCE 8131-8136

Lied ohne Worte No 22 in F op 53 no 4

London
September 1956

LP: Columbia 33CX 1479
LP: Angel 35428
LP: EMI 1C 047 00451/3C 053 00451
LP: EMI 3C 153 52434-52441M
LP: EMI RLS 143 6203
CD: Toshiba TOCE 8131-8136

Lied ohne Worte No 25 in G op 62 no 1

London
September 1956

LP: Columbia 33CX 1479
LP: Angel 35428
LP: EMI 1C 047 00451/3C 053 00451
LP: EMI 3C 153 52434-52441M
LP: EMI RLS 143 6203
CD: Toshiba TOCE 8131-8136

Lieder ohne Worte/continued

Lied ohne Worte No 29 in A minor op 62 no 5 "Venezianisches Gondellied"

London
September 1956

LP: Columbia 33CX 1479
LP: Angel 35428
LP: EMI 1C 047 00451/3C 053 00451
LP: EMI 3C 153 52434-52441M
CD: Toshiba TOCE 8131-8136

Lied ohne Worte No 30 in A op 62 no 6 "Frühlingslied"

Zürich
June 1951

78: Columbia LB 139

London
September 1956

LP: Columbia 33CX 1479/33CX 1761
LP: Angel 35428/35488
LP: EMI 1C 047 00451/3C 053 00451
LP: EMI 3C 153 52434-52441M
LP: EMI RLS 143 6203
CD: Toshiba TOCE 8131-8136

Lied ohne Worte No 33 in B flat op 67 no 3

London
September 1956

LP: Columbia 33CX 1479
LP: Angel 35428
LP: EMI 1C 047 00451/3C 053 00451
LP: EMI 3C 153 52434-52441M
CD: Toshiba TOCE 8131-8136

Lied ohne Worte No 34 in C op 67 no 4 "Spinnerlied"

London
September 1956

LP: Columbia 33CX 1479
LP: Angel 35428
LP: EMI 1C 047 00451/3C 053 00451
LP: EMI 3C 153 52434-52441M
LP: EMI RLS 143 6203
CD: Toshiba TOCE 8131-8136

Lied ohne Worte No 40 in D op 85 no 4

London
September 1956

LP: Columbia 33CX 1479
LP: Angel 35428
LP: EMI 1C 047 00451/3C 053 00451
LP: EMI 3C 153 52434-52441M
CD: Toshiba TOCE 8131-8136

Lied ohne Worte No 42 in B flat op 85 no 6

London
September 1956

LP: Columbia 33CX 1479
LP: Angel 35428
LP: EMI 1C 047 00451/3C 053 00451
LP: EMI 3C 153 52434-52441M
CD: Toshiba TOCE 8131-8136

Lieder ohne Worte/concluded

Lied ohne Worte No 45 in C op 102 no 3

London
September 1956

LP: Columbia 33CX 1479
LP: Angel 35428
LP: EMI 1C 047 00451/3C 053 00451
LP: EMI 3C 153 52434-52441M
LP: EMI RLS 143 6203
CD: Toshiba TOCE 8131-8136

Lied ohne Worte No 47 in A op 102 no 5 "Kinderstück"

London
September 1956

LP: Columbia 33CX 1479
LP: Angel 35428
LP: EMI 1C 047 00451/3C 053 00451
LP: EMI 3C 153 52434-52441M
LP: EMI RLS 143 6203
CD: Toshiba TOCE 8131-8136

Mozart

Adagio in C K356

London
March 1954

LP: Columbia 33CX 1453
LP: Angel 35078
LP: Columbia (Germany) C 90547
LP: EMI 3C 153 00997-01007M
LP: EMI 1C 197 43020-43024M
CD: EMI CHS 763 6882

Adagio in B minor K540

London
August 1953

LP: Columbia 33CX 1160
LP: Angel 35070
LP: Columbia (Germany) C 90365
LP: EMI 3C 153 00997-01007M
LP: EMI 1C 197 43020-43024M
CD: EMI CHS 763 6882

Adagio K617a for mechanical organ or glass harmonica, arranged for piano

London
March 1954

Columbia unpublished

Allegro in B flat K3

London
August 1953

LP: Columbia 33CX 1128
LP: Angel 35068
LP: EMI 3C 153 00997-01007M
LP: EMI 1C 197 43020-43024M
CD: EMI CHS 763 6882

Allegro in G minor K312 (Sonatensatz)

London
August 1953

LP: Columbia 33CX 1271
LP: Columbia (Germany) C 90441
LP: Angel 35073
LP: EMI 3C 153 00997-01007M
LP: EMI 1C 197 43020-43024M
CD: EMI CHS 763 6882

Allegro in B flat K400 (Sonatensatz)

London
March 1954

LP: Columbia 33CX 1453
LP: Columbia (Germany) C 90547
LP: Angel 35078
LP: EMI 3C 153 00997-01007M
LP: EMI 1C 197 43020-43024M
CD: EMI CHS 763 6882

Andante in F K616 for mechanical organ, arranged for piano

London
August 1953

LP: Columbia 33CX 1128
LP: Angel 35068
LP: EMI 3C 153 00997-01007M
LP: EMI 1C 197 43020-43024M
CD: EMI CHS 763 6882

Andantino in E flat K236

London
August 1953

LP: Columbia 33CX 1142
LP: Angel 35069
LP: Columbia (Germany) 90356
LP: EMI 3C 153 00997-01007M
LP: EMI 1C 197 43020-43024M
CD: EMI CHS 763 6882

Capriccio in C K395

London
March 1954

LP: Columbia 33CX 1453
LP: Angel 35078
LP: Columbia (Germany) C 90547
LP: EMI 3C 153 00997-01007M
LP: EMI 1C 197 43020-43024M
CD: EMI CHS 763 6882

Eine kleine Gigue K574

London
August 1953

LP: Columbia 33CX 1315/33CX 1761
LP: Angel 35074/35488
LP: Columbia (Germany) C 90473
LP: EMI 3C 153 00997-01007M
LP: EMI 1C 197 43020-43024M
CD: EMI CHS 763 6882

Fantasy with Fugue in C K394

London
August 1953

LP: Columbia 33CX 1242
LP: Columbia (Germany) C 90417
LP: Angel 35072
LP: EMI 3C 153 00997-01007M
LP: EMI 1C 197 43020-43024M
CD: EMI CHS 763 6882

Fantasy in C minor K396

London
August 1953

LP: Columbia 33CX 1358
LP: Angel 35076
LP: EMI 3C 153 00997-01007M
LP: EMI 1C 197 43020-43024M
CD: EMI CHS 763 6882

Fantasy in D minor K397

London
August 1953

LP: Columbia 33CX 1142
LP: Columbia (Germany) C 90356
LP: Angel 35069
LP: EMI 3C 153 00997-01007M
LP: EMI 1C 197 43020-43024M
CD: EMI CHS 763 6882

Fantasy in C minor K475

London
August 1953

LP: Columbia 33CX 1220
LP: Angel 35071
LP: EMI 3C 153 00997-01007M
LP: EMI 1C 197 03133-03137M
CD: EMI CHS 763 6882

Fugue in G minor K401

London
August 1953

LP: Columbia 33CX 1271
LP: Columbia (Germany) C 90441
LP: Angel 35073
LP: EMI 3C 153 00997-01007M
LP: EMI 1C 197 43020-43024M
CD: EMI CHS 763 6882

6 German Dances with Trios K509

London
March 1954

LP: Columbia 33CX 1453
LP: Columbia (Germany) C 90547
LP: Angel 35078
LP: EMI 3C 153 00997-01007M
LP: EMI 1C 197 43020-43024M
CD: EMI CHS 763 6882

Abendempfindung

London   Schwarzkopf
April 1955

LP: Columbia 33CX 1321
LP: Columbia (Germany) C 90478
LP: Angel 35270
LP: EMI 2C 061 01578
LP: EMI 3C 153 52700-52705M
LP: EMI ASD 3858
LP: Toshiba EAC 81060
CD: EMI CDC 747 3262/CDH 763 7022

Lieder/continued

Als Luise die Briefe

| London
April 1955 | Schwarzkopf | LP: Columbia 33CX 1321
LP: Columbia (Germany) C 90478
LP: Angel 35270
LP: EMI 2C 061 01578
LP: EMI 3C 153 52700-52705M
LP: EMI ASD 3858
LP: Toshiba EAC 81060
CD: EMI CDC 747 3262/CDH 763 7022 |

Die Alte

| London
April 1955 | Schwarzkopf | LP: Columbia 33CX 1321
LP: Columbia (Germany) C 90478
LP: Angel 35270
LP: EMI 2C 061 01578
LP: EMI 3C 153 52700-52705M
LP: EMI ASD 3858
LP: Toshiba EAC 81060
CD: EMI CDH 763 7022 |

An Chloé

| London
April 1955 | Schwarzkopf· | LP: Columbia 33CX 1321
LP: Columbia (Germany) C 90478
LP: Angel 35270
LP: EMI 2C 061 01578
LP: EMI 3C 153 52700-52705M
LP: EMI ASD 3858
LP: Toshiba EAC 81060
CD: EMI CDC 747 3262/CDH 763 7022 |

Dans un bois solitaire

| London
April 1955 | Schwarzkopf | LP: Columbia 33CX 1321
LP: Columbia (Germany) C 90478
LP: Angel 35270
LP: EMI 2C 061 01578
LP: EMI 3C 153 52700-52705M
LP: EMI ASD 3858
LP: Toshiba EAC 81060
CD: EMI CDH 763 7022 |
| London
April 1955 | Schwarzkopf | LP: Columbia 33CX 1321
LP: Columbia (Germany) C 90478
LP: Angel 35270
LP: EMI 2C 061 01578
LP: EMI 3C 153 52700-52705M
LP: EMI ASD 3858
LP: Toshiba EAC 81060
CD: EMI CDC 747 3262/CDH 763 7022 |

Lieder/continued

Im Frühlingsanfange

London
April 1955 | Schwarzkopf

LP: Columbia 33CX 1321
LP: Columbia (Germany) C 90478
LP: Angel 35270
LP: EMI 2C 061 01578
LP: EMI 3C 153 52700-52705M
LP: EMI ASD 3858
LP: Toshiba EAC 81060
CD: EMI CDC 747 3262/CDH 763 7022

Das Kinderspiel

London
April 1955 | Schwarzkopf

LP: Columbia 33CX 1321
LP: Columbia (Germany) C 90478
LP: Angel 35270
LP: EMI 2C 061 01578
LP: EMI 3C 153 52700-52705M
LP: EMI ASD 3858
LP: Toshiba EAC 81060
CD: EMI CDC 747 3262/CDH 763 7022

Die kleine Spinnerin

London
April 1955 | Schwarzkopf

LP: Columbia 33CX 1321
LP: Columbia (Germany) C 90478
LP: Angel 35270
LP: EMI 2C 061 01578
LP: EMI 3C 153 52700-52705M
LP: EMI ASD 3858
LP: Toshiba EAC 81060
CD: EMI CDC 747 3262/CDH 763 7022

Das Lied der Trennung

London
April 1955 | Schwarzkopf

LP: Columbia 33CX 1321
LP: Columbia (Germany) C 90478
LP: Angel 35270
LP: EMI 2C 061 01578
LP: EMI 3C 153 52700-52705M
LP: EMI ASD 3858
LP: Toshiba EAC 81060
CD: EMI CDH 763 7022

Un moto di gioia

London
April 1955 | Schwarzkopf

Columbia unpublished

Lieder/continued

Nehmt meinen Dank

London April 1955	Schwarzkopf	Columbia unpublished

Oiseaux, si tous les ans

London   Schwarzkopf   LP: Columbia 33CX 1321
April 1955   LP: Columbia (Germany) C 90478
                                     LP: Angel 35270
                                     LP: EMI 2C 061 01578
                                     LP: EMI 3C 153 52700-52705M
                                     LP: EMI ASD 3858
                                     LP: Toshiba EAC 81060
                                     CD: EMI CDC 747 3262/CDH 763 7022

Ridente la calma

London   Schwarzkopf   LP: Columbia 33CX 1321
April 1955   LP: Columbia (Germany) C 90478
                                     LP: Angel 35270
                                     LP: EMI 2C 061 01578
                                     LP: EMI 3C 153 52700-52705M
                                     LP: EMI ASD 3858
                                     LP: Toshiba EAC 81060
                                     CD: EMI CDC 747 3262/CDH 763 7022

Sehnsucht nach dem Frühlinge

London   Schwarzkopf   LP: Columbia 33CX 1321
April 1955   LP: Columbia (Germany) C 90478
                                     LP: Angel 35270
                                     LP: EMI 2C 061 01578
                                     LP: EMI 3C 153 52700-52705M
                                     LP: EMI ASD 3858
                                     LP: Toshiba EAC 81060
                                     CD: EMI CDC 747 3262/CDH 763 7022

Lieder/concluded

Das Traumbild

London   Schwarzkopf
April 1955

LP: Columbia 33CX 1321
LP: Columbia (Germany) C 90478
LP: Angel 35270
LP: EMI 2C 061 01578
LP: EMI 3C 153 52700-52705M
LP: EMI ASD 3858
LP: Toshiba EAC 81060
CD: EMI CDH 763 7022

Das Veilchen

London   Schwarzkopf
April 1955

LP: Columbia 33CX 1321
LP: Columbia (Germany) C 90478
LP: Angel 35270
LP: EMI 2C 061 01578
LP: EMI 3C 153 52700-52705M
LP: EMI ASD 3858
LP: Toshiba EAC 81060
CD: EMI CDH 763 7022

Die Verschweigung

London   Schwarzkopf
April 1955

LP: Toshiba EAC 81060
Previously unpublished

Warnung

London   Schwarzkopf
April 1955

Columbia unpublished

Der Zauberer

London   Schwarzkopf
April 1955

LP: Columbia 33CX 1321
LP: Columbia (Germany) C 90478
LP: Angel 35270
LP: EMI 2C 061 01578
LP: EMI 3C 153 52700-52705M
LP: EMI ASD 3858
LP: Toshiba EAC 81060
CD: EMI CDC 747 3262/CDH 763 7022

Die Zufriedenheit

London
April 1955

LP: Columbia 33CX 1321
LP: Columbia (Germany) C 90478
LP: Angel 35270
LP: EMI 2C 061 01578
LP: EMI 3C 153 52700-52705M
LP: EMI ASD 3858
LP: Toshiba EAC 81060
CD: EMI CDC 747 3262/CDH 763 7022

Minuet and Trio in G K1

London
August 1953

LP: Columbia 33CX 1128
LP: Angel 35068
LP: EMI 3C 153 00997-01007M
LP: EMI 1C 197 43020-43024M
CD: EMI CHS 763 6882

Minuet in F K2

London
August 1953

LP: Columbia 33CX 1128
LP: Angel 35068
LP: EMI 3C 153 00997-01007M
LP: EMI 1C 197 43020-43024M
CD: EMI CHS 763 6882

Minuet in F K4

London
August 1953

LP: Columbia 33CX 1128
LP: Angel 35068
LP: EMI 3C 153 00997-01007M
LP: EMI 1C 197 43020-43024M
CD: EMI CHS 763 6882

Minuet in F K5

London
August 1953

LP: Columbia 33CX 1128
LP: Angel 35068
LP: EMI 3C 153 00997-01007M
LP: EMI 1C 197 43020-43024M
CD: EMI CHS 763 6882

Minuet in D K94

London
August 1953

LP: Columbia 33CX 1128
LP: Angel 35068
LP: EMI 3C 153 00997-01007M
LP: EMI 1C 197 43020-43024M
CD: EMI CHS 763 6883

8 Minuets with Trios K315a

London	LP: Columbia 33CX 1453
March 1954	LP: Columbia (Germany) C 90547
	LP: Angel 35078
	LP: EMI 3C 153 00997-01007M
	LP: EMI 1C 197 43020-43024M
	CD: EMI CHS 763 6882

Minuet in D K355

London	LP: Columbia 33CX 1142
August 1953	LP: Columbia (Germany) C 90356
	LP: Angel 35069
	LP: EMI 3C 153 00997-01007M
	LP: EMI 1C 197 43020-43024M
	CD: EMI CHS 763 6882

Piano Concerto No 9 K271

Berlin	Staatskapelle	78: Columbia LX 559-562
1936	Rosbaud	78: Columbia (France) LFX 460-463
		78: Columbia (USA) M 291
		78: Columbia (Australia)
		LOX 335-338
		LP: Discocorp RR 411
		LP: EMI 3C 153 52425-52431M

Frankfurt	Orchestra of	Unpublished radio broadcast
December 1952	Hessischer Rundfunk	
	Schröder	

Montreux	Orchestre National	CD: Pearl GEMMCD 9038
September 1955	Markevitch	

Piano Concerto No 20 K466

London	Philharmonia	LP: Columbia 33CX 1235
August 1953	Rosbaud	LP: Angel 35215
		LP: EMI 3C 153 52425-52431M
		CD: EMI CHS 763 7092

Piano Concerto No 21 K467

Frankfurt	Orchestra of	Unpublished radio broadcast
February 1947	Hessischer Rundfunk	
	Schröder	

New York	NYPO	LP: Toscanini Society ATSGC 1217
March 1955	Cantelli	LP: Discocorp MLG 70/IGI 349
		LP: CLS MDRL 12823/ARPCL 22022
		CD: AS-Disc AS 529
		AS-Disc misdated; Toscanini
		Society never published

Piano Concerto No 23 K488

Zürich June 1949	Tonhalle-Orchester V.Andreae	LP: Discocorp IGI 363

London
June 1951

Philharmonia
Karajan

78: Columbia LX 1510-1513/
    LX 8894-8897 auto
LP: Columbia 33C 1012
LP: Columbia (USA) ML 4536
LP: Odyssey 3216 0371
LP: Toshiba EAC 37001-37019
LP: EMI 3C 153 52425-52431M
CD: EMI CHS 763 7092

Frankfurt
October 1951

Orchestra of
Hessischer Rundfunk
Schröder

Unpublished radio broadcast

Piano Concerto No 24 K491

London
August 1953

Philharmonia
Karajan

LP: Columbia 33CX 1526
LP: Angel 35501
LP: EMI 3C 153 52425-52431M
LP: Toshiba EAC 37001-37019
CD: EMI CHS 763 7092

Piano Concerto No 25 K503

London
August 1953

Philharmonia
Rosbaud

LP: Columbia 33CX 1235
LP: Angel 35215
LP: EMI 3C 153 52425-52431M
CD: EMI CHS 763 7092

Piano Concerto No 27 K595

LP: Discocorp IGI 349
Also published by International
Piano Archive

Piano and Wind Quintet K452

London
April 1955

Sutcliffe, Walton,
Brain, James

LP: Columbia 33CX 1322
LP: Angel 35303
LP: EMI 3C 153 52700-52705M
LP: EMI 1C 047 01242
CD: EMI CHS 763 7092

Piano Sonata No 1 in C K279

London
August 1953

LP: Columbia 33CX 1242
LP: Columbia (Germany) C 90417
LP: Angel 35072
LP: EMI 3C 153 00997-01007M
LP: EMI 1C 197 03133-03137M
CD: EMI CHS 763 6882

Piano Sonata No 2 in F K280

London
August 1953

LP: Columbia 33CX 1160
LP: Columbia (Germany) C 90365
LP: Angel 35070
LP: EMI 3C 153 00997-01007M
LP: EMI 1C 197 03133-03137M
CD: EMI CHS 763 6882

Piano Sonata No 3 in B flat K281

London
August 1953

LP: Columbia 33CX 1315
LP: Columbia (Germany) C 35074
LP: Angel 35074
LP: EMI 3C 153 00997-01007M
LP: EMI 1C 197 03133-03137M
CD: EMI CHS 763 6882

Piano Sonata No 4 in E flat K282

London
August 1953

LP: Columbia 33CX 1142
LP: Columbia (Germany) C 90356
LP: Angel 35069
LP: EMI 3C 153 00997-01007M
LP: EMI 1C 197 03133-03137M
CD: EMI CHS 763 6882

Piano Sonata No 5 in G K283

London
August 1953

LP: Columbia 33CX 1345
LP: Columbia (Germany) C 90492
LP: Angel 35075
LP: EMI 3C 153 00997-01007M
LP: EMI 1C 197 03133-03137M
CD: EMI CHS 763 6882

Piano Sonata No 6 in D K284

London
August 1953

LP: Columbia 33CX 1271
LP: Columbia (Germany) C 90441
LP: Angel 35073
LP: EMI 3C 153 00997-01007M
LP: EMI 1C 197 03133-03137M
CD: EMI CHS 763 6882

Piano Sonatas/continued

Piano Sonata No 7 in C K309

London
August 1953

LP: Columbia 33CX 1428
LP: Columbia (Germany) C 90535
LP: Angel 35077
LP: EMI 3C 153 00997-01007M
LP: EMI 1C 197 03133-03137M
CD: EMI CHS 763 6882

Piano Sonata No 8 in A minor K310

London
August 1953

LP: Columbia 33CX 1160
LP: Columbia (Germany) C 90365
LP: Angel 35070
LP: EMI 3C 153 00997-01007M
LP: EMI 1C 197 03133-03137M
CD: EMI CHS 763 6882

Piano Sonata No 9 in D K311

London
August 1953

LP: Columbia 33CX 1242
LP: Columbia (Germany) C 90417
LP: Angel 35072
LP: EMI 3C 153 00997-01007M
LP: EMI 1C 197 03133-03137M
CD: EMI CHS 763 6882

Piano Sonata No 10 in C K330

London
August 1953

LP: Columbia 33CX 1428
LP: Columbia (Germany) C 90535
LP: Angel 35077
LP: EMI 3C 153 00997-01007M
LP: EMI 1C 197 03133-03137M
CD: EMI CHS 763 6882

Piano Sonatas/continued

Piano Sonata No 11 in A minor K331

Frankfurt
October 1947

Unpublished radio broadcast

Saarbrücken
November 1949

CD: Music and Arts CD 612

London
August 1953

LP: Columbia 33CX 1142
LP: Columbia (Germany) C 90356
LP: Angel 35069
LP: EMI 3C 153 00997-01007M
LP: EMI 1C 197 03133-03137M
CD: EMI CHS 763 6882

Alla turca (Piano Sonata No 11)

London
1934

78: Columbia LX 514
78: Columbia (Germany) LWX 117
78: Columbia (USA) 68595D

Piano Sonata No 12 in F K332

London
August 1953

LP: Columbia 33CX 1358
LP: Angel 35076
LP: EMI 3C 153 00997-01007M
LP: EMI 1C 197 03133-03137M
CD: EMI CHS 763 6882

Piano Sonata No 13 in B flat K333

London
August 1953

LP: Columbia 33CX 1220
LP: Angel 35071
LP: EMI 3C 153 00997-01007M
LP: EMI 1C 197 03133-03137M
CD: EMI CHS 763 6882

Piano Sonata No 14 in C minor K457

Berlin
1937

78: Columbia LX 615-616
78: Columbia (France) LFX 492-493
78: Columbia (USA) X 93
78: Columbia (Australia)
    LOX 492-493

London
August 1953

LP: Columbia 33CX 1220
LP: Angel 35071
LP: EMI 3C 153 00997-01007M
LP: EMI 1C 197 03133-03137M
CD: EMI CHS 763 6882

Piano Sonatas/continued

Piano Sonata No 15 in C K545

Paris
1949

78: Columbia LX 1304
78: Columbia (France) LFX 887

London
August 1953

LP: Columbia 33CX 1358
LP: Angel 35076
LP: EMI 3C 153 00997-01007M
LP: EMI 1C 197 03133-03137M
LP: EMI CHS 763 6882

Berlin
October 1955

Unpublished radio broadcast

Piano Sonata No 16 in B flat K570

Berlin
1937

78: Columbia LX 572-573
78: Columbia (Germany) LWX 160-161
78: Columbia (USA) X 79

London
August 1953

LP: Columbia 33CX 1128
LP: Angel 35068
LP: EMI 3C 153 00997-01007M
LP: EMI 1C 197 03133-03137M
CD: EMI CHS 763 6882

Piano Sonata No 17 in D K576

Zürich
August 1944

CD: Music and Arts CD 612

Frankfurt
March 1949

Unpublished radio broadcast

London
August 1953

LP: Columbia 33CX 1345
LP: Angel 35075
LP: EMI 3C 153 00997-01007M
LP: EMI 1C 197 03133-03137M
CD: EMI CHS 763 6882

Piano Sonatas/concluded

Piano Sonata No 18 in F K533/K494

London
August 1953

LP: Columbia 33CX 1271
LP: Columbia (Germany) C 90441
LP: Angel 35073
LP: EMI 3C 153 00997-01007M
LP: EMI 1C 197 03133-03137M
CD: EMI CHS 763 6882

Piano Sonata No 19 in F K547a

London
August 1953

LP: Columbia 33CX 1315
LP: Columbia (Germany) C 90473
LP: Angel 35074
LP: EMI 3C 153 00997-01007M
LP: EMI 1C 197 03133-03137M
CD: EMI CHS 763 6882

Rondo in D K485

London
August 1953

LP: Columbia 33CX 1428
LP: Columbia (Germany) C 90535
LP: Angel 35077
LP: EMI 3C 153 00997-01007M
LP: EMI 1C 197 43020-43024M
CD: EMI CHS 763 6882

Rondo in A minor K511

London
August 1953

LP: Columbia 33CX 1315
LP: Columbia (Germany) C 90473
LP: Angel 35074
LP: EMI 3C 153 00997-01007M
LP: EMI 1C 197 43020-43024M
CD: EMI CHS 763 6882

Sonatensatz and Minuet in B flat K498a

London
March 1954

LP: Columbia 33CX 1453
LP: Columbia (Germany) C 90547
LP: Angel 35078
LP: EMI 3C 153 00997-01007M
LP: EMI 1C 197 03133-03137M
CD: EMI CHS 763 6882

Suite in C in the style of Handel K399

London
August 1953

LP: Columbia 33CX 1142
LP: Columbia (Germany) C 90356
LP: Angel 35069
LP: EMI 3C 153 00997-01007M
LP: EMI 1C 197 43020-43024M
CD: EMI CHS 763 6882

Kleiner Trauermarsch in C minor K453a

London
March 1954

LP: Columbia 33CX 1160
LP: Columbia (Germany) C 90365
LP: Angel 35070
LP: EMI 3C 153 00997-01007M
LP: EMI 1C 197 43020-43024M
CD: EMI CHS 763 6882

8 Variations in G on a Dutch song K24

London
August 1953

LP: Columbia 33CX 1128
LP: Angel 35068
LP: EMI 3C 153 00997-01007M
LP: EMI 1C 197 43020-43024M
CD: EMI CHS 763 6882

7 Variations in D on "Willem van Nassau" K25

London
August 1953

LP: Columbia 33CX 1128
LP: Angel 35068
LP: EMI 3C 153 00997-01007M
LP: EMI 1C 197 43020-43024M
CD: EMI CHS 763 6882

6 Variations in F K54

London
March 1954

LP: Columbia 33CX 1160
LP: Columbia (Germany) C 90365
LP: Angel 35070
LP: EMI 3C 153 00997-01007M
LP: EMI 1C 197 43020-43024M
CD: EMI CHS 763 6882

12 Variations in C on a minuet by J.Chr. Fischer K179

London
March 1954

LP: Columbia 33CX 1160
LP: Columbia (Germany) C 90365
LP: Angel 35070
LP: EMI 3C 153 00997-01007M
LP: EMI 1C 197 43020-43024M
CD: EMI CHS 763 6882

6 Variations in G on "Caro mio Adone" K180

London
August 1953

LP: Columbia 33CX 1142
LP: Columbia (Germany) C 90356
LP: Angel 35069
LP: EMI 3C 153 00997-01007M
LP: EMI 1C 197 43020-43024M
CD: EMI CHS 763 6882

9 Variations in C on "Lison dormait" K264

London
August 1953

LP: Columbia 33CX 1345
LP: Columbia (Germany) C 90492
LP: Angel 35075
LP: EMI 3C 153 00997-01007M
LP: EMI 1C 197 43020-43024M
CD: EMI CHS 763 6882

12 Variations in C on "Ah, vous dirai-je Mamam" K265

London
August 1953

LP: Columbia 33CX 1142
LP: Columbia (Germany) C 90356
LP: Angel 35069
LP: EMI 3C 153 00997-01007M
LP: EMI 1C 197 43020-43024M
CD: EMI CHS 763 6882

8 Variations in F on a march from Grétry's "Les Mariages samnites" K352

London
August 1953

LP: Columbia 33CX 1128
LP: Angel 35068
LP: EMI 3C 153 00997-01007M
LP: EMI 1C 197 43020-43024M
CD: EMI CHS 763 6882

12 Variations in E flat on "La belle Francoise" K353

London
August 1953

LP: Columbia 33CX 1220
LP: Angel 35071
LP: EMI 3C 153 00997-01007M
LP: EMI 1C 197 43020-43024M
CD: EMI CHS 763 6882

12 Variations in E flat on "Je suis Lindor" K354

London
August 1953

LP: Columbia 33CX 1358
LP: Angel 35076
LP: EMI 3C 153 00997-01007M
LP: EMI 1C 197 43020-43024M
CD: EMI CHS 763 6882

Variations/concluded

6 Variations in F on "Salve tu, Domine" K398

London
August 1953

LP: Columbia 33CX 1315
LP: Columbia (Germany) C 90473
LP: Angel 35074
LP: EMI 3C 153 00997-01007M
LP: EMI 1C 197 43020-43024M
CD: EMI CHS 763 6882

10 Variations in G on "Unser dummer Pöbel meint" K455

London
August 1953

LP: Columbia 33CX 1345
LP: Columbia (Germany) C 90492
LP: Angel 35075
LP: EMI 3C 153 00997-01007M
LP: EMI 1C 197 43020-43024M
CD: EMI CHS 763 6882

8 Variations in A on "Come un' agnello" K460

London
August 1953

LP: Columbia 33CX 1358
LP: Angel 35076
LP: EMI 3C 153 00997-01007M
LP: EMI 1C 197 43020-43024M
CD: EMI CHS 763 6882

Berlin
September 1955

Unpublished radio broadcast

12 Variations in B flat on an Allegretto K500

London
August 1953

LP: Columbia 33CX 1315
LP: Columbia (Germany) C 90473
LP: Angel 35074
LP: EMI 3C 153 00997-01007M
LP: EMI 1C 197 43020-43024M
CD: EMI CHS 763 6882

9 Variations in D on a Minuet by Duport K573

London
August 1953

LP: Columbia 33CX 1315
LP: Columbia (Germany) C 90473
LP: Angel 35074
LP: EMI 3C 153 00997-01007M
LP: EMI 1C 197 43020-43024M
CD: EMI CHS 763 6882

8 Variations in F on "Ein Weib ist das herrlichste Ding" K613

London
August 1953

LP: Columbia 33CX 1242
LP: Columbia (Germany) C 90417
LP: Angel 35072
LP: EMI 3C 153 00997-01007M
LP: EMI 1C 197 43020-43024M
CD: EMI CHS 763 6882

Pfitzner

Piano Concerto op 31

Hamburg December 1943	Philharmonisches Staatsorchester Bittner	LP: Discocorp IGI 363

Piston

Concerto for piano and chamber orchestra

Frankfurt April 1947	Orchestra of Hessischer Rundfunk Schröder	Unpublished radio broadcast

Poulenc

Mouvements perpetuels

1924-1925	78: Homochord 1-8679 CD: Pearl GEMMCD 9930

Rachmaninov

Piano Concerto No 2

| Amsterdam
October 1940 | Concertgebouw
Orchestra
Mengelberg | LP: Discocorp IGI 234
CD: Music and Arts CD 250
Also issued on LP by International
Piano Archive |

Piano Concerto No 3

| New York
February 1939 | NYPO
Barbirolli | LP: International Piano Archive
    IPA 505 |
| Amsterdam
March 1940 | Concertgebouw
Orchestra
Mengelberg | CD: Music and Arts CD 250 |

Ravel

Ondine (Gaspard de la nuit)

London
1937

78: Columbia LX 623
78: Columbia (France) LFX 539
78: Columbia (USA) X 141
78: Columbia (Australia) LOX 354

Zürich
August 1944

CD: Music and Arts CD 612

London
December 1954

LP: Columbia 33CX 1351
LP: Angel 35273
LP: EMI 3C 053 01249
LP: EMI 3C 153 52331-52440M

Berlin
October 1955

CD: Pearl GEMMCD 9449

Le gibet (Gaspard de la nuit)

Berlin
1938

78: Columbia LX 772
78: Columbia (France) LFX 580
78: Columbia (Australia) LOX 509

London
December 1954

LP: Columbia 33CX 1351
LP: Angel 35273
LP: EMI 3C 053 01249
LP: EMI 3C 153 52331-52440M

Berlin
October 1955

CD: Pearl GEMMCD 9449

Gaspard de la nuit/concluded

Scarbo (Gaspard de la nuit)

Berlin
1939

78: Columbia LX 813
78: Columbia (Germany) LWX 282
78: Columbia (Australia) LOX 432

London
December 1954

LP: Columbia 33CX 1351
LP: Angel 35273
LP: EMI 3C 053 01249
LP: EMI 3C 153 52331-52440M

Berlin
October 1955

CD: Pearl GEMMCD 9449

Jeux d'eau

December
1923

78: Homochord 1-8446
CD: Pearl GEMMCD 9038

Frankfurt
October 1947

Unpublished radio broadcast

London
December 1954

45: Columbia SEL 1701
LP: Columbia 33CX 1352/33CX 1761
LP: Angel 35274/35488
LP: EMI 2C 061 01566/3C 053 01249
LP: EMI 3C 153 52331-52440M
LP: EMI HQM 1225/RLS 143 6203

Menuet antique

London
December 1954

LP: Columbia 33CX 1352
LP: Angel 35274
LP: EMI 2C 061 01566/3C 053 01249
LP: EMI 3C 153 52331-52440M

Menuet sur le nom de Haydn

London
December 1954

LP: Columbia 33CX 1352
LP: Angel 35274
LP: EMI 3C 153 52331-52440M

Noctuelles (Miroirs)

Berlin
1939

78: Columbia (France) LFX 893

Berlin
May 1950

Unpublished radio broadcast

London
December 1954

LP: Columbia 33CX 1352
LP: Angel 35274
LP: EMI 3C 053 01250
LP: EMI 3C 153 52331-52440M

Miroirs/continued

Oiseaux tristes (Miroirs)

Berlin
1939

78: Columbia (France) LFX 893

Berlin
May 1950

Unpublished radio broadcast

London
December 1954

LP: Columbia 33CX 1352
LP: Angel 35274
LP: EMI HQM 1225/3C 053 01250
LP: EMI 3C 153 52331-52440M

Une barque sur l'océan (Miroirs)

Berlin
1939

78: Columbia (France) LFX 894

Berlin
May 1950

Unpublished radio broadcast

London
December 1954

LP: Columbia 33CX 1352
LP: Angel 35274
LP: EMI 3C 053 01250

Alborada del gracioso (Miroirs)

Berlin
1938

78: Columbia LB 53
78: Columbia (Germany) LW 24
78: Columbia (USA) 17137D
78: Columbia (Australia) LO 29
LP: EMI RLS 143 6203
CD: Pearl GEMMCD 9449

Berlin
1939

78: Columbia (France) LFX 894

Berlin
May 1950

Unpublished radio broadcast

London
December 1954

45: Columbia SEL 1697
LP: Columbia 33CX 1352
LP: Angel 35274
LP: EMI 3C 053 01250
LP: EMI 3C 153 52331-52440M
LP: EMI RLS 143 6203

La vallée des cloches (Miroirs)

Berlin
1938

78: Columbia LX 772
78: Columbia (France) LFX 580
78: Columbia (Australia) LOX 509

Berlin
1939

78: Columbia (France) LFX 895

Berlin
May 1950

Unpublished radio broadcast

London
December 1954

LP: Columbia 33CX 1352
LP: Angel 35274
LP: EMI 3C 053 01250
LP: EMI 3C 153 52331-52440M

A la manière de Borodin

London
December 1954

LP: Columbia 33CX 1352/33CX 1761
LP: Angel 35274/35488
LP: EMI 3C 053 01250
LP: EMI 3C 153 52331-52440M

A la manière de Chabrier

London
December 1954

LP: Columbia 33CX 1352
LP: Angel 35274
LP: EMI 3C 053 01250
LP: EMI 3C 153 52331-52440M

Pavane pour une infante défunte

London
December 1954

LP: Columbia 33CX 1352
LP: Angel 35274
LP: EMI 2C 061 01566/3C 053 01250
LP: EMI 3C 153 52331-52440M
LP: EMI RLS 143 6203

Piano Trio in A minor

Frankfurt   Taschner, Hoelscher   Unpublished radio broadcast
November 1948

Prélude in A minor

London
December 1954

45: Columbia SEL 1701
LP: Columbia 33CX 1352
LP: Angel 35274
LP: EMI 3C 053 01250
LP: EMI 3C 153 52331-52440M

Sonatine

London
December 1954

LP: Columbia 33CX 1351
LP: Angel 35273
LP: EMI 2C 061 01566/3C 053 01249
LP: EMI 3C 153 52331-52440M
LP: EMI RLS 143 6203

Berlin
September 1955

Unpublished radio broadcast

Prélude (Le tombeau de Couperin)

London
December 1954

LP: Columbia 33CX 1350
LP: Angel 35272
LP: EMI 2C 061 01565/3C 053 01248
LP: EMI 3C 153 52331-52440M

Rigaudon (Le tombeau de Couperin)

London
December 1954

LP: Columbia 33CX 1350
LP: Angel 35272
LP: EMI 2C 061 01565/3C 053 01248
LP: EMI 3C 153 52331-52440M

Fugue (Le tombeau de Couperin)

London
December 1954

LP: Columbia 33CX 1350
LP: Angel 35272
LP: EMI 2C 061 01565/3C 053 01248
LP: EMI 3C 153 52331-52440M

Menuet (Le tombeau de Couperin)

London
December 1954

LP: Columbia 33CX 1350
LP: Angel 35272
LP: EMI 2C 061 01565/3C 053 01248
LP: EMI 3C 153 52331-52440M

Le tombeau de Couperin/concluded

Forlane (Le tombeau de Couperin)

London
December 1954

LP: Columbia 33CX 1350
LP: Angel 35272
LP: EMI HQM 1225
LP: EMI 2C 061 01565/3C 053 01248
LP: EMI 3C 153 52331-52440M

Toccata (Le tombeau de Couperin)

London
December 1954

LP: Columbia 33CX 1350
LP: Angel 35272
LP: EMI 2C 061 01565/3C 053 01248
LP: EMI 3C 153 52331-52440M

Valses nobles et sentimentales

London
December 1954

LP: Columbia 33CX 1351
LP: Angel 35373
LP: EMI 2C 061 01566/3C 053 01249
LP: EMI 3C 153 52331-52440M

Roussel

Les joueurs de flûte, Aria and M. de la Péjaudie for flute and piano

Berlin   Scheck   Columbia unpublished
1937   Intended as fill-up for the
                                           unpublished recording of
                                           Gieseking's own Flute Sonatina

Samazeuilh

Naiades au soir

Frankfurt   Unpublished radio broadcast
September 1948

Domenico Scarlatti

Sonata in E L23

Zürich
August 1944

CD: Music and Arts CD 612

Frankfurt
April 1947

LP: Discocorp IGI 272/RR 493

London
September 1951

78: Columbia LB 144
LP: Columbia (USA) ML 4646
LP: EMI 3C 153 52434-52441M

Sonata in E minor L275

London
September 1951

78: Columbia LB 136
LP: Columbia (USA) ML 4646
LP: EMI 3C 153 52434-52441M

Sonata L286

Zürich
August 1944

CD: Music and Arts CD 612

Sonata in D minor L413

London
September 1951

78: Columbia LB 136
LP: Columbia (USA) ML 4646
LP: EMI 3C 153 52434-52441M

Sonata in D L424

Frankfurt
April 1947

LP: Discocorp IGI 272/RR 493

London
September 1951

78: Columbia LB 144
LP: Columbia (USA) ML 4646
LP: EMI 3C 153 52434-52441M

Sonata in C L443

Frankfurt
April 1947

LP: Discocorp IGI 272/RR 493

London
September 1951

LP: Columbia (USA) ML 4646
LP: EMI 3C 153 52434-52441M

A group of unspecified Scarlatti Sonatas are also preserved in an unpublished radio broadcast from Frankfurt in October 1947

Schubert

Impromptu in C minor D899 no 1

London
September 1955

LP: Columbia 33CX 1611
LP: Angel 35533
LP: EMI 3C 153 52434-52441M
CD: Toshiba TOCE 8131-8136

Impromptu in E flat D899 no 2

London
September 1955

LP: Columbia 33CX 1611
LP: Angel 35533
LP: EMI 3C 153 52434-52441M
CD: Toshiba TOCE 8131-8136

Impromptu in G D899 no 3

London
September 1955

LP: Columbia 33CX 1611
LP: Angel 35533
LP: EMI 3C 153 52434-52441M
CD: Toshiba TOCE 8131-8136

Impromptu in A flat D899 no 4

London
September 1955

LP: Columbia 33CX 1611
LP: Angel 35533
LP: EMI 3C 153 52434-52441M
CD: Toshiba TOCE 8131-8136

Berlin
September-October
1955

Unpublished radio broadcast

Impromptus/concluded

Impromptu in F minor D935 no 1

London
September 1955

LP: Columbia 33CX 1611
LP: Angel 35533
LP: EMI 3C 153 52434-52441M
CD: Toshiba TOCE 8131-8136

Impromptu in A flat D935 no 2

London
September 1955

45: Columbia SEL 1615
LP: Columbia 33CX 1611
LP: Angel 35533
LP: EMI 3C 153 52434-52441M
CD: Toshiba TOCE 8131-8136

Impromptu in B flat D935 no 3

London
September 1955

LP: Columbia 33CX 1612
LP: Angel 35534
LP: EMI 3C 153 52434-52441M
CD: Toshiba TOCE 8131-8136

Berlin
September-October
1955

Unpublished radio broadcast

Impromptu in F minor D935 no 4

London
September 1955

45: Columbia SEL 1615
LP: Columbia 33CX 1612
LP: Angel 35534
LP: EMI 3C 153 52434-52441M
CD: Toshiba TOCE 8131-8136

Klavierstück in E flat minor D946 no 1

London
October 1956

LP: Columbia 33CX 1612
LP: Angel 35534
LP: EMI 3C 153 52434-52441M
CD: Toshiba TOCE 8131-8136

Klavierstück in E flat D946 no 2

London
October 1956

LP: Columbia 33CX 1612
LP: Angel 35534
LP: EMI 3C 153 52434-52441M
CD: Toshiba TOCE 8131-8136

Klavierstück in C D946 no 3

London
October 1956

LP: Columbia 33CX 1612
LP: Angel 35534
LP: EMI 3C 153 52434-52441M
CD: Toshiba TOCE 8131-8136

Moment musical in C D780 no 1

London
September 1951

78: Columbia LX 1588
LP: Columbia (France) FCX 373
LP: EMI 3C 153 52434-52441M
CD: Toshiba TOCE 8131-8136

Moment musical in A flat D780 no 2

London
September 1951

78: Columbia LX 1589
LP: Columbia (France) FCX 373
LP: EMI 3C 153 52434-52441M
CD: Toshiba TOCE 8131-8136

Moment musical in F minor D780 no 3

London
1934

78: Columbia LB 31
78: Columbia (Germany) LW 18
78: Columbia (USA) 17079D
78: Columbia (Australia) LO 19

London
September 1951

78: Columbia LX 1589
LP: Columbia (France) FCX 373
LP: EMI 3C 153 52434-52441M
CD: Toshiba TOCE 8131-8136

Moments musicaux/concluded

Moment musical in C sharp minor D780 no 4

London
September 1951

78: Columbia LX 1588
LP: Columbia (France) FCX 373
LP: EMI 3C 153 52434-52441M
CD: Toshiba TOCE 8131-8136

Moment musical in F minor D780 no 5

London
September 1951

78: Columbia LX 1591
LP: Columbia (France) FCX 373
LP: EMI 3C 153 52434-52441M
CD: Toshiba TOCE 8131-8136

Moment musical in A flat D780 no 6

London
September 1951

78: Columbia LX 1588
LP: Columbia (France) FCX 373
LP: EMI 3C 153 52434-52441M
CD: Toshiba TOCE 8131-8136

Piano Sonata No 18 in G D894

September
1947

LP: Discocorp IGI 380
LP: Movimento Musica 01.063

Piano Trio in B flat D898

Frankfurt   Taschner, Hoelscher   Unpublished radio broadcast
November 1947

Schumann

Piano Concerto

Berlin
March 1942

BPO
Furtwängler

LP: Melodiya M10 36605-36606
LP: Everest SDBR 8434
LP: Discocorp IGI 348
LP: French Furtwängler Society
    SWF 7701
LP: Columbia (Japan) OZ 7596
CD: DG 427 7792/427 7732
CD: Melodiya (Japan) MEL 719

Dresden
1942

Dresden
Staatskapelle
Böhm

78: Columbia (Germany) LWX 356-359
LP: EMI 1C 137 53505-53507M

Baden-Baden
1944

BPO
Heger

LP: Discocorp IGI 363

Frankfurt
November 1949

Orchestra of
Hessischer Rundfunk
Schröder

Unpublished radio broadcast

Cologne
January 1951

WDR Orchestra
Wand

CD: Hunt CDHP 588

London
August 1953

Philharmonia
Karajan

LP: Columbia 33C 1033
LP: EMI 1C 047 01401M
LP: EMI 3C 153 52425-52431M
LP: Toshiba EAC 37001-37019

Album für die Jugend, Book 1 nos. 3,8,10,13,16 and 17

Berlin
October 1955

Unpublished radio broadcast

Carnaval

London
September 1951

78: International Columbia
    LCX 5013-5015
LP: Columbia (USA) ML 4772
LP: EMI 3C 153 52434-52441M
CD: Toshiba TOCE 8131-8136

Davidsbündlertänze

Location and
date uncertain

LP: Urania URLP 7106
LP: Saga XID 5148

Fantasia in C

Frankfurt
October 1947

LP: Melodiya M10 43395-43398

Berlin
September 1955

Unpublished radio broadcast

Kinderszenen

Location uncertain
1939-1940

78: Columbia (Germany) LWX 342-343
78: Columbia (France) LFX 858-859

Saarbrücken
November 1950

Unpublished radio broadcast

London
September 1951

78: Columbia LX 8913-8914 auto
LP: Columbia 33C 1014
LP: Columbia (USA) ML 4540
LP: Angel 35321
LP: EMI 1C 047 01401M
LP: EMI 1C 153 52434-52441M
CD: Toshiba TOCE 8131-8136
Träumerei only
LP: Columbia 33CX 1761
LP: Angel 35488

London
August 1955

Columbia unpublished

Kreisleriana

Saarbrücken
July 1951

Unpublished radio broadcast

Piano Sonata No 1 in F sharp minor

Berlin
1942

LP: Melodiya M10 43395-43398

3 Romanzen

Saarbrücken
July 1951

LP: Discocorp RR 492
CD: Music and Arts CD 743

Schlummerlied (Albumblätter)

London
August 1955

45: Columbia SCD 2163
LP: Columbia 33CX 1761
LP: Angel 35488
LP: EMI 3C 153 52434-52441M

Symphonic Studies

Saarbrücken
July 1951

LP: Discocorp RR 492
CD: Music and Arts CD 743

Waldszenen

Saarbrücken
July 1951

LP: Discocorp RR 492
CD: Music and Arts CD 743

Vogel als Prophet (Waldszenen)

London
October 1956

LP: Columbia 33CX 1761
LP: Angel 35488
LP: EMI 3C 153 52434-52441M

Scriabin

Piano Sonata No 5 in F sharp op 53

Frankfurt
October 1947

CD: Pearl GEMMCD 9011

4 Pieces op 51 (Fragilité; Prélude; Poème ailé; Danse languide)

Frankfurt
October 1947

CD: Pearl GEMMCD 9930

Poème op 32 no 1

Frankfurt
October 1947

Unpublished radio broadcast

London
October 1956

LP: Columbia 33CX 1761
LP: Angel 35488
LP: EMI 3C 153 52434-52441M

Poème op 32 no 2

Frankfurt
October 1947

Unpublished radio broadcast

Prélude op 15 no 4

London
October 1956

LP: Columbia 33CX 1761
LP: Angel 35488
LP: EMI 3C 153 52434-52441M

24 Préludes op 11

Berlin
October 1955

Unpublished radio broadcast

Sinding

Rustle of Spring op 32 no 3

London
June 1951

78: Columbia LX 1506/LX 8891
LP: Columbia 33CX 1761
LP: EMI 3C 153 52700-52705M

Zürich
June 1951

78: Columbia LB 139
78: Columbia (Germany) LW 64

It is not entirely clear why Gieseking should have commercially recorded this piece twice within a few weeks, firstly as the 12-inch fill-up to his 1951 version of the Grieg Piano Concerto and then as a 10-inch side to be coupled with a piece from Mendelssohn's Songs without Words

Richard Strauss

Lieder, arranged for piano solo: Freundliche Vision; Ständchen

1920s

78: Homochord 4-3003
78: Odeon 25228
78: Parlophone R 1077
78: Decca (USA) 20053
LP: EMI 3C 153 52700-52705M

Tansman

Blues

London
October 1956

Columbia unpublished

Villa-Lobos

3 Piano pieces

Frankfurt
September 1948

Unpublished radio broadcast

PHILHARMONIE

Montag, den 29. Oktober 1923, abends 7½ Uhr

II. Philharmonisches Konzert

Dirigent: Wilhelm Furtwängler
Solist: Walter Gieseking

Vortragsfolge:

I. Brandenburgisches Konzert Nr. 3 G-Dur   J. S. Bach

> I. Allegro (für Streichorchester) (Einlage: Andante für 2 Flöten mit Streichorchester aus dem Konzert Nr. 4)
>
> II. Allegro (für Streichorchester)

II. Symphonie H-Moll (unvollendet) - - - F. Schubert

> Allegro moderato — Andante con moto

III. Konzert für Klavier in Es-Dur mit Begleitung des Orchesters op. 31 - - Hans Pfitzner

> I. Pomphaft, mit Kraft und Schwung
> II. Heiterer Satz
> III. Äußerst ruhig, versonnen, schwärmerisch
> IV. Rasch, ungeschlacht, launig

IV. Ouverture zur Oper „Benvenuto Cellini"   H. Berlioz

Konzertflügel: GROTRIAN STEINWEG

III. Philharmonisches Konzert: Montag, den 12. November 1923
Dirigent: Wilhelm Furtwängler

Edwin Fischer
1886-1960

With valuable assistance and an introduction
by Roger Smithson

Discography compiled by John Hunt

Introduction

Edwin Fischer was born on 6 October 1886 in Basel. Both his parents came from musical families; his father, a self-styled "contemporary of Beethoven" born in 1826, played the oboe in the Basel orchestra and viola in a string quartet. The first sign of the young Edwin's talents came when he played a note on his parents' piano and announced "That's G". By the age of 10 he was sufficiently advanced to be accepted at the Basel Conservatory.

His father died when Edwin was about three years old (the exact date is uncertain), and his mother took charge of his development. She was ambitious for him, but wisely concentrated his efforts into training and study rather than forcing him to become a prodigy. In 1904 she took him to Berlin to study at the Stern Conservatory with Martin Krause, a former pupil and assistant of Liszt. Fischer himself subsequently became a professor at the Stern Conservatory, though probably later than 1905, the date sometimes cited for this appointment.

By the early 1920s Fischer had developed an enthusiastic following as a soloist, but he never cared to make this his only activity. He formed a celebrated trio with Georg Kulenkampff and Enrico Mainardi. He pursued a secondary career as a conductor, directing the Lübeck Musikverein from 1926 and the Munich Bachverein from 1928, and formed his own chamber orchestra to perform baroque and classical works. He researched and published editions of Bach keyboard works, Mozart piano sonatas, and (with Kulenkampff) the Beethoven violin sonatas, seeking to remove earlier editors' "improvements" and to restore the Urtext. Like many interpreters of his generation he was also a composer; his works include songs, piano pieces, and cadenzas (not beyond criticism) for some of the Mozart and Beethoven concertos. And he was an inspiring teacher, still remembered with respect and affection by former students including Alfred Brendel and Paul Badura-Skoda.

Fischer lived and worked in Berlin until 1942. While he seems to have had no particular interest in politics, he was far from being an admirer of the Nazi regime and resigned from the Hochschule für Musik in 1933 when his Jewish colleagues were expelled. He finally returned to Switzerland after his house was destroyed in an air raid, continuing his teaching work at the Lucerne Conservatory. Deteriorating health impaired his playing in later life, and he gave up recording and regular public appearances after 1954. He died in a Zürich hospital on 24 January 1960.

The records which he made for HMV and Electrola between 1931 and 1942 are in general his most successful; the complete "Well-Tempered Clavier" is a landmark in the history of recording. These discs show that his technique, though certainly never perfect, was far more secure than it was to become towards the end of his career. From 1947 onwards he visited the studio more reluctantly and with less consistent results. The best of these later records are perhaps those in which sympathetic partners compensated for the absence of an audience: the Philharmonia in Bach, Gioconda de Vito in Brahms, Furtwängler in the Beethoven Emperor Concerto. Fortunately this legacy is complemented by a number of inspired performances from live broadcasts, some of which also preserve his interpretations of works which he never recorded for commercial release.

Fischer's repertoire was far more extensive than his recordings suggest. Recital programmes show him performing the following works among others :

Beethoven: 27 of the 32 Sonatas; Eroica and Diabelli Variations

Chopin: Etudes op 10, Préludes op 28, Barcarolle, Fantasia op 49, Sonatas opp 35 and 58 and selected Ballades, Nocturnes, Polonaises, etc.

Liszt: Au bord d'une source Rapsodie espagnole, B minor Sonata

Schubert: Sonata D784 (op 42) and D845 (op 143)

Schumann: Carnaval, Fantasiestücke, Sonata op 11, Symphonic Etudes, Toccata

Other composers represented included Debussy, Mendelssohn, Scriabin and Schoenberg (the 6 Klavierstücke), and in the 1920s he played the concertos of Tchaikovsky (No 1), Reger and D'Albert. His conducting ranged from his exploration of the German and Italian baroque with his Chamber Orchestra to several of the symphonies of Bruckner, though he never achieved a lifelong ambition to conduct the St Matthew Passion.

Fischer's writings show how carefully he considered the interpreter's role. In his youth, he writes, he learned a tradition in which "the score was a strict law, the time inviolable, the form sacred", admirable in many ways yet susceptible to pedantry and philistinism. Then came Romanticism: "What Schumann and Liszt sowed, we have harvested; much that is imaginative, free and dreamlike, but also much excess of feeling, variation of tempo, arpeggios and use of pedal". (It is interesting to note that distinct classical and romantic styles existed side by side in Fischer's youth.) In the context of his time he was an advocate of authentic performance, and he welcomed the purifying influence of artists such as Busoni and Toscanini.

But he also saw the potential sterility of the trend, already current in his day, towards literalism and mechanical perfection. For Fischer, interpretation was fundamentally a spiritual quest. He adhered to the concept of the masterpiece in composition (his essays on the Beethoven sonatas have a firm musicological basis) but his thinking on the relationship between score and performance took him close to the intuitive, non-didactic world of Eastern philosophy. Technique, textual fidelity and analysis were all indispensible, but so were experience of life, closeness to nature, the capacity for humility. Ronald Smith, in an illuminating account of the recording of the Bach C major triple concerto, emphasises that "the whole idea of·a definitive performance would have been alien to Fischer". But perhaps Fischer's own words, from a lecture to his students, best convey his conception of the relationship between score and performance and of the ultimate goal of the performer:

"A piano piece well played merely in the pianistic sense is worthless. Only art experienced within, in which the personality plays a creative role, can be of interest or have validity. You must find yourselves."

Copyright 1994   Roger Smithson

Bach

Adagio (Concerto BWV 974, after Marcello)

London
November 1933

78: HMV DA 1389
78: Victor 1693
LP: HMV COLH 45
LP: Toshiba GR 2023
LP: EMI 2C 061 01226/29 12221
CD: Pearl GEMMCD 9481
78 edition coupled with
Mozart Minuet K1

Air (Suite No 3 BWV 1068)

Berlin
October 1936

Fischer Chamber
Orchestra
Fischer conducts

78: HMV DB 3002 and 3085/
    8258-8260 auto
78: Victor M 479
LP: EMI 29 12221
78 version coupled with Mozart
Symphony No 33

Brandenburg Concerto No 1 in F BWV 1046

Berlin 1942	Fischer Chamber Orchestra Fischer conducts	Electrola unpublished

Brandenburg Concerto No 2 in F BWV 1047

Berlin 1942	Fischer Chamber Orchestra Fischer conducts	78: Electrola DB 7612-7613 CD: Koch Historic 3-7701-2
London February 1953	Philharmonia Fischer conducts	LP: HMV ALP 1084 LP: Victor LHMV 8 LP: Electrola E 90056 LP: Toshiba GR 2213 LP: EMI 29 06261 CD: EMI CDH 763 0392/764 9282

Brandenburg Concerto No 5 in D BWV 1050

Berlin April 1942	Fischer Chamber Orchestra Other soloists unnamed Fischer also conducts	Electrola unpublished
Lausanne October 1948	Lausanne Chamber Orchestra Defrancesco, Wachsmuth-Loew Fischer also conducts	Swiss Radio unpublished
London October 1952	Philharmonia Morris, Parikian Fischer also conducts	LP: HMV ALP 1084 LP: Victor LHMV 8 LP: Electrola E 90056 LP: Toshiba GR 2213 LP: EMI 29 06261 CD: EMI CDH 763 0392

Brandenburg Concerto No 6 in B flat BWV 1051

Berlin
1942

Fischer Chamber
Orchestra
Fischer conducts

Electrola unpublished

Chorale Prelude "O Mensch bewin' dein' Sünde gross" BWV 622

London
May 1949

HMV unpublished
Matrix lost

Chorale Prelude "Ich ruf' zu Dir Herr Jesu Christ" BWV 639, arr. Busoni

Berlin
1941

78: Electrola DB 5688
LP: HMV COLH 45
LP: Toshiba GR 2023
LP: EMI 2C 061 01226/29 12221

Chromatic Fantasia and Fugue in D minor BWV 903

Berlin
October 1931

78: HMV DB 4403-4404
78: Victor 8680-8681
LP: HMV COLH 45/HQM 1174
LP: EMI 2C 061 01226/29 12221
CD: EMI CDH 764 9282

Lucerne
August 1954

Private recording unpublished
Recording incomplete

Concerto in A minor for flute, violin and piano BWV 1044

Lausanne
October 1945

Lausanne Chamber
Orchestra
Defrancesco,
Bagarotti
Fischer also conducts

Swiss Radio unpublished

Lausanne
November 1945

Lausanne Chamber
Orchestra
Defrancesco,
Bagarotti
Fischer also conducts

Swiss Radio unpublished
Parts of 1st and 3rd
movements only

Concerto No 1 in D minor for piano BWV 1052

Berlin January 1933	Fischer Chamber Orchestra Fischer also conducts	78: HMV DB 4420-4422/ 7335-7337 auto 78: Victor M 252 LP: HMV COLH 15 LP: Electrola E 80730 LP: World Records SH 108 LP: Toshiba GR 2009 LP: EMI 2C 051 01421/061 01421 LP: EMI 1C 049 01421/101 4211 CD: EMI CDH 763 0392

Concerto No 2 in E for piano BWV 1053

Lausanne October 1945	Lausanne Chamber Orchestra Fischer also conducts	Swiss Radio unpublished
London May 1950	Philharmonia Fischer also conducts	CD: EMI CDH 764 9282

Concerto No 4 in A for piano BWV 1055

Berlin October 1936	Fischer Chamber Orchestra Fischer also conducts	78: HMV DB 3081-3082 78: Victor M 368 LP: HMV COLH 15 LP: Electrola E 80730 LP: World Records SH 108 LP: Toshiba GR 2009 LP: EMI 2C 051 01421/061 01421 LP: EMI 1C 049 01421/101 4211 CD: EMI CDH 763 0392
Lausanne October 1948	Lausanne Chamber Orchestra Fischer also conducts	Swiss Radio unpublished

Concerto No 5 in F minor for piano BWV 1056

Berlin 1938 or 1939	Fischer Chamber Orchestra Fischer also conducts	78: HMV 4679-4680 78: Victor M 786 LP: HMV COLH 15 LP: Electrola E 80730 LP: World Records SH 108 LP: Toshiba GR 2009 LP: EMI 2C 051 01421/061 01421 LP: EMI 1C 049 01421/101 4211 CD: EMI CDH 763 0392 Roger Smithson considers that this recording was made later than the April 1938 date usually stated
Lausanne October 1948	Lausanne Chamber Orchestra Fischer also conducts	Swiss Radio unpublished 2nd & 3rd movements only

Concerto in C for 2 pianos BWV 1061

Munich May 1951	Winterthur Chamber Orchestra Gebhardt Fischer also conducts	Bavarian Radio unpublished

Concerto in D minor for 3 pianos BWV 1063

Lausanne October 1945	Lausanne Chamber Orchestra Baumgartner, Aeschbacher Fischer also conducts	Swiss Radio unpublished

Concerto in C for 3 pianos BWV 1064

Berlin 1932	Fischer Chamber Orchestra Hansen, Aschaffenburg Fischer also conducts	Electrola unpublished
London May 1950	Philharmonia R.Smith, Matthews Fischer also conducts	78: HMV DB 21180-21182/ DB 9573-9575 auto 45: Victor WHMV 1004 LP: Victor LHMV 1004 LP: HMV ALP 1103 LP: Electrola E 90066 LP: EMI 29 06261 CD: EMI CDH 764 9282

Fantasia and Fugue in A minor BWV 904

London
March 1937

78: HMV DB 3286
LP: HMV COLH 45
LP: Toshiba GR 2023
LP: EMI 2C 061 01226/29 12221
CD: EMI CDH 764 9282

Fantasia in C minor BWV 906

London
May 1949

78: HMV DB 21180-21182/
    DB 9573-9575 auto
LP: HMV COLH 45
LP: Toshiba GR 2023
LP: EMI 2C 061 01226/29 12221
CD: EMI CDH 764 9282
78 version coupled with Concerto
for 3 pianos BWV 1064

Fantasia in A minor BWV 922

London
March 1937

78: HMV DB 3287
LP: HMV COLH 45
LP: Toshiba GR 2023
LP: EMI 2C 061 01226/29 12221

Italian Concerto in F BWV 971, first movement

1909

Welte Mignon piano roll

Prelude and Fugue in E flat BWV 552, arr. Busoni

London
April 1933

78: HMV DB 1991-1992
78: Victor 7960-7961
LP: HMV COLH 50
LP: Toshiba GR 2036-2040/GR 2187
LP: EMI 2C 061 01304
LP: EMI 2C 151 54045-54049
LP: EMI 137 290991
CD: Pearl GEMMCD 9481

Prelude and Fugue No 1 in C BWV 846 (Well-Tempered Clavier, Book 1)

London
September 1933

78: HMV DB 2079
LP: HMV COLH 46
LP: Toshiba GR 70028-70029
LP: Toshiba GR 2036-2040/GR 2183
LP: EMI 2C 061 01300/29 06211
LP: EMI 2C 151 54045-54049
CD: EMI CHS 763 1882

Prelude and Fugue No 2 in C minor BWV 847 (Well-Tempered Clavier, Book 1)

London
April 1933

78: HMV DB 2079
LP: HMV COLH 46
LP: Toshiba GR 70028-70029
LP: Toshiba GR 2036-2040/GR 2183
LP: EMI 2C 061 01300/29 06211
LP: EMI 2C 151 54045-54049
CD: EMI CHS 763 1882

Prelude and Fugue No 3 in C sharp BWV 848 (Well-Tempered Clavier, Book 1)

London
April 1933

78: HMV DB 2080
LP: HMV COLH 46
LP: Toshiba GR 70028-70029
LP: Toshiba GR 2036-2040/GR 2183
LP: EMI 2C 061 01300/29 06211
LP: EMI 2C 151 54045-54049
CD: EMI CHS 763 1882

Prelude and Fugue No 4 in C sharp minor BWV 849 (Well-Tempered Clavier, Book 1)

1909

Welte Mignon piano roll 1834

London
April 1933

78: HMV DB 2081
78: HMV COLH 46
LP: Toshiba GR 70028-70029
LP: Toshiba GR 2036-2040/GR 2183
LP: EMI 2C 061 01300/29 06211
LP: EMI 2C 151 54045-54049
CD: EMI CHS 763 1882

Prelude and Fugue No 5 in D BWV 850 (Well-Tempered Clavier, Book 1)

1909	Welte Mignon piano roll 1836
Berlin October 1931	78: Electrola DB 4404 78: Victor 8681 LP: HMV HQM 1174
London April 1933	HMV unpublished Matrix lost
London September 1933	78: HMV DB 2080 LP: HMV COLH 46 LP: Toshiba GR 70028-70029 LP: Toshiba GR 2036-2040/GR 2183 LP: EMI 2C 061 01300/29 06211 LP: EMI 2C 151 54045-54049 CD: EMI CHS 763 1882

Prelude and Fugue No 6 in D minor BWV 851 (Well-Tempered Clavier, Book 1)

London April 1933	78: HMV DB 2080 LP: HMV COLH 46 LP: Toshiba GR 70028-70029 LP: Toshiba GR 2036-2040/GR 2183 LP: EMI 2C 061 01300/29 06211 LP: EMI 2C 151 54045-54049 CD: EMI CHS 763 1882

Prelude and Fugue No 7 in E flat BWV 852 (Well-Tempered Clavier, Book 1)

London September 1933	78: HMV DB 2083 LP: HMV COLH 46 LP: Toshiba GR 70028-70029 LP: Toshiba GR 2036-2040/GR 2183 LP: EMI 2C 061 01300/29 06211 LP: EMI 2C 151 54045-54049 CD: EMI CHS 763 1882

Prelude and Fugue No 8 in E flat minor BWV 853 (Well-Tempered Clavier, Book 1)

London September 1933	78: HMV DB 2084 LP: HMV COLH 46 LP: Toshiba GR 70028-70029 LP: Toshiba GR 2036-2040/GR 2183 LP: EMI 2C 061 01300/29 06211 LP: EMI 2C 151 45045-54049 CD: EMI CHS 763 1882

Prelude and Fugue No 9 in E BWV 854 (Well-Tempered Clavier, Book 1)

London
September 1933

78: HMV DB 2085
LP: HMV COLH 46
LP: Toshiba GR 70028-70029
LP: Toshiba GR 2036-2040/GR 2183
LP: EMI 2C 061 01300/29 06211
LP: EMI 2C 151 45045-54049
CD: EMI CHS 763 1882

Prelude and Fugue No 10 in E minor BWV 855 (Well-Tempered Clavier, Book 1)

London
April 1933

78: HMV DB 2085
LP: HMV COLH 46
LP: Toshiba GR 70028-70029
LP: Toshiba GR 2036-2040/GR 2183
LP: EMI 2C 061 01300/29 06211
LP: EMI 2C 151 54045-54049
CD: EMI CHS 763 1882

Prelude and Fugue No 11 in F BWV 856 (Well-Tempered Clavier, Book 1)

London
September 1933

78: HMV DB 2085
LP: HMV COLH 46
LP: Toshiba GR 70028-70029
LP: Toshiba GR 2036-2040/GR 2183
LP: EMI 2C 061 01300/29 06211
LP: EMI 2C 151 54045-54049
CD: EMI CHS 763 1882

Prelude and Fugue No 12 in F minor BWV 857 (Well-Tempered Clavier, Book 1)

London
September 1933

78: HMV DB 2082
LP: HMV COLH 46
LP: Toshiba GR 70028-70029
LP: Toshiba GR 2036-2040/GR 2183
LP: EMI 2C 061 01300/29 06221
LP: EMI 2C 151 54045-54049
CD: EMI CHS 763 1882

Prelude and Fugue No 13 in F sharp BWV 858 (Well-Tempered Clavier, Book 1)

London
April 1933

78: HMV DB 2292
LP: HMV COLH 47
LP: Toshiba GR 70028-70029
LP: Toshiba GR 2036-2040/GR 2184
LP: EMI 2C 061 01300/29 06221
LP: EMI 2C 151 54045-54049
CD: EMI CHS 763 1882

ROYAL ALBERT HALL

Manager - C. S. Taylor

PHILHARMONIA CONCERT SOCIETY

(President: H.H. The Maharaja of Mysore)

presents

PHILHARMONIA ORCHESTRA

(Leader: MANOUG PARIKIAN)

EDWIN FISCHER
DENIS MATTHEWS
RONALD SMITH
MAX SALPETER
GARETH MORRIS

BACH PROGRAMME

Concerto for Pianoforte in A major

Concerto for Two Pianofortes in C major

Concerto for Pianoforte, Violin and Flute

Concerto for Three Pianofortes

Thursday, May 11th, at 7.30 p.m.

KINGSWAY HALL
KINGSWAY, W.C.2

PHILHARMONIA CONCERT SOCIETY
(President: H.H. The Maharaja of Mysore)

presents

MYSORE CONCERTS
Bach Concert

EDWIN FISCHER

PHILHARMONIA ORCHESTRA
Led by MAX SALPETER

HAROLD JACKSON
(Trumpet)

GARETH MORRIS
(Flute)

MANOUG PARIKIAN
(Violin)

ELISABETH SCHWARZKOPF
(Soprano)

Clavier Concerto in D minor
Cantata No. 51: "Jauchzet Gott"
Clavier Concerto in E major
Brandenburg Concerto No. 5 in D major
for Clavier, Flute and Violin

———STEINWAY PIANOFORTE———

MONDAY, NOVEMBER 20th, 1950
at 7.30 p.m.

Management. IBBS & TILLETT LTD., 124 WIGMORE STREET, W.1

Prelude and Fugue No 14 in F sharp minor BWV 859 (Well-Tempered Clavier, Book 1)

London
May 1934

78: HMV DB 2292
LP: HMV COLH 47
LP: Toshiba GR 70028-70029
LP: Toshiba GR 2036-2040/GR 2184
LP: EMI 2C 061 01301/29 06221
LP: EMI 2C 151 54045-54049
CD: EMI CHS 763 1882

Prelude and Fugue No 15 in G BWV 860 (Well-Tempered Clavier, Book 1)

London
May 1934

78: HMV DB 2293
LP: HMV COLH 47
LP: Toshiba GR 70028-70029
LP: Toshiba GR 2036-2040/GR 2184
LP: EMI 2C 061 01301/29 06221
LP: EMI 2C 151 54045-54049
CD: EMI CHS 763 1882

Prelude and Fugue No 16 in G minor BWV 861 (Well-Tempered Clavier, Book 1)

London
May 1934

78: HMV DB 2293
LP: HMV COLH 47
LP: Toshiba GR 70028-70029
LP: Toshiba GR 2036-2040/GR 2184
LP: EMI 2C 061 01301/29 06221
LP: EMI 2C 151 54045-54049
CD: EMI CHS 763 1882

Prelude and Fugue No 17 in A flat BWV 862 (Well-Tempered Clavier, Book 1)

London
April 1933

78: HMV DB 2294
LP: HMV COLH 47
LP: Toshiba GR 70028-70029
LP: Toshiba GR 2036-2040/GR 2184
LP: EMI 2C 061 01301/29 06221
LP: EMI 2C 151 54045-54049
CD: EMI CHS 763 1882

Prelude and Fugue No 18 in G sharp minor BWV 863 (Well-Tempered Clavier, Book 1)

London
May 1934

78: HMV DB 2294
LP: HMV COLH 47
LP: Toshiba GR 70028-70029
LP: Toshiba GR 2036-2040/GR 2184
LP: EMI 2C 061 01301/29 06221
LP: EMI 2C 151 54045-54049
CD: EMI CHS 763 1882

Prelude and Fugue No 19 in A BWV 864 (Well-Tempered Clavier, Book 1)

London
August 1934

78: HMV DB 2295
LP: HMV COLH 47
LP: Toshiba GR 70028-70029
LP: Toshiba GR 2036-2040/GR 2184
LP: EMI 2C 061 01301/29 06221
LP: EMI 2C 151 54045-54049
CD: EMI CHS 763 1882

Prelude and Fugue No 20 in A minor BWV 865 (Well-Tempered Clavier, Book 1)

London
August 1934

78: HMV DB 2295
LP: HMV COLH 47
LP: Toshiba GR 70028-70029
LP: Toshiba GR 2036-2040/GR 2184
LP: EMI 2C 061 01301/29 06221
LP: EMI 2C 151 54045-54049
CD: EMI CHS 763 1882

Berlin
February 1939

Fischer Chamber
Orchestra
Fischer conducts

Fugue only arranged by Fischer
and prefaced by his arrangement
of Prelude in A minor BWV 944
78: HMV DA 4461
LP: EMI 29 12221
CD: Koch Historic 3-7701-2

Prelude and Fugue No 21 in B flat BWV 866 (Well-Tempered Clavier, Book 1)

London
May 1934

78: HMV DB 2296
LP: HMV COLH 47
LP: Toshiba GR 70028-70029
LP: Toshiba GR 2036-2040/GR 2184
LP: EMI 2C 061 01301/29 06221
LP: EMI 2C 151 54045-54049
CD: EMI CHS 763 1882

Prelude and Fugue No 22 in B flat minor BWV 867 (Well-Tempered Clavier, Book 1)

1909	Welte Mignon piano roll 1835
London April 1933	78: HMV DB 2297 LP: HMV COLH 47 LP: Toshiba GR 70028-70029 LP: Toshiba GR 2036-2040/GR 2184 LP: EMI 2C 061 01301/29 06231 LP: EMI 2C 151 54045-54049 CD: EMI CHS 763 1882

Prelude and Fugue No 23 in B BWV 868 (Well-Tempered Clavier, Book 1)

London May 1934	78: HMV DB 2296 LP: HMV COLH 47 LP: Toshiba GR 70028-70029 LP: Toshiba GR 2036-2040/GR 2184 LP: EMI 2C 061 01301/29 06231 LP: EMI 2C 151 54045-54049 CD: EMI CHS 763 1882

Prelude and Fugue No 24 in B minor BWV 869 (Well-Tempered Clavier, Book 1)

London May 1934	HMV unpublished Matrix lost
London August 1934	78: HMV DB 2298 LP: HMV COLH 47 LP: Toshiba GR 70028-70029 LP: Toshiba GR 2036-2040/GR 2184 LP: EMI 2C 061 01301/29 06231 LP: EMI 2C 151 54045-54049 CD: EMI CHS 763 1882

Prelude and Fugue No 25 in C BWV 870 (Well-Tempered Clavier, Book 2)

London February 1935	HMV unpublished
London June 1935	78: HMV DB 2532 LP: HMV COLH 48 LP: Toshiba GR 70030-70031 LP: Toshiba GR 2036-2040/GR 2185 LP: EMI 2C 061 01302/29 06231 LP: EMI 2C 151 54045-54049 CD: EMI CHS 763 1882

Prelude and Fugue No 26 in C minor BWV 871 (Well-Tempered Clavier, Book 2)

London
February 1935

78: HMV DB 2532
LP: HMV COLH 48
LP: Toshiba GR 70030-70031
LP: Toshiba GR 2036-2040/GR 2185
LP: EMI 2C 061 01302/29 06231
LP: EMI 2C 151 54045-54049
CD: EMI CHS 763 1882

Prelude and Fugue No 27 in C sharp BWV 872 (Well-Tempered Clavier, Book 2)

London
February 1935

HMV unpublished

London
June 1935

78: HMV DB 2533
LP: HMV COLH 48
LP: Toshiba GR 70030-70031
LP: Toshiba GR 2036-2040/GR 2185
LP: EMI 2C 061 01302/20 06231
LP: EMI 2C 151 54045-54049
CD: EMI CHS 763 1882

Prelude and Fugue No 28 in C sharp minor BWV 873 (Well-Tempered Clavier, Book 2)

Berlin
April 1935

Electrola unpublished

London
June 1935

78: HMV DB 2533-2534
LP: HMV COLH 48
LP: Toshiba GR 70030-70031
LP: Toshiba GR 2036-2040/GR 2185
LP: EMI 2C 061 01302/29 06231
LP: EMI 2C 151 54045-54049
CD: EMI CHS 763 1882

Prelude and Fugue No 29 in D BWV 874 (Well-Tempered Clavier, Book 2)

Berlin
April 1935

Electrola unpublished
Matrix lost

London
June 1935

78: HMV DB 2535
LP: HMV COLH 48
LP: Toshiba GR 70030-70031
LP: Toshiba GR 2036-2040/GR 2185
LP: EMI 2C 061 01302/29 06231
LP: EMI 2C 151 54045-54049
CD: EMI CHS 763 1882

Prelude and Fugue No 30 in D minor BWV 875 (Well-Tempered Clavier, Book 2)

Berlin
April 1935

Electrola unpublished
Matrix lost

London
June 1935

78: HMV DB 2536
LP: HMV COLH 48
LP: Toshiba GR 70030-70031
LP: Toshiba GR 2036-2040/GR 2185
LP: EMI 2C 061 01302/29 06241
LP: EMI 2C 151 54045-54049
CD: EMI CHS 763 1882

Prelude and Fugue No 31 in E flat BWV 876 (Well-Tempered Clavier, Book 2)

Berlin
April 1935

Electrola unpublished
Matrix lost

London
June 1935

78: HMV DB 2536
LP: HMV COLH 48
LP: Toshiba GR 70030-70031
LP: Toshiba GR 2036-2040/GR 2185
LP: EMI 2C 061 01302/29 06241
LP: EMI 2C 151 54045-54049
CD: EMI CHS 763 1882

Prelude and Fugue No 32 in E flat minor BWV 877 (Well-Tempered Clavier, Book 2)

Berlin
April 1935

Electrola unpublished
Matrix lost

London
June 1935

78: HMV DB 2534
LP: HMV COLH 48
LP: Toshiba GR 70030-70031
LP: Toshiba GR 2036-2040/GR 2185
LP: EMI 2C 061 01302/29 06241
LP: EMI 2C 151 54045-54049
CD: EMI CHS 763 1882

Prelude and Fugue No 33 in E BWV 878 (Well-Tempered Clavier, Book 2)

Berlin
April 1935

Electrola unpublished
Matrix lost

London
June 1935

78: HMV DB 2537
LP: HMV COLH 48
LP: Toshiba GR 70030-70031
LP: Toshiba GR 2036-2040/GR 2185
LP: EMI 2C 061 01302/29 06241
LP: EMI 2C 151 54045-54049
CD: EMI CHS 763 1882

Prelude and Fugue No 34 in E minor BWV 879 (Well-Tempered Clavier, Book 2)

London
June 1935

78: HMV DB 2538
LP: HMV COLH 48
LP: Toshiba GR 70030-70031
LP: Toshiba GR 2036-2040/GR 2185
LP: EMI 2C 061 01302/29 06241
LP: EMI 2C 151 54045-54049
CD: EMI CHS 763 1882

Prelude and Fugue No 35 in F BWV 880 (Well-Tempered Clavier, Book 2)

London
June 1936

78: HMV DB 2944
78: Victor M 334
LP: HMV COLH 49
LP: Toshiba GR 70030-70031
LP: Toshiba GR 2036-2040/GR 2186
LP: EMI 2C 061 01303/29 06241
LP: EMI 2C 151 54045-54049
CD: EMI CHS 763 1882

Prelude and Fugue No 36 in F minor BWV 881 (Well-Tempered Clavier, Book 2)

Berlin
April 1935

Electrola unpublished
Matrix lost

London
June 1936

78: HMV DB 2944
78: Victor M 334
LP: HMV COLH 49
LP: Toshiba GR 70030-70031
LP: Toshiba GR 2036-2040/GR 2186
LP: EMI 2C 061 01303/29 06241
LP: EMI 2C 151 54045-54049
CD: EMI CHS 763 1882

Prelude and Fugue No 37 in F sharp BWV 882 (Well-Tempered Clavier, Book 2)

London
June 1936

78: HMV DB 2945
78: Victor M 334
LP: HMV COLH 49
LP: Toshiba GR 70030-70031
LP: Toshiba GR 2036-2040/GR 2186
LP: EMI 2C 061 01303/29 06241
LP: 2C 151 54045-54049
CD: EMI CHS 763 1882

Prelude and Fugue No 38 in F sharp minor BWV 883 (Well-Tempered Clavier, Book 2)

London
June 1936

78: HMV DB 2946
78: Victor M 334
LP: HMV COLH 49
LP: Toshiba GR 70030-70031
LP: Toshiba GR 2036-2040/GR 2186
LP: EMI 2C 061 01303/29 06241
LP: EMI 2C 151 54045-54049
CD: EMI CHS 763 1882

Prelude and Fugue No 39 in G BWV 884 (Well-Tempered Clavier, Book 2)

London
June 1936

78: HMV DB 2947
78: Victor M 334
LP: HMV COLH 49
Lp: Toshiba GR 70030-70031
LP: Toshiba GR 2036-2040/GR 2186
LP: EMI 2C 061 01303/29 06251
LP: EMI 2C 151 54045-54049
CD: EMI CHS 763 1882

Prelude and Fugue No 40 in G minor BWV 885 (Well-Tempered Clavier, Book 2)

London
June 1936

78: HMV DB 2947-2948
78: Victor M 334
LP: HMV COLH 49
LP: Toshiba GR 70030-70031
LP: Toshiba GR 2036-2040/GR 2186
LP: EMI 2C 061 01303/29 06251
LP: EMI 2C 151 54045-54049
CD: EMI CHS 763 1882

Prelude and Fugue No 41 in A flat BWV 886 (Well-Tempered Clavier, Book 2)

London
June 1936

78: HMV DB 2948-2949
78: Victor M 334
LP: HMV COLH 49
LP: Toshiba GR 70030-70031
LP: Toshiba GR 2036-2040/GR 2186
LP: EMI 2C 061 01303/29 06251
LP: EMI 2C 151 54045-54049
CD: EMI CHS 763 1882

Prelude and Fugue No 42 in G sharp minor BWV 887 (Well-Tempered Clavier, Book 2)

London
June 1936

78: HMV DB 2949-2950
78: Victor M 334
LP: HMV COLH 49
LP: Toshiba GR 70030-70031
LP: Toshiba GR 2036-2040/GR 2186
LP: EMI 2C 061 01303/29 06251
LP: EMI 2C 151 54045-54049
CD: EMI CHS 763 1882

Prelude and Fugue No 43 in A BWV 888 (Well-Tempered Clavier, Book 2)

London
June 1936

78: HMV DB 2950
78: Victor M 334
LP: HMV COLH 49
LP: Toshiba GR 70030-70031
LP: Toshiba GR 2036-2040/GR 2186
LP: EMI 2C 061 01303/29 06251
LP: EMI 2C 151 54045-54049
CD: EMI CHS 763 1882

Prelude and Fugue No 44 in A minor BWV 889 (Well-Tempered Clavier, Book 2)

London
June 1936

78: HMV DB 3236/DB 8276
78: Victor M 447
LP: HMV COLH 49
LP: Toshiba GR 70030-70031
LP: Toshiba GR 2036-2040/GR 2186
LP: EMI 2C 061 01303/29 06251
LP: EMI 2C 151 54045-54049
CD: EMI CHS 763 1882

Prelude and Fugue No 45 in B flat BWV 890 (Well-Tempered Clavier, Book 2)

London
June 1936

78: HMV DB 3236-3237/
    BD 8277-8278 auto
78: Victor M 447
LP: HMV COLH 50
LP: Toshiba GR 70030-70031
LP: Toshiba GR 2036-2040/GR 2187
LP: EMI 2C 061 01304/29 06251
LP: EMI 2C 151 54045-54049
CD: EMI CHS 763 1882

Prelude and Fugue No 46 in B flat minor BWV 891 (Well-Tempered Clavier, Book 2)

London
June 1936

78: HMV DB 3237-3238/
       DB 8279-8281 auto
78: Victor M 447
LP: HMV COLH 50
LP: Toshiba GR 70030-70031
LP: Toshiba GR 2036-2040/GR 2187
LP: EMI 2C 061 01304/29 06251
LP: EMI 2C 151 54045-54049
CD: EMI CHS 763 1882

Prelude and Fugue No 47 in B BWV 892 (Well-Tempered Clavier, Book 2)

London
June 1936

78: HMV DB 3239/DB 8281
78: Victor M 447
LP: HMV COLH 50
LP: Toshiba GR 70030-70031
LP: Toshiba GR 2036-2040/GR 2187
LP: EMI 2C 061 01304/29 06251
LP: EMI 2C 151 54045-54049
CD: EMI CHS 763 1882

Prelude and Fugue No 48 in B minor BWV 893 (Well-Tempered Clavier, Book 2)

London
June 1936

78: HMV DB 3239/DB 8280
78: Victor M 447
LP: HMV COLH 50
LP: Toshiba GR 70030-70031
LP: Toshiba GR 2036-2040/GR 2187
LP: EMI 2C 061 01304/29 06251
LP: EMI 2C 151 54045-54049
CD: EMI CHS 763 1882

Ricerare à 6 arr. Fischer (The Musical Offering)

~~Potsdam~~ June 1930	Fischer Chamber Orchestra Fischer conducts	Electrola unpublished
Berlin January 1933	Fischer Chamber Orchestra Fischer conducts	78: HMV DB 4419 78: Victor 8660 CD: Pearl GEMMCD 9481
Lausanne October 1948	Lausanne Chamber Orchestra Fischer conducts	Swiss Radio unpublished

Toccata No 3 in D BWV 912

Berlin
January 1942

78: Electrola DB 5687-5688
LP: HMV COLH 45
LP: Toshiba GR 2023
LP: EMI 2C 061 01226/29 12221

Beethoven

Fantasia in G minor op 77

Munich
November 1952

LP: Discocorp RR 450
CD: Orfeo C 270921 B

Grosse Fuge op 133 arr. Fischer

Berlin
October 1939

Fischer Chamber
Orchestra
Fischer conducts

78: Electrola DB 5547-5548
CD: Koch Histroric 3-7701-2
CD: Nuova Era HMT 90024

Piano Concerto No 1

Berlin 1943	Fischer Chamber Orchestra <u>Fischer also conducts</u>	LP: Discocorp RR 450
Salzburg July 1951	VPO <u>Fischer also conducts</u>	Unpublished radio broadcast

Piano Concerto No 3

Copenhagen March 1954	Royal Danish Orchestra King Frederik IX	Unpublished private recording <u>Parts of rehearsal also</u> <u>recorded</u>
London May 1954	Philharmonia <u>Fischer also conducts</u>	LP: HMV BLP 1063 LP: Electrola E 70039/E 91411 LP: Electrola SMVP 8044 LP: EMI 1C 047 01404M *LP: EMI RLS 29 00013 *Also names <u>orchestra leader</u> <u>(Manoug Parikian) as directing</u> <u>the performance</u>

Piano Concerto No 4

Munich November 1951	Bavarian RO Jochum	CD: Orfeo C 270921 A
London May 1954	Philharmonia <u>Fischer also conducts</u>	LP: HMV BLP 1067 LP: Electrola E 70041/E 91411 LP: Electrola SMVP 8007 LP: EMI 1C 047 00842M *LP: EMI RLS 29 00013 LP: EMI 137 290992 *Also names <u>orchestra leader</u> <u>(Manoug Parikian) as directing</u> <u>the performance</u>

Piano Concerto No 5 "Emperor"

| Berlin
May 1930 | Berlin RO
Scherchen | Unpublished RRG recording
<u>May be incomplete</u> |

| Berlin
October 1932 | Berlin RO
Jochum | RRG recording untraced
<u>Opening of 1st movement only</u> |

Dresden
June 1939

Dresden
Staatskapelle
Böhm

78: Electrola DB 5511-5515
LP: EMI 1C 137 53500-53504M
LP: EMI 2C 051 45660
CD: Dante HPC 007

London
February 1951

Philharmonia
Furtwängler

78: HMV DB 21315-21319/
    DB 9661-9665 auto
LP: Pathé FALP 121
LP: HMV ALP 1051/HLM 7027
LP: Electrola SMVP 8039
LP: EMI 1C 047 00803
LP: EMI 2C 153 52540-52551M
LP: Toshiba WF 60013/WF 70046
LP: Turnabout THS 65072
LP: EMI RLS 29 00013
CD: Toshiba CE28-5578
CD: EMI CDH 761 0052

Piano Sonata No 7 in D op 10 no 3

1909

Welte Mignon piano roll
    1839-1840

Hamburg
February 1948

LP: Cetra LO 528/DOC 38
CD: Hunt CD 514

London
May 1954

LP: HMV ALP 1271
LP: Electrola E 90107/E 80673
LP: EMI 1C 147 01674-01675M
CD: EMI CDH 761 0052

Piano Sonata No 8 in C minor op 13 "Pathetique"

1909	Welte Mignon piano roll 1837-1838
London November 1938	78: HMV DB 3666-3667 CD: Piano Time (Italy) PTC 2003 CD: Nuova Era HMT 90024 CD: Appian APR 5502
London October 1952	LP: HMV ALP 1094 LP: Electrola E 90060/E 80673 LP: EMI 1C 047 00842M LP: EMI 1C 147 01674-01675M LP: Toshiba GR 70013
Munich November 1952	CD: Hunt CD 513 CD: Orfeo C 270921 B

Piano Sonata No 14 in C sharp minor op 27 no 2 "Moonlight"

Berlin May 1928	Electrola unpublished

Piano Sonata No 15 in D op 28 "Pastoral"

Salzburg July 1954	LP: Discocorp RR 435 LP: Cetra LO 528/DOC 38 CD: Hunt CD 514

Piano Sonata No 21 in C op 53 "Waldstein"

Salzburg July 1954	LP: Discocorp RR 435 LP: Cetra LO 528/DOC 38 CD: Hunt CD 513

Piano Sonata No 23 in F minor op 57 "Appassionata"

London
February and
June 1935

78: HMV DB 2517-2519/
    DB 7899-7901 auto
78: Victor M 279
CD: Piano Time (Italy) PTC 2003
CD: Nuova Era HMT 90024
CD: Appian APR 5502

London
October 1952

LP: HMV ALP 1094
LP: Victor LHMV 1055
LP: Electrola E 90060/E 80673
LP: EMI 1C 147 01674-01675M
LP: Toshiba GR 70013

Piano Sonata No 30 in E op 109

Turin
December 1954

CD: Hunt CD 513
Incorrectly dated June 1952

Piano Sonata No 31 in A flat op 110

1909

Welte Mignon piano roll
    1841-1842

London
November 1938

78: HMV DB 3707-3708
LP: EMI 1C 147 01674-01675M
LP: Discocorp DIS 714
CD: Pearl GEMMCD 9481
CD: Dante HPC 007
CD: Appian APR 5502

Piano Sonata No 32 in C minor op 111

London
May 1954

LP: HMV ALP 1271
LP: Electrola E 90107
LP: EMI 1C 147 01674-01675M
LP: Discocorp DIS 714
LP: Toshiba GR 70013

Salzburg
July 1954

LP: Cetra DOC 38
CD: Hunt CD 514

Piano Trio No 5 in D op 70 no 1 "Ghost"

Salzburg
August 1953

Schneiderhan,
Mainardi

LP: Discocorp BWS 735
LP: Cetra DOC 35
CD: Hunt CD 568

Piano Trio No 6 in B flat op 97 "Archduke"

Salzburg
August 1952

Schneiderhan
Mainardi

LP: Discocorp BWS 735
LP: Cetra LO 518

Brahms

Piano Concerto No 1, bars 123-245 from first movement only

Basle	Basle Orchestra	Unpublished fragment
December 1945	H.Münch	

Piano Concerto No 2

Berlin
November 1942

BPO
Furtwängler

LP: Melodiya D 09883-09884
LP: Unicorn UNI 102
LP: French Furtwängler Society
    SWF 6901
LP: Turnabout TV 4324
LP: Columbia (Japan) DXM 108
LP: EMI 1C 149 53420-53426M
LP: EMI 2C 153 53420-53426M
LP: EMI 3C 153 53660-53669M
LP: Toshiba WF 60053/WF 70011
CD: Priceless D 14236
CD: Toshiba CE28-5756
CD: DG 427 7782/427 7732
CD: Music and Arts CD 804

Basle
February 1943

Basle Orchestra
H.Münch

LP: Discocorp RR 503
Incorrectly dated 1945

Piano Quartet No 1 in G minor op 25

Berlin
September 1939

Members of
Breronel String
Quartet

78: Electrola DB 5532-5536
LP: Discocorp MLG 74
CD: Koch Historic 3-7701-3

Piano Sonata No 3 in F minor op 5

1916-1925

Duo Art piano roll
LP: Everest X 920

Zürich
July 1946

HMV unpublished
Matrices lost

London
May 1949

78: HMV DB 21213-21215/
    DB 9645-9647 auto
45: Victor WHMV 1065
LP: Victor LHMV 1065
LP: HMV BLP 1017
LP: Electrola E 70025
LP: EMI 29 05751/137 290993

Rhapsody in G minor op 79 no 2

London
October 1946

HMV unpublished
Matrix lost

London
February 1947

78: HMV DB 6437
CD: Piano Time (Italy) PTC 2003

Intermezzo in E flat op 117 no 1

London
November 1933

HMV unpublished
Matrix lost

London
February 1947

78: HMV DB 6478
CD: Piano Time (Italy) PTC 2003

Intermezzo in B flat minor op 117 no 2

London
October 1946

HMV unpublished
Matrix lost

London
February 1947

78: HMV DB 6478
CD: Piano Time (Italy) PTC 2003

Ballade in G minor op 118 no 3

London
October 1946

HMV unpublished
Matrix lost

London
February 1947

78: HMV DB 6437
CD: Piano Time (Italy) PTC 2003

Intermezzo in F minor op 118 no 4

1949
Location uncertain

Unpublished radio broadcast
Authenticity uncertain

Romanze in F op 118 no 5

1949
Location uncertain

Unpublished radio broadcast
Authenticity uncertain

Intermezzo in E flat minor op 118 No 6

1949
Location uncertain

Unpublished radio broadcast
Authenticity uncertain

Piano Trio No 1 in B op 8

Salzburg August 1953	Schneiderhan, Mainardi	LP: Cetra DOC 35
Munich November 1953	Schneiderhan, Mainardi	LP: Discocorp BWS 739 CD: Music and Arts CD 739
Rome December 1953	Schneiderhan, Mainardi	Unpublished radio broadcast
Salzburg August 1954	Schneiderhan, Mainardi	LP: Cetra DOC 55 CD: Hunt CD 568

Piano Trio No 2 in C op 87

Munich December 1951	Schneiderhan, Mainardi	LP: Discocorp BWS 739 CD: Music and Arts CD 739
Salzburg August 1952	Schneiderhan, Mainardi	Unpublished radio broadcast
Rome December 1953	Schneiderhan, Mainardi	Unpublished radio broadcast
Salzburg August 1954	Schneiderhan, Mainardi	LP: Cetra DOC 55 CD: Hunt CD 568

Piano Trio No 3 in C minor op 101

Salzburg August 1954	Schneiderhan, Mainardi	LP: Cetra DOC 55 CD: Hunt CD 568

Variations on an original theme op 21 no 1

1953 Location uncertain	LP: Discocorp RR 503

Violin Sonata No 1 in G op 78

London May 1954	de Vito	LP: HMV ALP 1282 LP: Toshiba EAC 77350-77360 LP: EMI 29 02571 CD: Toshiba CE25 5876-5885 CD: Testament SBT 1024

Violin Sonata No 3 in D minor op 108

London October 1954	de Vito	LP: HMV ALP 1282 LP: Toshiba EAC 77350-77360 LP: EMI 29 02571 CD: Toshiba CE25 5876-5885 CD: Testament SBT 1024

Da unten im Tale (Deutsche Volkslieder)

Turin
February 1954   Schwarzkopf   CD: Hunt CD 535/CDHP 535

Der Tod, das ist die kühle Nacht

Turin
February 1954   Schwarzkopf   CD: Hunt CD 535/CDHP 535

Feldeinsamkeit

Turin
February 1954   Schwarzkopf   CD: Hunt CD 535/CDHP 535

In stiller Nacht (Deutsche Volkslieder)

Turin
February 1954   Schwarzkopf   CD: Hunt CD 535/CDHP 535

Liebestreu

Turin
February 1954   Schwarzkopf   CD: Hunt CD 535/CDHP 535

Meine Liebe ist grün

Turin
February 1954   Schwarzkopf   CD: Hunt CD 535/CDHP 535

Therese

Turin
February 1954   Schwarzkopf   CD: Hunt CD 535/CDHP 535

Vergebliches Ständchen

Turin
February 1954   Schwarzkopf   CD: Hunt CD 535/CDHP 535

Von ewiger Liebe

Turin
February 1954   Schwarzkopf   CD: Hunt CD 535/CDHP 535

Wiegenlied

Turin
February 1954   Schwarzkopf   CD: Hunt CD 535/CDHP 535

Wie Melodien zieht es mir

Turin
February 1954   Schwarzkopf   CD: Hunt CD 535/CDHP 535

ROYAL FESTIVAL HALL
General Manager: T. E. Bean

PHILHARMONIA CONCERT SOCIETY

Artistic Director:
WALTER LEGGE

presents

PHILHARMONIA
ORCHESTRA
Leader: MAX SALPETER

EDWIN FISCHER

PROGRAMME

MOZART: Pianoforte Concerto in D minor, K.466

MOZART: Symphony in G minor, K.550

INTERVAL

BEETHOVEN: Piano Concerto No. 4 in G

Monday, April 26, 1954
at 8 p.m.

Management: IBBS & TILLETT LTD., 124 WIGMORE STREET, W.1

ROYAL FESTIVAL HALL

General Manager: T. E. Bean

PHILHARMONIA CONCERT SOCIETY

Artistic Director:

WALTER LEGGE

presents

ELISABETH SCHWARZKOPF
EDWIN FISCHER

LIEDER RECITAL

BEETHOVEN, SCHUBERT, BRAHMS

Friday, April 30, 1954
at 8 p.m.

Management: IBBS & TILLETT LTD., 124 WIGMORE STREET, W.1

Dall'Abaco

Concerto Grosso in B flat op 2 no 9

Berlin	Fischer Chamber	78: HMV DB 3175
October and	Orchestra	78: Victor 14418
November 1936	Fischer conducts	

Edwin Fischer

10 Lieder nach Gedichten von Hermann Hesse

Location	Schey	Unpublished radio broadcast
and date		
uncertain		

Foerster

Ariette variée, arr. Fischer

London	HMV unpublished
February 1947	

Furtwängler

Symphonic Concerto in B minor

Berlin	BPO	CD: Pilz CD 78004
January 1939	Furtwängler	

Adagio (Symphonic Concerto in B minor)

Berlin	BPO	78: Electrola DB 4696-4697
April 1939	Furtwängler	LP: Japan JP 1101-1102
		LP: French Furtwängler Society
		SWF 7101
		LP: HMV HLM 7027
		LP: Discocorp MLG 74
		LP: EMI 1C 047 01415M
		LP: Toshiba WF 70046
		CD: Toshiba TOCE 6072
		CD: Biddulph WHL 006-007

Handel

Chaconne in G

Berlin
May 1928

Electrola unpublished

Berlin
October 1931

78: HMV DA 4401
78: Victor 1597
LP: HMV HQM 1174
CD: Pearl GEMMCD 9481

Hamburg
February 1948

Unpublished radio broadcast

Suite No 3 in D minor, movements 1, 5 and 6

London
August 1934

78: HMV DB 2378
78: Victor 8693
LP: HMV HQM 1174
CD: Appian APR 5502
Appian incorrectly dates the
recording as 1928 on the
back liner

Haydn

Piano Concerto in D

Vienna
October 1942

VPO
Fischer also conducts

78: Electrola DB 7657-7658
LP: Discocorp MLG 74
LP: EMI 137 290991
CD: Piano Time (Italy) PTC 2003

Symphony No 104 "London"

Berlin
April 1938

Fischer Chamber
Orchestra
Fischer conducts

78: HMV DB 4615-4617/
    DB 8669-8671 auto
78: Victor M 617

Salzburg
July 1951

VPO
Fischer conducts

Unpublished radio broadcast

Mozart

Concerto for 2 pianos K365, arrangement of 2nd movement only

1909   Welte Mignon piano roll 1846

Contredanse in D K534 "Das Donnerwetter"

Berlin   Fischer Chamber   78: HMV DB 4680
April 1938   Orchestra   78: Victor M 786
                  Fischer conducts   LP: Victor LM 6130

Fantasia in C minor K396

1909   Welte Mignon piano roll 1843

Berlin   Electrola unpublished
May 1928

London   78: HMV DB 2377
August 1934   78: Victor 8696
                                             LP: HMV COLH 309/HQM 1174
                                             LP: EMI 143 6741
                                             CD: EMI CHS 763 7192

Fantasia in D minor K397

ca. 1951   Unpublished radio recording
Location uncertain

Fantasia in C minor K475

Berlin   78: Electrola DB 5637-5638
1941   LP: Discocorp RR 450

London   LP: EMI 143 6741
February 1947   CD: EMI CHS 763 7192

Minuet No 1 in G K1, arr. Fischer

London   78: HMV DA 1389
November 1933   78: Victor 1689
                                             LP: EMI 143 6741
                                             CD: EMI CHS 763 7192
                                             78 version coupled with
                                             Bach Adagio BWV 974

Piano Concerto No 9 K271, 3rd movement bar 150 to end

Berlin June 1932	Fischer Chamber Orchestra Fischer also conducts	RRG recording untraced

Piano Concerto No 17 K453

Berlin May 1937	Fischer Chamber Orchestra Fischer also conducts	78: HMV DB 3362-3364/ DB 8465-8467 auto 78: Victor M 481 LP: Victor LCT 6013 LP: HMV COLH 44 LP: Toshiba GR 2047 LP: EMI 2C 061 01423 LP: EMI 2C 051 43326 CD: EMI CHS 763 7192

Piano Concerto No 20 K466

Berlin September 1932	Unspecified orchestra Jochum	Electrola unpublished
London November 1933	LPO Fischer also conducts	78: HMV DB 2118-2121/ DB 7629-7632 auto 78: Victor M 223 LP: Victor LCT 6013 LP: EMI 2C 061 01408/29 10881 CD: EMI CHS 763 7192
London May 1954	Philharmonia Fischer also conducts	LP: HMV BLP 1055 LP: Electrola E 70040 LP: Toshiba GR 2159
Munich December 1954	Bavarian RO Jochum	LP: Discocorp IGI 290 CD: Memories HR 4246

Piano Concerto No 22 K482

London June 1935	Orchestra Barbirolli	78: HMV DB 2681-2684/ DB 8015-8018 auto 78: Victor M 316 78: Victor LCT 6013 LP: HMV COLH 94 LP: EMI 2C 061 01422 LP: Turnabout THS 65094 LP: EMI 29 10851 CD: EMI CHS 763 7192
Salzburg August 1946	VPO Fischer also conducts	Unpublished radio broadcast
Turin November 1954	Royal Danish Orchestra Fischer also conducts	LP: Discocorp IGI 329 LP: Cetra LO 502/DOC 51 CD: Hunt CDLSMH 34009

Piano Concerto No 24 K491

London March 1937	LPO Collingwood	78: HMV DB 3339-3342/ DB 8410-8413 auto 78: Victor M 482 LP: Victor LCT 6013 LP: HMV COLH 44 LP: Toshiba GR 2047 LP: EMI 2C 061 01423 CD: EMI CHS 763 7192
Salzburg July 1951	VPO Fischer also conducts	Unpublished radio broadcast
Turin November 1954	Royal Danish Orchestra Fischer also conducts	LP: Discocorp IGI 329 LP: Cetra LO 502/DOC 51 LP: Turnabout THS 65123 CD: Hunt CDLSMH 34009

Piano Concerto No 25 K503

Salzburg August 1946	VPO Fischer also conducts	LP: Discocorp IGI 290
London October 1947	Philharmonia Krips	78: HMV DB 6604-6607/ DB 9287-9290 auto 45: Victor WHMV 1004 LP: Victor LHMV 1004 LP: Turnabout THS 65094 LP: EMI 2C 061 01408 LP: EMI 2C 051 43328 CD: EMI CHS 763 7192

Piano Concerto No 26 K537 "Coronation", brief extract

Salzburg August 1948	VPO Fischer also conducts	Unpublished video extract Possibly the only existing film of Fischer in action

Piano Quartet No 1 in G minor K478

Berlin
1940

Members of
Breronel String
Quartet

Electrola unpublished

Piano Quintet in E flat K452

Vienna
1943

Meyer, Blöcher,
Burdach, Zutter

Unpublished radio broadcast

Piano Sonata No 10 K330

London
March 1937

78: HMV DB 3424-3425
LP: HMV COLH 309
LP: EMI 143 6741
CD: EMI CHS 763 7192

Piano Sonata No 11 K331

Berlin
May 1928

Electrola unpublished
Only the first movement
appears to have been
recorded

London
April 1933

78: HMV DB 1993-1994
LP: HMV COLH 309
LP: EMI 143 6741
CD: EMI CHS 763 7192
CD: Pearl GEMMCD 9481
3rd movement only
LP: HMV HLM 7008

Piano Sonata No 15 K545

London
March 1937

HMV unpublished
Matrix of side 1 lost

Piano Sonata, unspecified

Berlin
January 1942

Electrola unpublished

Piano Trio No 5 in C K548

Salzburg
August 1952

Schneiderhan,
Mainardi

LP: Discocorp BWS 735

Romanze in A flat KAnh. 205 (attributed)

1909	Welte Mignon piano roll 1844 CD: Autographe 158003-158005
London March 1938	78: HMV DB 3425 LP: HMV COLH 309 78 version coupled with Piano Sonata No 10
Berlin 1941	78: Electrola DB 5638 Coupled with Fantasia K475
London February 1947	LP: EMI 143 6741 CD: EMI CHS 763 7192

Rondo for piano and orchestra K382

Berlin October and November 1936	Fischer Chamber Orchestra Fischer also conducts	78: HMV DB 3110 78: Victor 15185/110031 LP: HMV COLH 94 LP: EMI 2C 061 01422 LP: EMI 2C 051 43326 CD: EMI CHS 763 7192
Würzburg June 1954	Bavarian RO Jochum	Unpublished radio broadcast
Turin November 1954	Royal Danish Orchestra Fischer also conducts	LP: Cetra DOC 51 CD: Hunt CDLSMH 34009

Serenade No 10 for 13 wind instruments, movements 1, 3, 4, 6 and 7

Berlin 1939	Fischer Chamber Orchestra Fischer conducts	78: HMV DB 4693-4695 78: Victor M 743

Symphony No 33

Berlin October 1936	Fischer Chamber Orchestra Fischer conducts	78: HMV DB 3000-3002/3083-3085/ DB 8258-8260 auto 78: Victor M 479

Symphony No 35 "Haffner"

Turin November 1954	Royal Danish Orchestra Fischer conducts	LP: Discocorp IGI 329 LP: Cetra LO 502/DOC 51 LP: Turnabout THS 65123

Symphony No 40

Strassburg June 1953	Strasbourg PO Fischer conducts	Unpublished private recording

Pergolesi

Concerto in F minor, arr. Franco

Lausanne
October 1948

Lausanne Chamber
Orchestra
Fischer conducts

Swiss Radio unpublished

Reger

Telemann Variations op 134

Berlin
1941

Electrola unpublished
Recording probably incomplete

Schubert

Fantasia in C D760 "Wanderer"

London
May 1934

78: HMV DB 2276-2278/
    DB 7787-7789 auto
78: Victor 8373-8375
LP: HMV HQM 1174
LP: Toshiba GR 2199
LP: EMI 2C 061 01333/29 00953

Impromptu in C minor D899 no 1

London
March 1938

78: HMV DB 3484/
    DB 8524-8529 auto
78: Victor M 494
LP: HMV COLH 68
LP: Toshiba GR 2030
LP: World Records SH 195
LP: EMI 2C 061 01230/29 00953
CD: Dante HPC 006

Impromptu in E D899 no 2

Berlin
May 1928

Electrola unpublished

London
March 1938

78: HMV DB 3485/
    DB 8524-8529 auto
78: Victor M 494
LP: HMV COLH 68
LP: Toshiba GR 2030
LP: World Records SH 195
LP: EMI 2C 061 01230/29 00953
CD: Dante HPC 006

Impromptu in G flat D899 no 3

London
March 1938

78: HMV DB 3485/
    DB 8524-8529 auto
78: Victor M 494
LP: HMV COLH 68
LP: Toshiba GR 2030
LP: World Records SH 195
LP: EMI 2C 061 01230/29 00953
CD: Dante HPC 006

Impromptu in A flat D899 no 4

London
March 1938

78: HMV DB 3486/
    DB 8524-8529 auto
78: Victor M 494
LP: HMV COLH 68
LP: Toshiba GR 2030
LP: World Records SH 195
LP: EMI 2C 061 01230/29 00953
CD: Dante HPC 006

Impromptu in F minor D935 no 1

London
March 1938

78: HMV DB 3487/
    DB 8524-8529 auto
78: Victor M 494
LP: HMV COLH 68
LP: Toshiba GR 2030
LP: World Records SH 195
LP: EMI 2C 061 01230/29 00953
CD: Dante HPC 006

Impromptu in A flat D935 no 2

London
March 1938

78: HMV DB 3488/
    DB 8524-8529 auto
78: Victor M 494
LP: HMV COLH 68
LP: Toshiba GR 2030
LP: World Records SH 195
LP: EMI 2C 061 01230/29 00953
CD: Dante HPC 006

Impromptu in B flat D935 no 3

London
March 1938

78: HMV DB 3489/
    DB 8524-8529 auto
78: Victor M 494
LP: HMV COLH 68
LP: Toshiba GR 2030
LP: World Records SH 195
LP: EMI 2C 061 01230/29 00953
CD: Dante HPC 006
CD: Pearl GEMMCD 9481

Impromptu in F minor D935 no 4

London
March 1938

78: HMV DB 3488/
    DB 8524-8529 auto
78: Victor M 494
LP: HMV COLH 68
LP: Toshiba GR 2030
LP: World Records SH 195
LP: EMI 2C 061 01230/29 00953
CD: Dante HPC 006

Impromptus D935, unspecified

Berlin
May 1928

Electrola unpublished
Total of 3 78rpm sides known
to have been recorded

PHILHARMONIE

Freitag den 13. Februar 1920, abends 7¹|₂ Uhr

KONZERT

mit dem Philharmonischen Orchester

Wilhelm Furtwängler

Solist:

Edwin Fischer

Vortrags-Folge:

I. Symphonie c-moll, Nr. 8 . . . Anton Bruckner

Allegro moderato
Scherzo (Allegro moderato)
Adagio
Feierlich (nicht schnell)

II. Klavier-Konzert Nr. II, B-dur, op. 83   Joh. Brahms

mit Begleitung des Orchesters

Allegro non troppo
Allegro appassionato
Andante
Allegretto grazioso

Konzertflügel: BECHSTEIN

Während der Vorträge bleiben die Saaltüren geschlossen.

Bernburger Str. 22 PHILHARMONIE Bernburger Str. 22

Montag, den 24. Januar 1927, abends 7¹/₂ Uhr

9. Philharmonisches Konzert

Dirigent: Wilhelm Furtwängler

Solist: Edwin Fischer

L. van Beethoven:

1. Ouvertüre zu „Coriolan" op. 62

2. Konzert für Klavier und Orchester
   Nr. IV G-dur op. 58
   Allegro moderato
   Andante con moto
   Rondo (Vivace)

— PAUSE —

3. Symphonie Nr. VII A-dur op. 92
   Poco sostenuto; vivace
   Allegretto
   Scherzo (Presto)
   Allegro con brio

Konzertflügel STEINWAY & SONS
aus dem Veraulsmagazin
BERLIN W 9, Friedrich-Ebert-Straße 6

PHILHARMONIE, Montag, 25. April 1927, abends 7¹/₂ Uhr
10. (letztes) PHILHARMONISCHES KONZERT
Dirigent: Wilhelm Furtwängler

Moment musical in C D780 no 1

London
May 1950

78: HMV DB 21551
LP: Victor LHMV 1055
LP: HMV ALP 1103
LP: Electrola E 90066
LP: Toshiba GR 2199
LP: EMI 2C 061 01333
LP: EMI 29 00953/137 2909913

Moment musical in A flat D780 no 2

London
May 1950

78: HMV DB 21568
LP: Victor LHMV 1055
LP: HMV ALP 1103
LP: Electrola E 90066
LP: Toshiba GR 2199
LP: EMI 2C 061 01333
LP: EMI 29 00953/137 2909913

Moment musical in F minor D780 no 3

London
May 1950

78: HMV DB 21568
45: Electrola 7EGW 9600
LP: Victor LHMV 1055
LP: HMV ALP 1103
LP: Electrola E 90066
LP: Toshiba GR 2199
LP: EMI 2C 061 01333
LP: EMI 29 00953/137 2909913

Moment musical in C sharp minor D780 no 4

London
May 1950

78: HMV DB 21551
45: Electrola 7EGW 9600
LP: Victor LHMV 1055
LP: HMV ALP 1103
LP: Electrola E 90066
LP: Toshiba GR 2199
LP: EMI 2C 061 01333
LP: EMI 29 00953/137 2909913

Moment musical in F minor D780 no 5

London
May 1950

78: HMV DB 21578
LP: Victor LHMV 1055
LP: HMV ALP 1103
LP: Electrola E 90060
LP: Toshiba GR 2199
LP: EMI 2C 061 01333
LP: EMI 29 00953/137 2909913

Moment musical in A flat D780 no 6

London
May 1950

78: HMV DB 21578
45: Electrola 7EGW 9600
LP: Victor LHMV 1055
LP: HMV ALP 1103
LP: Electrola E 90066
LP: Toshiba GR 2199
LP: EMI 2C 061 01333
LP: EMI 29 00953/137 2909913

Piano Trio No 2 in E flat D927

Lucerne   Schneiderhan,   Unpublished recording of
August 1954   Mainardi   rehearsal performance

An die Musik

London
October 1952

Schwarzkopf

45: Columbia SEL 1564
45: Columbia (Germany) C 50581
45: Electrola E 50157
LP: Columbia 33CX 1040
LP: Columbia (Germany) C 90305
LP: EMI 2C 053 00404
LP: EMI 1C 137 53032-53036M
LP: EMI ALP 3843
CD: EMI CDC 747 3262/
    CDH 764 0262

An Sylvia

London
October 1952

Schwarzkopf

45: Columbia SEL 1564
45: Columbia (Germany) C 50581
45: Electrola E 50157
LP: Columbia 33CX 1040
LP: Columbia (Germany) C 90305
LP: EMI 2C 053 00404
LP: EMI 1C 137 53032-53036M
LP: EMI ALP 3843
CD: EMI CDC 747 3262/
    CDH 764 0262

Auf dem Wasser zu singen

London
October 1952

Schwarzkopf

45: Columbia SEL 1582
LP: Columbia 33CX 1040
LP: Columbia (Germany) C 90305
LP: EMI 2C 053 00404
LP: EMI 1C 137 53032-53036M
LP: EMI ALP 3843
CD: EMI CDC 747 3262/
    CDH 764 0262

Das Lied im Grünen

London
October 1952

Schwarzkopf

45: Columbia SEL 1564
45: Electrola E 50157
LP: Columbia 33CX 1040
LP: Columbia (Germany) C 90305
LP: EMI 2C 053 00404
LP: EMI 1C 137 53032-53036M
LP: EMI ALP 3843
CD: EMI CDC 747 3262/
    CDH 764 0262

Der Musensohn

London
October 1952
Schwarzkopf

45: Columbia SEL 1582
45: Columbia (Germany) C 50581
LP: Columbia 33CX 1040
LP: Columbia (Germany) C 90305
LP: EMI 2C 053 00404
LP: EMI 1C 137 53032-53036M
LP: EMI ALP 3843
CD: EMI CDC 747 3262/
    CDH 764 0262

Die junge Nonne

London
October 1952
Schwarzkopf

45: Columbia SEL 1570
LP: Columbia 33CX 1040
LP: Columbia (Germany) C 90305
LP: EMI 2C 053 00404
LP: EMI 1C 137 53032-53036M
LP: EMI ALP 3843
CD: EMI CDC 747 3262/
    CDH 764 0262

Ganymed

London
October 1952
Schwarzkopf

LP: Columbia 33CX 1040
LP: Columbia (Germany) C 90305
LP: EMI 2C 053 00404
LP: EMI 1C 137 53032-53036M
LP: EMI ALP 3843
CD: EMI CDC 747 3262/
    CDH 764 0262

Gretchen am Spinnrade

London
October 1952
Schwarzkopf

45: Columbia SEL 1564
45: Columbia (Germany) C 50581
45: Electrola E 50157
LP: Columbia 33CX 1040
LP: Columbia (Germany) C 90305
LP: EMI 2C 053 00404
LP: EMI 1C 137 53032-53036M
LP: EMI ALP 3843
CD: EMI CDC 747 3262/
    CDH 764 0262

Im Frühling

London
October 1952

Schwarzkopf

45: Columbia SEL 1582
LP: Columbia 33CX 1040
Lp: Columbia (Germany) C 90305
LP: EMI 2C 053 00404
LP: EMI 1C 137 53032-53036M
LP: EMI ALP 3843
CD: EMI CDC 747 3262/
     CDH 764 0262

Nachtviolen

London
October 1952

Schwarzkopf

45: Columbia SEL 1582
LP: Columbia 33CX 1040
LP: Columbia (Germany) C 90305
LP: EMI 2C 053 00404
LP: EMI 1C 137 53032-53036M
LP: EMI ALP 3843
CD: EMI CDC 747 3262
     CDH 764 0262

Nähe des Geliebten

London
October 1952

Schwarzkopf

45: Columbia SEL 1570
45: Columbia (Germany) C 50581
LP: Columbia 33CX 1040
LP: Germany (Columbia) C 90305
LP: EMI 2C 053 00404
LP: EMI 1C 137 53032-53036M
LP: EMI ALP 3843
CD: EMI CDC 747 3262/
     CDH 764 0262

Wehmut

London
October 1952

Schwarzkopf

45: Columbia SEL 1570
LP: Columbia 33CX 1040
LP: Columbia (Germany) C 90305
LP: EMI 2C 053 00404
LP: EMI 1C 137 53032-53036M
LP: EMI ALP 3843
CD: EMI CDC 747 3262/
     CDH 764 0262

Schumann

Fantasia in C op 17

London
May 1949

78: HMV DB 6959-6961/
      DB 9419-9421 auto
45: Victor WHMV 1065
LP: Victor LHMV 1065
*LP: EMI 29 05751
*LP: EMI 137 2909913
*Contains some different 78 takes

Piano Trio No 1 in D minor op 63

Salzburg   Schneiderhan,
August 1953   Mainardi

LP: Cetra DOC 35
LP: Discocorp BWS 735
CD: Hunt CD 568

Interviews

Interviews between Fischer and Henri Jaton

Lucerne
September 1954

Swiss Radio unpublished

Fischer speaks to students at a masterclass

Lucerne
August 1944

Swiss Radio unpublished

Clara Haskil
1895-1960

With valuable assistance and an introduction
by Roger Smithson

Discography compiled by John Hunt

Introduction

Clara Haskil's biographer Jérôme Spycket begins his book (1) by asking why it took so long for her to be recognised. The chronology of her recordings tells its own story. At the age of 50 she had recorded just four 78rpm sides; if she had died before she was 55 we would never have heard of her.

It is all to easy to see Haskil's life as a succession of troubles and disappointments. She was born on 7 January 1895 in Bucharest into a Sephardic Jewish family originally from Spain; her parents owned a modest shop. She had the classic prodigy's aptitude for performance. At the age of six she played a Mozart sonata after a single hearing, then transposed it into another key. She also played the violin as a child. These gifts, however, brought with them the disrupted childhood of the prodigy and its long-term psychological damage.

Clara began studying at the Bucharest Conservatory in 1901, and in 1902 went to study in Vienna under the care of her uncle, Avram Moscona. In 1905 they moved on to Paris, where she attended Cortot's classes at the Conservatoire, but she felt that she learned little there. She was expected to begin a brilliant career, but the outbreak of war in 1914 forced the cancellation of tours of Europe and the USA. In her teens she also began to suffer from scoliosis, a progressive spinal deformation, and for some years endured a painful but ineffective attempt to correct the disorder by means of a tight plaster cast.

Returning to public performance in 1920, she soon established a high reputation among her fellow musicians, performing with Ysaye, Casals and Szigeti among others, and she was well received by the public and critics when she appeared in her own right. Programmes from this period (2) show a repertoire ranging from the then little-known works of Rameau and Scarlatti to virtuoso pieces by Liszt and Rachmaninov. Yet her career did not flourish, and she gave only a few performances each year. There were several reasons for this. She made little impact in Paris, where she lived, and in the other main musical centres she was no more than an occasional impressive visitor. She had no recording contract (three short pieces for Polydor in 1934 passed largely unnoticed). She was critical almost to the point of disgust with her own playing, and did not seek engagements or promote herself in any way. She began to suffer badly from stage fright. Her scoliosis not only caused her physical pain but also made her very self-conscious about her appearance. Finally, it is clear that her uncle's tutelage was oppressive. Avram was by all accounts a difficult man, strict, irritable and increasingly bitter over his own lack of success, but Clara remained loyal to him until his death in 1934.

This frustrating stage of Haskil's career ended with the outbreak of war. She escaped from occupied Paris to Marseille in 1941 with the French Radio orchestra and their conductor Inghelbrecht. In 1942 she had to have an operation to remove a brain tumour. Just before the Nazi occupation of Vichy France she was allowed into Switzerland, making her home in Vevey for the rest of her life.

Success came only after these years of obscurity. She began recording for Philips in 1951, finding a new audience through the expanding medium of the LP, and belatedly embarked on the star performer's demanding life of travel - 25 appearances in 1950, 50 in 1952, 60 in 1954, 80 in 1956. She bought the first piano she had ever owned in 1953. The familiar image of the frail saint dates from this period. It does little justice to either her complex personality or her technique; she programmed Liszt's La leggierezza until 1950, and her record of the Schumann Abegg Variations demonstrates a remarkable virtuosity. It is indisputable, however, that in these last years she gradually reduced her basic repertoire to a handful of works by Beethoven, Chopin, Mozart, Schubert and Schumann, where many felt that her art found its greatest fulfilment.

On 6 December 1960 she went to Brussels for a recital with Arthur Grumiaux. Characteristically refusing help down a flight of steps at the station, she fell heavily and suffered a cerebral haemmorhage. An emergency operation was unsuccessful and she died during the night.

Haskil was as dissatisfied with most of her records as she was with her public appearances, but they show clearly enough why she inspired such admiration. One might cite her beauty of tone, fluency, nuancing or rubato, but the final impression is not of any specific characteristic of performance but the elusive quality of absolute naturalness. Comparisons between her studio and live recordings are often illuminating. The latter are particularly helpful in our appreciation of her concerto work, since contractual constraints prevented her from making records with many conductors whom she admired: Karajan, Kubelik, Ackermann and Giulini among others. Her recordings with Fricsay, both commercial and live, are testaments of a close friendship allied to profound mutual respect. She shared a similar affinity with Arthur Grumiaux, and was uncharacteristically enthusiastic about their classic recordings of the Beethoven violin sonatas and six by Mozart. Again, there are complementary live versions; they also gave some of the Brahms sonatas and Schubert violin-piano duos in concert.

Most of the works in Haskil's restricted latter-day solo repertoire are represented by both live and studio recordings, but sadly there are few recordings of the other solo pieces which she programmed up to the early 1950s - among them sonatas by Beethoven and Haydn and selections from Brahms' Capriccios and Intermezzi and the Chopin Mazurkas. Strangely, Chopin almost vanished from her solo repertoire after 1953, though she played the F minor concerto right to the end of her life.

References:

(1) Jérôme Spycket: Clara Haskil. Payot Lausanne, 1975. This excellent study is likely to remain definitive; an English translation would be welcome.

(2) Compiled by Peter Feuchtwanger and published in Recorded Sound, no. 63-63 (July-October 1976). This issue was largely devoted to Haskil; it also includes the text of a lecture by Dr. Feuchtwanger, who knew Haskil well and has studied her career in detail, and shorter recollections by Etienne Amyot and Sheridan Russell.

Bach

Concerto No 5 in F minor for piano BWV 1056

Prades June 1950	Prades Festival Orchestra Casals	LP: Columbia 33CX 1109 LP: Columbia (USA) ML 4353 LP: Philips A 01511 L LP: CBS (France) 76082 CD: Sony SMK 58982

Concerto in C for 2 pianos BWV 1061

London April 1956	Philharmonia Anda (1st piano) Galliera	LP: Columbia 33CX 1403 LP: Angel 35380 LP: EMI SXLP 30175 LP: EMI 1C 053 00439 CD: EMI CDH 763 4922

Toccata in E minor BWV 914

Hilversum February 1952	Unpublished radio broadcast
Ludwigsburg April 1953	LP: Rococo 2089 LP: Discocorp RR 213 LP: Melodram MEL 207 CD: AS-Disc AS 124 CD: Stradivarius STR 13602

Beethoven

Piano Concerto No 3

Winterthur 1950	Winterthur Symphony Orchestra Swoboda	LP: Westminster WL 5057 LP: Westminster XWN 18379 LP: Ricordi MRC 5022 LP: Heliodor (USA) 478 005 CD: Warner Pioneer (Japan) WPCC 41912
Boston November 1956 (1 November)	Boston SO Münch	LP: Rococo LP: Discocorp RR 553 LP: Columbia (Japan) OS 7116 CD: Music and Arts CD 716
Boston November 1956 (2 November)	Boston SO Münch	Unpublished radio broadcast
Paris November 1959	Lamoureux Orchestra Markevitch	LP: Philips 899 019/6500 324 LP: Epic LC 3726 LP: Philips 6733 002/6747 055 LP: Philips SFM 23006 CD: Philips 434 1682
Montreux August 1960	Suisse Romande Orchestra Ansermet	Unpublished radio broadcast

Piano Concerto No 4

London June 1947	LPO Zecchi	78: Decca K 1944-1947/ AK 1944-1947 auto LP: Decca ACL 168 LP: Telefunken 641.904 AJ LP: Decca 417 4651 According to Jared Weinberger in his discography in the Italian periodical Musica, LP issues use different 78 takes of sides 4 and 5 of the original edition
Vienna October 1952	VSO Karajan	Unpublished radio broadcast
Paris December 1955	Orchestre National Cluytens	LP: Discocorp RR 232 CD: Disques Montaigne TCE 8780
Turin April 1960	RAI Turin Orchestra Rossi	LP: Discocorp RR 497 LP: Cetra LAR 2

Piano Sonata No 17 in D minor op 31 no 2 "Tempest"

Vevey
September 1960

LP: Philips A 02073 L
LP: Epic BC 1168
LP: Philips 6733 002/6747 055
CD: Philips 420 0882

Piano Sonata No 18 in E flat op 31 no 3

Besançon
September 1956

LP: Rococo
LP: Columbia (Japan) OS
     7077-7078
LP: Replica RPL 2473-2474
LP: Discocorp RR 542
LP: FNAC Rappel 01/1-2
CD: Columbia (Japan) 30C 37-7920
CD: Music and Arts CD 542
Some editions incorrectly attribute
this performance to Zürich May 1956

Salzburg
August 1957

Unpublished radio broadcast

Edinburgh
August 1957

Unpublished radio broadcast

Vevey
September 1960

LP: Philips A 02073 L
LP: Epic BC 1168
LP: Philips 6733 002/6747 055
CD: Philips 420 0882/434 1682

Piano Sonata No 32 in C minor op 111

Ludwigsburg
April 1953

LP: Columbia (Japan) OS 7117
LP: Discocorp RR 213
LP: Melodram MEL 207
CD: AS-Disc AS 124
CD: Stradivarius STR 13602

Violin Sonata No 1 in D op 12 no 1

Amsterdam   Grumiaux
January 1957

LP: Philips 836 962
LP: Epic SC 6030
LP: Philips GL 5858
LP: Philips 6580 090/6733 001
CD: Philips 422 1402

Besancon   Grumiaux
September 1957

LP: Discocorp RR 555
LP: Melodram MEL 219
CD: Melodram MEL 18001

Violin Sonata No 2 in A op 12 no 2

Amsterdam   Grumiaux
September 1956

LP: Philips 836 961
LP: Epic SC 6030
LP: Philips GL 5857
LP: Philips 6580 090/6733 001
CD: Philips 422 1402

Violin Sonata No 3 in E flat op 12 no 3

Amsterdam   Grumiaux
September 1956

LP: Philips 836 961
LP: Epic SC 6030
LP: Philips GL 5857
LP: Philips 6580 090/6733 001
CD: Philips 422 1402

Violin Sonata No 4 in A minor op 23

Amsterdam   Grumiaux
January 1957

LP: Philips 836 962
LP: Epic SC 6030
LP: Philips GL 5858/6733 001
CD: Philips 422 1402

Ascona   Grumiaux
August 1960

CD: Eremitage ERM 112

Violin Sonata No 5 in F op 24 "Spring"

Amsterdam   Grumiaux
January 1957

LP: Philips 836 962
LP: Epic SC 6030
LP: Philips GL 5858
LP: Philips 6580 032/6733 001
CD: Philips 422 1402

Violin Sonata No 6 in A op 30 no 1

Amsterdam   Grumiaux
September 1957

LP: Philips 836 944
LP: Epic SC 6030
LP: Philips GL 5860/6733 001
CD: Philips 422 1402

Violin Sonata No 7 in C minor op 30 no 2

Amsterdam   Grumiaux
December 1956

LP: Philips 836 963
LP: Epic SC 6030
LP: Philips GL 5859/6733 001
CD: Philips 422 1402

Violin Sonata No 8 in G op 30 no 3

Amsterdam   Grumiaux
September 1956

LP: Philips 836 961
LP: Epic SC 6030
LP: Philips GL 5857/6733 001
CD: Philips 422 1402

Violin Sonata No 9 in A op 47 "Kreutzer"

Amsterdam   Grumiaux
September 1957

LP: Philips 836 944
LP: Epic SC 6030
LP: Philips GL 5860
LP: Philips 6580 032/6733 001
CD: Philips 422 1402

Violin Sonata No 10 in G op 96

Amsterdam   Grumiaux
December 1956

LP: Philips 836 963
LP: Epic SC 6030
LP: Philips GL 5859/6733 001
CD: Philips 422 1402

Besancon   Grumiaux
September 1957

LP: Discocorp RR 555
LP: Melodram MEL 219
CD: Melodram MEL 18001

Ascona   Grumiaux
August 1960

CD: Eremitage ERM 112

Brahms

Piano Quintet in F minor op 34

Zürich 1949	Winterthur String Quartet	LP: Concert Hall Society CHC 46 LP: Nixa CLP 46

Busoni

Violin Sonata op 36a

London October 1947	Szigeti	LP: Discocorp WSA 700 CD: Music and Arts CD 720
Vevey December 1954	Rybar	Private recording made for the composer's widow

Chopin

Piano Concerto No 2

Paris April 1954	Orchestre National Cluytens	Unpublished radio broadcast
Montreux September 1954	Orchestre National Cluytens	Unpublished radio broadcast
Basel January 1955	Basel Orchestra H.Münch	Unpublished radio broadcast
Paris January 1960	Paris Conservatoire Orchestra Kubelik	LP: Discocorp RR 233 CD: Disques Montaigne TCE 8780
Vienna March 1960	VSO Giulini	Unpublished radio broadcast
Paris October 1960	Lamoureux Orchestra Markevitch	LP: Philips 839 582/6500 263 LP: Philips 6747 055 CD: Philips 416 4432/426 9642

Debussy

Etude No 7 (Pour les degrés chromatiques)

Ludwigsburg
April 1953

LP: Discocorp RR 213
LP: Melodram MEL 207
CD: AS-Disc AS 124
CD: Stradivarius STR 13602

Etude No 10 (Pour les sonorités opposées)

Ludwigsburg
April 1953

LP: Discocorp RR 213
LP: Melodram MEL 207
CD: AS-Disc AS 124
CD: Stradivarius STR 13602

Falla

Noches en los jardines de Espana

Paris
October 1960

Lamoureux Orchestra
Markevitch

LP: Philips 839 582/894 051
LP: Philips 6500 263/6747 055
CD: Philips 416 4432/426 9642
CD: Philips 432 8292/434 2092

Haydn

Piano Sonata No 37 in D

Hilversum
February 1952

Unpublished radio broadcast

Variations in F minor

Paris
1934

78: Polydor (France) 522 864
78: Brunswick 35035
One variation missing from
this recording

Hindemith

Die 4 Temperamente (Theme & Variations for piano & string orchestra)

Baden-Baden March 1953	Südwestfunk- Orchester Rosbaud	LP: Rococo LP: Columbia (Japan) OS 7117
Munich July 1955	Bavarian RO Rosbaud	Unpublished radio broadcast
Montreux September 1957	Orchestre National Hindemith	LP: Discocorp RR 230 CD: Stradivarius STR 13603

Liszt

Capriccio

Paris or Berne 1936	Private recording belonging to Clara Haskil

Mendelssohn

Charakterstück op 7 no 4

Paris or Berne 1936	Private recording belonging to Clara Haskil

Mozart

Concerto for 2 pianos in E flat K365

London April 1956	Philharmonia Anda (2nd piano) Galliera	LP: Columbia 33CX 1403 LP: Angel 35380 LP: EMI SXLP 30175 LP: EMI 1C 053 00439 CD: EMI CDH 763 4922
Salzburg August 1957	Camerata Academica Anda (2nd piano) Paumgartner	CD: Stradivarius STR 13603

Piano Concerto No 9 K271 "Jeunehomme"

Stuttgart May 1952	SDR Orchestra Schuricht	LP: CLS Records ARPCL 22046 LP: International Piano Library IPG 7618 CD: Preludio PMC 2140 /ITM 950021
Prades June 1953	Prades Festival Orchestra Casals	CD: Lyrinx CD 102
Cologne June 1954	WDR Orchestra Ackermann	LP: Rococo LP: Columbia (Japan) OS 7077-7078 CD: Music and Arts CD 715 CD: Stradivarius STR 13596 Some editions incorrectly attributed Hamburg 1954
Vienna October 1954	VSO Sacher	LP: Philips 836 935 LP: Epic LC 3162 LP: Philips 6599 068/6747 055 LP: Philips 6768 366 LP: Melodiya M10 52589-52590 CD: Philips 420 7822/426 9642

Piano Concerto No 13 K415

Berlin March 1953	Berlin RO Fricsay	LP: Discocorp RR 232
Lucerne May 1960	Lucerne Festival Strings Baumgartner	LP: DG LPM 18 670/ SLPM 138 670 LP: DG 135 137/2535 116 LP: DG 2538 139 LP: Philips 6768 366 LP: Longanesi periodici GCL 36 CD: DG 437 6762 <u>Longanesi issue incorrectly</u> <u>labelled Berlin RO/Fricsay</u> <u>and incorrectly dated</u> <u>January 1953</u>

Piano Concerto No 19 K459

Winterthur September 1950	Winterthur Symphony Orchestra Swoboda	LP: Westminster XWN 18380 LP: Nixa WLP 5054 LP: Ducretet LPG 8329 LP: Ricordi MRC 5023 LP: Heliodor (USA) 478 059 LP: Whitehall WH 20087 CD: Warner Pioneer (Japan) WPCC 41912
Cologne May 1952	WDR Orchestra Fricsay	Unpublished radio broadcast
Berlin January 1953	Berlin RO Fricsay	LP: Rococo 2086 LP: Longanesi periodici GCL 36
Berlin September 1955	BPO Fricsay	LP: DG LPM 18 383 LP: DG LPM 18 554-18 555 LP: Decca (USA) 9830 LP: DG 2548 032/2548 209/2535 830 LP: Philips 6768 366 CD: DG 431 8722
Ludwigsburg July 1956	SDR Orchestra Schuricht	LP: Teichiku ULS 3104 LP: International Piano Library IPG 7618 CD: Preludio PMC 2140/ITM 950021
Besancon September 1956	Paris Conservatoire Orchestra Katlowicz	Unpublished radio broadcast
Lausanne October 1957	Lausanne Chamber Orchestra Desarzens	LP: CLS Records ARPCL 22046 LP: Discocorp RR 232
Paris February 1959	Orchestre National Silvestri	CD: Disques Montaigne TCE 8780

Piano Concerto No 20 K466

Winterthur September 1950	Winterthur Symphony Orchestra Swoboda	LP: Westminster XWN 18380 LP: Nixa WLP 5054 LP: Ducretet LPG 8329 LP: Ricordi MRC 5023 LP: Heliodor (USA) 478 059 LP: Whitehall WH 20087
Berlin January 1954 (10 January)	Berlin RO Fricsay	LP: Discocorp RR 230 CD: Myto 92361 Discocorp dated October 1954
Berlin January 1954 (11 January)	Berlin RO Fricsay	LP: DG 2535 708 CD: DG 437 6762
Vienna October 1954	VSO Paumgartner	LP: Philips A 00752 L/ABL 3129 LP: Epic LC 3163 LP: Philips G 05334 R LP: Mercury SR 90413
Salzburg January 1956	Philharmonia Karajan	Unpublished radio broadcast
Montreux September 1956	Orchestre National Hindemith	LP: Discocorp RR 230 CD: Stradivarius STR 13596
Boston November 1956	Boston SO Münch	LP: Rococo 2086 CD: Music and Arts CD 715
Lucerne September 1959	Philharmonia Klemperer	LP: Discocorp RR 545 LP: CLS ARPCL 22046 LP: Columbia (Japan) OS 7079 CD: AS-Disc AS 612
Paris November 1960	Lamoureux Orchestra Markevitch	LP: Philips 839 585/6500 265 LP: Epic BC 1143 LP: Philips 6527 093/6733 002 LP: Philips 6747 055/6768 366 CD: Philips 412 2542/426 9642

Piano Concerto No 23 K488

Lugano June 1953	Swiss-Italian Radio Orchestra Nussio	Unpublished radio broadcast
Vienna October 1954	VSO Sacher	LP: Philips 836 935/A 00653 R LP: Philips ABL 3129 LP: Epic LC 3163 LP: Philips 6527 093/6599 068 LP: Philips 6747 055/6768 366 CD: Philips 420 7822/426 9642
Montreux September 1959	Orchestre National Munch	Unpublished radio broadcast

AMICI DELLA MUSICA
FIRENZE

TEATRO DELLA PERGOLA
Concerto inaugurale della Stagione 1959-1960

Sabato 31 Ottobre 1959 ore 17

CLARA HASKIL
pianoforte

MOZART - Sonata in *fa* maggiore K 332
Allegro - Adagio - Assai allegro

SCHUBERT - Sonata in la maggiore, op. 42
Moderato - Andante, poco mosso - Scherzo
(allegro vivace) e *Trio* (un poco più lento)
- *Rondò* (allegro vivace)

BEETHOVEN - Sonata in re maggiore, op. 10, n. 3
Presto - Largo e mesto - Minuetto (allegro)
e *Trio - Rondò* (allegro)

BRAHMS - Tre Capricci, op. 76

Concertdir. Johan Koning - Ruychrocklaan 32, Tel. 776518-776768, Den Haag

Concertgebouw, grote zaal, Zaterdag 25 November, 8.15 uur

Piano-recital

CLARA HASKIL

1.	Toccata in e	J. S. Bach
2.	Drie sonates	D. Scarlatti
3.	Sonate in Bes op. posth.	F. Schubert

Molto moderato
Andante sostenuto
Scherzo: Allegro vivace con delicatezza
Allegro ma non troppo

Pauze

4. Waldszenen op. 82   R. Schumann

Eintritt - Jäger auf der Lauer - Einsame Blumen -
Verrufene Stelle - Freundliche Landschaft -
Herberge - Vogel als Prophet - Jagdlied - Abschied

5. Sonate in Es op. 31 no. 3   L. van Beethoven

Allegro
Scherzo: allegretto vivace
Menuetto: moderato grazioso
Presto con fuoco

Steinway & Sons' concertvleugel

Agenda:

Kleine zaal:	Grote zaal:
Dinsdag 28 November, 8.15 uur	Donderdag 7 December, 8.15 uur
Schubert-avond	*Frankrijks grootste pianist*
Adrian Aeschbacher	**Alfred Cortot**

Piano Concerto No 24 K491

| Paris
February 1956 | Orchestre National
Cluytens | LP: Discocorp RR 497
CD: Disques Montaigne TCE 8780 |

| Lausanne
June 1956 | Lausanne Chamber
Orchestra
Desarzens | LP: Discocorp RR 232 |

| Paris
November 1960 | Lamoureux Orchestra
Markevitch | LP: Philips 835 075/839 585
LP: Epic BC 1143
LP: Philips 6500 265/6733 002
LP: Philips 6747 055/6768 366
CD: Philips 412 2542/426 9642 |

Piano Concerto No 27 K595

| Montreux
September 1956 | Gürzenich-Orchester
Klemperer | LP: CLS Records ARPCL 22046
LP: Discocorp RR 232/RR 545
LP: Columbia (Japan) OS 7079
CD: AS-Disc AS 612
CD: Music and Arts CD 716 |

| Munich
May 1957 | Bavarian State
Orchestra
Fricsay | LP: DG LPM 18 383
LP: DG 2548 032/2548 209
LP: Philips 6768 366
CD: DG 431 8722 |

Piano Sonata No 2 in F K280

| Lucerne
May 1960 | | LP: DG LPM 18 670/
    SLPM 138 670
LP: DG 2535 115/2538 139/2535 830
LP: Philips 6768 366
CD: DG 437 6762 |

Piano Sonata No 10 in C K330

| Amsterdam
May 1954 | | LP: Philips 695 090/A 00724 R
LP: Philips 6733 002/6768 366
CD: Philips (Japan) PHCP 1308 |

| Salzburg
August 1957 | | CD: Stradivarius STR 13603 |

| Edinburgh
August 1957 | | Unpublished radio broadcast |

Rondo for piano and orchestra K386

Vienna
October 1954

VSO
Paumgartner

LP: Philips S 06100 R
LP: Philips A 00259 L/SBR 6200
LP: Epic LC 3162
LP: Philips 6747 055/6768 366
CD: Philips 420 7822/426 9642

Variations on "Ah, vous dirai-je, Maman" K265

Lucerne
May 1960

LP: DG LPM 18 670/
    SLPM 138 670
LP: DG 2535 115
LP: DG 2538 079/2538 139
LP: Philips 6768 366
CD: DG 437 6762

Variations on a Minuet by Duport K573

Amsterdam
May 1954

LP: Philips A 00724 R
LP: Philips 6747 055/6768 366
CD: Philips (Japan) PHCP 1308

Besançon
September 1956

LP: Rococo
LP: Columbia (Japan)
    OS 7077-7078
LP: Replica RPL 2473-2474
LP: Discocorp RR 542
LP: Melodram MEL 207
LP: FNAC Rappel 01/1-2
CD: Columbia (Japan) 30C 37-7920
CD: Music and Arts CD 542
Some editions incorrectly attribute
this performance to Zürich May 1956

Violin Sonata No 18 in G K301

Amsterdam
November 1958

Grumiaux

LP: Philips 835 103
LP: Epic LC 3602
LP: Philips 6768 366/6780 017
CD: Philips 412 2532

Violin Sonata No 21 in E minor K304

Besancon
September 1957

Grumiaux

LP: Discocorp RR 555
LP: Melodram MEL 219
CD: Melodram MEL 18001

Amsterdam
November 1958

Grumiaux

LP: Philips 835 103
LP: Epic LC 3602
LP: Philips 6768 366/6780 017
CD: Philips 412 2532

Violin Sonata No 24 in F K376

Amsterdam   Grumiaux
November 1958

LP: Philips 835 103
LP: Epic LC 3602
LP: Philips 6768 366/6780 017
CD: Philips 412 2532

Violin Sonata No 26 in F K378

Amsterdam   Grumiaux
November 1958

LP: Philips 835 103
LP: Epic LC 3602
LP: Philips 6768 366/6780 017
CD: Philips 412 2532

Ascona
August 1960

CD: Eremitage ERM 112

Violin Sonata No 32 in B flat K454

Amsterdam   Grumiaux
May 1954

LP: Philips 802 841/6500 323
LP: Epic LC 3299
LP: Philips 6768 366/6780 017
CD: Philips 416 4782

Besancon   Grumiaux
September 1957

LP: Discocorp RR 555
LP: Melodram MEL 219
CD: Melodram MEL 18001

Violin Sonata No 34 in A K526

Amsterdam   Grumiaux
May 1954

LP: Philips 802841/6500 323
LP: Epic LC 3299
LP: Philips 6768 366/6780 017
CD: Philips 416 4782

Pescetti

Piano Sonata in D minor

Paris
1934

78: Polydor (France) 522 836

Poulenc

Presto in B flat

Paris or Berne
1936

Private recording belonging
to Clara Haskil

Ravel

Sonatine

Amsterdam
October 1951

LP: Philips A 00143 R/695 090
LP: Philips 6747 055
LP: Melodiya M10 42589-42590

Ludwigsburg
April 1953

LP: Rococo 2089
LP: Discocorp RR 213
LP: Melodram MEL 207
CD: Stradivarius STR 13602

Domenico Scarlatti

Sonata in B minor L33

Winterthur
October 1950

LP: Westminster XWN 18381
LP: Westminster WL 5072
LP: Ricordi MRC 5037
LP: Heliodor (USA) 479 019
LP: Columbia (Japan) OW 8057
CD: Warner Pioneer (Japan)
    WPCC 41912

Amsterdam
October 1951

LP: Philips 2087/A 00143 R
LP: Philips 695 090/6747 055
LP: Melodiya M10 42589-42590

Ludwigsburg
April 1953

LP: Discocorp RR 213
LP: Melodram MEL 207
CD: AS-Disc AS 124
CD: Stradivarius STR 13602

Sonata in E flat L142

Winterthur
October 1950

LP: Westminster XWN 18381
LP: Westminster WL 5072
LP: Ricordi MRC 5037
LP: Heliodor (USA) 479 019
LP: Columbia (Japan) OW 8057
CD: Warner Pioneer (Japan)
    WPCC 41912

Amsterdam
October 1951

LP: Philips 2087/A 00143 R
LP: Philips 695 090/6747 055

Ludwigsburg
April 1953

LP: Rococo 2089
LP: Discocorp RR 213
LP: Melodram MEL 207
CD: AS-Disc AS 124
CD: Stradivarius STR 13602

Sonata in F minor L 171

Winterthur
October 1950

LP: Westminster XWN 18381
LP: Westminster WL 5072
LP: Ricordi MRC 5037
LP: Heliodor (USA) 479 019
LP: Columbia (Japan) OW 8057
CD: Warner Pioneer (Japan)
    WPCC 41912

Amsterdam
October 1951

LP: Philips 2087/A 00143 R
LP: Philips 695 090/6747 055
LP: Melodiya M10 42589-42590

Sonatas in C L255 and C sharp minor L256

Winterthur
October 1950

LP: Westminster XWN 18381
LP: Westminster WL 5072
LP: Ricordi MRC 5037
LP: Heliodor (USA) 479 019
LP: Columbia (Japan) OW 8057
CD: Warner Pioneer (Japan)
    WPCC 41912

Sonatas in G minor L386 and G L388

Winterthur
October 1950

LP: Westminster XWN 18381
LP: Westminster WL 5072
LP: Ricordi MRC 5037
LP: Heliodor (USA) 479 019
LP: Columbia (Japan) OW 8057
CD: Warner Pioneer (Japan)
    WPCC 41912

Sonata in C L457

Winterthur
October 1950

LP: Westminster XWN 18381
LP: Westminster WL 5072
LP: Ricordi MRC 5037
LP: Heliodor (USA) 479 019
LP: Columbia (Japan) OW 8057
CD: Warner Pioneer (Japan)
    WPCC 41912

Ludwigsburg
April 1953

LP: Discocorp RR 213
LP: Melodram MEL 207
CD: AS-Disc AS 124
CD: Stradivarius STR 13602

Sonatas in F minor L475, in F L479 and in A L483

Winterthur
October 1950

LP: Westminster XWN 18381
LP: Westminster WL 5072
LP: Ricordi MRC 5037
LP: Heliodor (USA) 479 019
LP: Columbia (Japan) OW 8057
CD: Warner Pioneer (Japan)
    WPCC 41912

Schubert

Piano Sonata No 16 in A minor D845

Besançon
September 1956

LP: Rococo
LP: Columbia (Japan)
    OS 7077-7078
LP: Replica RPL 2473-2474
LP: Discocorp RR 542
LP: Movimento Musica 01.063
LP: FNAC Rappel 01/1-2
CD: Columbia (Japan) 30C 37-7920
CD: Music and Arts CD 542
<u>Some editions incorrectly attribute</u>
<u>this performance to Zürich May 1956</u>

Piano Sonata No 21 in B flat D960

Amsterdam
June 1951

LP: Philips 2087/ABL 3029
LP: Philips A 00108 L/A 00484 L
LP: Epic LC 3031
LP: Philips (USA) PHC 9076
LP: Philips 6733 002/6747 055
CD: Philips (Japan) PHCP 1308

Hilversum
February 1952

Unpublished radio broadcast

Salzburg
August 1957

Unpublished radio broadcast

Edinburgh
August 1957

Unpublished radio broadcast
<u>Recording may be incomplete</u>

Schumann

Abegg Variations op 1

Paris
1938

Polydor (France) 561 121

Amsterdam
October 1951

LP: Philips A 11213 G/A 00372 L
LP: Philips 835 936
LP: Philips 6590 088/6747 055
LP: Longanesi periodici GCL 54
CD: Philips 420 8512/426 9642
Longanesi incorrectly
attributed Berlin November 1954

Ludwigsburg
April 1953

LP: Rococo 2089
LP: Discocorp RR 213
LP: Melodram MEL 207
CD: AS-Disc AS 124
CD: Stradivarius STR 13602

Bunte Blätter op 99, nos. 1-8

Hilversum
February 1952

Unpublished radio broadcast

Amsterdam
April 1952

LP: Philips A 00108 L/A 00372 L
LP: Philips 835 936/ABL 3029
LP: Epic LC 3031
LP: Philips 6598 274/6747 055
LP: Longanesi periodici GCL 54
Longanesi incorrectly
attributed Berlin November 1954

Kinderszenen op 15

Amsterdam
May 1955

LP: Philips A 00372 L/835 936
LP: Philips LC 3031
LP: Philips 6598 274/6747 055
LP: Longanesi periodici GCL 54
CD: Philips 420 8512/426 9642
Longanesi incorrectly
attributed Berlin November 1954

Besançon
September 1956

LP: Rococo
LP: Columbia (Japan)
      OS 7077-7078
LP: Replica RPL 2473-2474
LP: Discocorp RR 542
LP: FNAC Rappel 01/1-2
CD: Columbia (Japan) 30C 37-7920
CD: Music and Arts CD 542
Some editions incorrectly attribute
this performance to Zürich May 1956

Piano Concerto

Amsterdam
May 1951

Hague Residentie
Orchestra
Van Otterloo

LP: Philips A 00134 L/695 088
LP: Epic LC 3020
LP: Philips ABR 4080/GBR 6504
LP: Philips 6598 274/6747 055
CD: Philips 420 8512/426 9642

Scheveningen
July 1953

Hague Residentie
Orchestra
Kletzki

Unpublished radio broadcast

Geneva
October 1956

Suisse Romande
Orchestra
Ansermet

LP: Rococo
LP: Columbia (Japan) OS 7116
LP: Discocorp RR 553

Waldszenen op 82

London
October 1947

78: Decca AK 2110-2111
78: London (USA) LA 127
LP: Decca 417 4651

Amsterdam
May 1954

LP: Philips A 00372 L
LP: Philips 695 089/835 936
LP: Philips 6747 055
CD: Philips 420 8512/426 9642

Soler

Sonata in D

Paris
1934

78: Polydor (France) 522 863

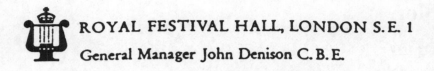

A TRIBUTE TO A GREAT PIANIST

CLARA HASKIL

1895 - 1960

An Exhibition of photographs, an oil-portrait
and drawings by

MICHAEL GARADY

December 4th - 14th 1970
on the red side of the main foyer

Open to the public from 6 p.m. in the evenings
(Sunday Dec 6th from 2 p.m. and 13th from 2.45 p.m.)

Wilhelm Backhaus
1884-1969

With valuable assistance from
Malcolm Walker

Discography compiled by John Hunt

Introduction

I recently came across the description of the playing of Wilhelm Backhaus as possessing a "gruff good humour". Over the enormous span of his recordings, made in a period of more than 60 years, there is certainly no indulgent lingering. What we have is a crystalline clarity and a boldness of statement, reminding us perhaps more than in the case of other great pianists that this instrument is a member of the percussion family.

Nor does Backhaus lack the grand manner or expansiveness of approach needed for the concerto repertory which he has embraced. Central points are the Beethoven concerti (recorded twice commercially for Decca) and the ones by Brahms (3 versions in a period of 30 years). The breadth of Backhaus' pedigree should not cause us to forget that it was he who first recorded the Grieg Piano Concerto (in abbreviated form, to start with) and who, at a very early stage in recording development, entrusted his art to the various forms of piano roll, where he even let his hair down in many piano showpieces such as were popular with audiences in the first decades of the 20th century.

Wilhelm Backhaus' finest memorial may well be his far-reaching survey of the Brahms solo piano music, recorded for HMV in the 1930s and recently reissued in its entirety for CD by the Biddulph label.

Backhaus' final London concerts (and amazingly he was a visitor to England over a period of 70 years) were concerto appearances with that other granite-like figure Otto Klemperer (Brahms 2, Mozart K595). The performances, if I remember correctly, were a unique combination of deep introspection and musical alertness.

John Hunt

ROYAL
OPERA HOUSE
COVENT GARDEN
(Sole Lessees—Messrs. BOOSEY & HAWKES LTD,)

Sunday, October 31st, at 7.30 p.m.

HAROLD HOLT LTD.
announce

BACKHAUS

ONLY RECITAL THIS SEASON

Programme

Italian Concerto - - - - - - -	*Bach*
Sonata in A flat major, Op. 26 (" Funeral March ") -	*Beethoven*
(Dedicated to Prince Carl von Lichnowsky)	
Sonata in C major, Op. 53 (" Waldstein ") - - -	*Beethoven*
(Dedicated to Count Waldstein)	
Impromptu No. 3 in B flat major, Op. 142 - - -	
(Theme and Variations)	*Schubert*
Impromptu No. 2 in E flat major, Op. 90 - - -	
Military March in E flat major (arranged by Backhaus) -	
Five Studies from Op. 10 - - - - - -	*Chopin*
Scherzo in C sharp minor - - - - - -	*Chopin*

TICKETS : **Boxes 50;- and 30/-** **Stalls 12/-, 9/-**

Stalls Circle 12;- **Grand Tier 12/-** **Balcony Stalls 7/6**

Amphitheatre 5/- **Gallery 2/6**

Albeniz

Tango, arr. Godowsky

London
June 1928

78: HMV DA 1018
LP: EMI EX 29 03453

Triana (Iberia)

London
June 1928

78: HMV DB 1125

Bach

English Suite No 6 in D minor BWV 811

Geneva
November 1956

LP: Decca LXT 5309/SXL 2205
CD: Decca 433 9012/433 9032

French Suite No 5 in G minor BWV 816

Zürich
March 1948

HMV unpublished

Geneva
November 1956

45: Decca CEP 691/SEC 5083
LP: Decca LXT 5309/SXL 2205
CD: Decca 433 9012/433 9032
Gavotte only
LP: Decca 414 4981

Italian Concerto BWV 971

Zürich
March 1948

78: HMV DB 6871-6872
78: Victor M 806

Pastorale (Christmas Oratorio), arr. Lucas

London
November 1934

78: HMV DB 2406
78: Victor 8736
LP: EMI EX 29 03453
<u>78 issue coupled with Beethoven</u>
<u>Piano Sonata No 14</u>

Prelude and Fugue No 1 in B BWV 846 (Well-Tempered Clavier, Book 1)

London
1936

78: HMV DB 3220
LP: Parnassus 3
<u>78 issue coupled with</u>
<u>Beethoven Sonata No 32</u>

Prelude and Fugue No 15 in G BWV 860 (Well-Tempered Clavier, Book 1)

Geneva
November 1956

LP: Decca LXT 5309/SXL 2205
CD: Decca 433 9012/433 9032

Prelude and Fugue No 21 in B flat BWV 866 (Well-Tempered Clavier, Book 1)

Zürich
March 1948

78: HMV DB 6872
78: Victor M 806
<u>Coupled with Italian Concerto</u>

Prelude and Fugue No 22 in B flat minor BWV 867 (Well-Tempered Clavier, Book 1)

London
November 1934

78: HMV DB 2408

Prelude and Fugue No 39 in G BWV 884 (Well-Tempered Clavier, Book 2)

Geneva
November 1956

45: Decca CEP 656/SEC 5062
LP: Decca LXT 5309/SXL 2205
CD: Decca 433 9012/433 9032

Diabelli Variations

Geneva
October 1954

LP: Decca LXT 5016/LXT 6014
LP: Decca 411 7451
CD: Decca 433 8912/433 9032

Piano Concerto No 1

Vienna April 1951	VPO Krauss	Decca unpublished
Vienna April 1958	VPO Schmidt-Isserstedt	LP: Decca LXT 5552/SXL 2178 LP: Decca BR 3001/SWL 8008 CD: Decca 433 8912/433 9032

Piano Concerto No 2

Vienna May 1951	VPO Krauss	LP: Decca LX 3083/ACL 148 LP: Decca ECM 524/ECS 524 LP: Telefunken 648.057 CD: London (Japan) POCL 3336
Vienna June 1959	VPO Schmidt-Isserstedt	LP: Decca LXT 5552/SXL 2178 LP: Decca BR 3073 CD: Decca 433 8912/433 9032

Piano Concerto No 3

Vienna September 1950	VPO Böhm	78: Decca AX 373-376 LP: Decca LXT 2553/LXT 5353 LP: Decca ACL 148 LP: Decca ECM 524/ECS 524 CD: London (Japan) POCL 3337
Vienna October 1958	VPO Schmidt-Isserstedt	LP: Decca BR 3038/SXL 2190 CD: Decca 433 8912/433 9032

Piano Concerto No 4

London 1930	LSO Ronald	78: HMV DB 1425-1428/ DB 7489-7492 auto LP: Japan PZ 2319
Vienna May 1951	VPO Krauss	78: Decca AKX 28542-28545 LP: Decca LXT 2629/LXT 5354 LP: Decca ACL 36 LP: Turnabout THS 65004-65006 LP: Telefunken 648.057/641.745 CD: Decca 425 9622
New York March 1956	NYPO Cantelli	LP: Toscanini Society ATSGC 1218 LP: Penzance PR 39 LP: Cetra LO 520/DOC 54 LP: Paragon DSV 52012 CD: AS-Disc AS 621
Vienna April 1958	VPO Schmidt-Isserstedt	LP: Decca LXT 5482/SXL 2010 LP: Decca 433 8912/433 9032
Vienna May 1962	VPO Knappertsbusch	Unpublished video recording

Piano Concerto No 5 "Emperor"

London 1927	Royal Albert Hall Orchestra Ronald	78: HMV D 1198-1201 78: Victor M 21
Vienna June 1953	VPO Krauss	LP: Decca LXT 2839/LXT 5355 LP: Decca ACL 98 LP: Turnabout THS 65004-65006 LP: Telefunken 648.057 CD: Decca 425 9622
Vienna June 1959	VPO Schmidt-Isserstedt	LP: Decca LXT 5553/SXL 2179 LP: Decca LXT 6292-6295/ SXL 6292-6295 CD: Decca 433 8912/433 9032
Munich December 1959	Bavarian State Orchestra Knappertsbusch	LP: Longanesi periodici GCL 17 LP: Laudis (Japan) RCL 3320 CD: Foyer CDS 16008 Incorrectly dated Berlin 1953
Stockholm 1959	Stockholm Radio Orchestra Keilberth	LP: Paragon DSV 52012

At time of going to press a version of the Emperor Concerto by Backhaus
with Böhm conducting is announced on the Datum CD label; further
details not yet to hand

Piano Sonata No 1 in F minor op 2 no 1

Geneva
November 1953

LP: Decca LXT 2902

Geneva
September and
October 1963

LP: Decca LXT 6097/SXL 6097
LP: Decca SXLA 6452-6461
CD: Decca 433 8822

Piano Sonata No 2 in A op 2 no 2

Geneva
November 1953

LP: Decca LXT 2920

Geneva
March 1968

LP: Decca SXL 6417/SXLA 6452-6461
CD: Decca 433 8822

Piano Sonata No 3 in C op 2 no 3

Geneva
May 1952

LP: Decca LXT 2747

Geneva
April 1969

LP: Decca SXL 6417/SXLA 6452-6461
CD: Decca 433 8822

Piano Sonata No 4 in E flat op 7

Geneva
November 1953

LP: Decca LXT 2809

Geneva
November 1967

LP: Decca LXT 6300/SXL 6300
LP: Decca SXLA 6452-6461
CD: Decca 433 8822

Piano Sonata No 5 in C minor op 10 no 1

Geneva
March 1951

LP: Decca LXT 2603

Geneva
September and
October 1963

LP: Decca LXT 6097/SXL 6097
LP: Decca SXLA 6452-6461
CD: Decca 433 8822

Piano Sonata No 6 in F op 10 no 2

Geneva
March 1951

LP: Decca LXT 2603

Geneva
September and
October 1963

LP: Decca LXT 6097/SXL 6097
LP: Decca SXLA 6452-6461
CD: Decca 433 8822

Vienna
May 1964

CD: Cetra 9075 027

Piano Sonata No 7 in D op 10 no 3

Geneva
November 1953

LP: Decca LXT 2809

Geneva
September and
October 1963

LP: Decca LXT 6097/SXL 6097
LP: Decca SXLA 6452-6461
CD: Decca 433 8822

Piano Sonata No 8 in C minor op 13 "Pathétique"

1925-1926

Duo-Art piano roll
CD: Bellaphon 690.07.013
First movement only

London
1928

78: HMV DB 1031-1032
78: Victor 6671-6672

New York
March 1954

LP: London (USA) LL 1109
LP: London (Japan) MZ 5099

Geneva
March 1954

LP: Decca LXT 2903

Vienna
October 1958

LP: Decca BR 3010/SWL 8016
LP: Decca SXLA 6452-6461
LP: Decca SPA 69
CD: Decca 433 8822

Piano Sonata No 9 in E op 14 no 1

Geneva
November 1953

LP: Decca LXT 2903

Geneva
March 1968

LP: Decca SXL 6358/SXLA 6452-6461
CD: Decca 433 8822

Piano Sonata No 10 in G op 14 no 2

Geneva
April 1952

LP: Decca LXT 2931

Geneva
March 1968

LP: Decca SXL 6358 /SXLA 6452-6461
CD: Decca 433 8822

Piano Sonata No 11 in B flat op 22

Geneva
November 1953

LP: Decca LXT 2920

Geneva
March 1968

LP: Decca SXL 6358 /SXLA 6452-6461
CD: Decca 433 8822

Piano Sonata No 12 in A flat op 26

Geneva
July 1950

78: Decca AX 428-430
LP: Decca LXT 2532

Geneva
February 1963

LP: Decca LXT 6064/SXL 6064
LP: Decca SXLA 6452-6461
CD: Decca 433 8822

Salzburg
August 1964

CD: Orfeo C300 921 B

Piano Sonata No 13 in E flat op 27 no 1

Geneva
November 1952

LP: Decca LXT 2780

Geneva
April 1969

LP: Decca SXL 6416 /SXLA 6452-6461
CD: Decca 433 8822

Piano Sonata No 14 in C minor op 27 no 2 "Moonlight"

London
November 1934

78: HMV DB 2405-2406
78: Victor 8735-8736

Geneva
October 1952

45: Decca CEP 561
LP: Decca LXT 2780

Vienna
October 1958

LP: Decca BR 3010/SWL 8016
LP: Decca SXL 2190/SPA 69
LP: Decca SXLA 6452-6461
CD: Decca 433 8822

Besancon
September 1959

LP: Paragon DSV 52102
CD: AS-Disc AS 303

Salzburg
August 1964

CD: Orfeo C300 921 B

Piano Sonata No 15 in D op 28 "Pastoral"

Geneva
November 1953

LP: Decca LXT 2903

Geneva
November 1961

LP: Decca BR 3107/SWL 8018
LP: Decca SXLA 6452-6461
CD: Decca 433 8822

Florence
June 1969

LP: Rococo 2116

Piano Sonata No 16 in G op 31 no 1

Geneva
November 1953

LP: Decca LXT 2950

Geneva
April 1969

LP: Decca SXL 6417/SXLA 6452-6461
CD: Decca 433 8822

Piano Sonata No 17 in D minor op 31 no 2 "Tempest"

Geneva
May 1952

LP: Decca LXT 2747

New York
March 1954

LP: London (USA) LL 1109
LP: London (Japan) MZ 5099

Geneva
October and
November 1959

LP: Decca LXT 6063/SXL 6063
LP: Decca SXLA 6452-6461
CD: Decca 433 8822

Lugano
May 1960

CD: Eremitage ERM 105

Salzburg
August 1964

CD: Orfeo C 300 921 B

Piano Sonata No 18 in E flat op 31 no 3

Zürich
March 1948

78: HMV DB 6788-6790/
DB 9303-9305 auto

Geneva
March 1954

LP: Decca LXT 2950

Geneva
February 1963

LP: Decca LXT 6064/SXL 6064
LP: Decca SXLA 6452-6461
CD: Decca 433 8822

Ossiach
June 1969

LP: Decca SET 441-442
LP: London (USA) CS 6666-6667
LP: Telefunken 641.505
SET 441-442 was not issued; final
movement of the sonata was not
performed

Piano Sonata No 19 in G minor op 49 no 1

Geneva
November 1952

LP: Decca LXT 2780

Geneva
March 1968

LP: Decca SXL 6359 /SXLA 6452-6461
CD: Decca 433 8822

Piano Sonata No 20 in G op 49 no 2

Geneva
April 1952

LP: Decca LXT 2780

Geneva
March 1968

LP: Decca SXLA 6452-6461
CD: Decca 433 8822

Piano Sonata No 21 in C op 53 "Waldstein"

Geneva
July 1950

78: Decca AX 428 and 431-432
LP: Decca LXT 2532

Salzburg
August 1954

CD: Cetra 9075 027

Salzburg
August 1959

CD: Laudis CDS 16008
CD: AS-Disc AS 303

Geneva
November 1959

LP: Decca LXT 5596/SXL 2241
LP: Decca SXLA 6452-6461
CD: Decca 433 8822

Ossiach
June 1969

LP: Decca SET 441-442
LP: London (USA) CS 6666-6667
SET 441-442 was not published

Piano Sonata No 22 in F op 54

Geneva
April 1952

LP: Decca LXT 2931

Geneva
April 1969

LP: Decca SXL 6358 /SXLA 6452-6461
CD: Decca 433 8822

Piano Sonata No 23 in F minor op 57 "Appassionata"

Geneva
April 1952

LP: Decca LXT 2715

Geneva
November 1959

LP: Decca LXT 5596/SXL 2241/SPA 69
LP: Decca SXLA 6452-6461
CD: Decca 433 8822

Piano Sonata No 24 in F op 78

Geneva
April 1952

LP: Decca LXT 2931

Geneva
April 1969

LP: Decca SXL 6416 /SXLA 6452-6461
CD: Decca 433 8822

Piano Sonata No 25 in G op 79

Geneva
March 1951

78: Decca X 53098/KX 28486
LP: Decca LXT 2603

New York
March 1954

LP: London (USA) LL 1109
LP: London (Japan) MZ 5099

Geneva
November 1963

LP: Decca LXT 6300/SXL 6300
LP: Decca SXLA 6452-6461
CD: Decca 433 8822

Vienna
May 1964

CD: Cetra 9075 027

Piano Sonata No 26 in E flat op 81a "Les adieux"

London
November 1934

78: HMV DB 2407-2408
78: Victor 8922-8923
LP: EMI QALP 10361
LP: Discocorp RR 315

Geneva
November 1953

LP: Decca LXT 2902

New York
March 1954

LP: London (USA) LL 1109
LP: London (Japan) MZ 5099

Geneva
December 1961

LP: Decca BR 3107/SWL 8018
LP: Decca SXLA 6452-6461
CD: Decca 433 8822

Salzburg
August 1968

CD: Orfeo C300 921 B

Florence
June 1969

LP: Rococo 2116
LP: Paragon DSV 52112

Piano Sonata No 27 in G minor op 90

Geneva
January 1954

LP: Decca LXT 2902

Geneva
April 1969

LP: Decca SXL 6417 /SXLA 6452-6461
CD: Decca 433 8822

Piano Sonata No 28 in A op 101

Geneva
April 1952

LP: Decca LXT 2715

Geneva
November 1961

LP: Decca LXT 6063/SXL 6063
LP: Decca SXLA 6452-6461
CD: Decca 433 8822

Piano Sonata No 29 in B flat op 106 "Hammerklavier"

Geneva
April 1952

LP: Decca LXT 2777/SXLA 6452-6461
CD: Decca 433 8822

Piano Sonata No 30 in E op 109

Geneva
July 1950

78: Decca AX 361-362
LP: Decca LXT 2535

Geneva
November 1961

LP: Decca BR 8500/SWL 8500
LP: Decca SXLA 6452-6461
CD: Decca 433 8822

Piano Sonata No 31 in A flat op 110

Geneva
November 1953

LP: Decca LXT 2939

Geneva
November 1963

LP: Decca LXT 6300/SXL 6300
LP: Decca SXLA 6452-6461
CD: Decca 433 8822

Piano Sonata No 32 in C minor op 111

London
1936

78: HMV DB 3218-3220

Geneva
November 1953

LP: Decca LXT 2939

New York
March 1954

LP: London (USA) LL 1109
LP: London (Japan) MZ 5099

Lugano
May 1960

CD: Eremitage ERM 128

Geneva
November 1961

LP: Decca BR 8500/SWL 8500
LP: Decca SXLA 6452-6461
CD: Decca 433 8822

Vienna
May 1964

CD: AS-Disc AS 303
CD: Orfeo C300 921 B

Brahms

Piano Concerto No 1

London November 1932	BBC SO Boult	78: HMV DB 1839-1843/ DB 7307-7311 LP: Discocorp RR 315 LP: EMI EX 29 03433 CD: Biddulph LWH 017
Vienna June 1953	VPO Böhm	LP: Decca LXT 2866/LXT 5364 LP: Decca (France) 592.135 CD: Decca 433 8952/433 9032

Piano Concerto No 2

Dresden June 1939	Dresden Staatskapelle Böhm	78: Electrola DB 5500-5505 78: HMV DB 3930-3935/ DB 8767-8772 auto LP: Toshiba GR 2078 LP: EMI 1C 053 01326M LP: EMI 2C 051 01326M LP: EMI 1C 137 53505-53507M CD: Memories HR 4442-4443 CD: Biddulph LWH 018
Vienna May 1952	VPO Schuricht	LP: Decca LXT 2723/LXT 5365 LP: Decca (France) 592.135 CD: London (Japan) POCL 3341
Lugano May 1958	Swiss-Italian RO Schuricht	LP: Melodram MEL 202 CD: Musica classica
Vienna May 1964	BPO Karajan	CD: Cetra CDE 1009 CD: Bellaphon 689.22002
Vienna April 1967	VPO Böhm	LP: Decca SXL 6322/JB 94 CD: Decca 414 1422 CD: Decca 433 8952/433 9032

Cello Sonata No 1 op 39

Geneva   Fournier
May 1955

LP: Decca LXT 5077
CD: Decca 425 9732

Cello Sonata No 2 op 99

Geneva   Fournier
May 1955

LP: Decca LXT 5077
CD: Decca 425 9732

Ballade in D minor op 10 no 1 "Edward"

London
December 1932

78: HMV DB 1894
78: Victor M 202
LP: Discocorp IGI 296
CD: Pearl GEMMCD 9385
CD: Memories HR 4442-4443
CD: Biddulph LWH 017
Memories incorrectly states
recording made in Berlin 1933

Ballade in D op 10 no 2

London
December 1932

78: HMV DB 1894
78: Victor M 202
LP: Discocorp IGI 296
CD: Pearl GEMMCD 9385
CD: Memories HR 4442-4443
CD: Biddulph LWH 017
Memories incorrectly states
recording made in Berlin 1933

Hungarian Dances Nos 6 in D flat and 7 in A, arranged for piano solo

London
April 1933

78: HMV DB 1896
78: Victor M 202
LP: Discocorp IGI 296
CD: Pearl GEMMCD 9385
CD: Memories HR 4442-4443
CD: Biddulph LWH 017
Pearl and Memories state that the
recording was made in 1934;
Memories incorrectly state that
the recording was made in Berlin

Scherzo in E flat minor op 4

London
December 1932

78: HMV DB 1895
78: Victor M 202
LP: Discocorp IGI 296
CD: Pearl GEMMCD 9385
CD: Memories HR 4442-4443
CD: Biddulph LWH 017
Pearl and Memories state that
recording was made in 1933

Capriccio in B minor op 76 no 2

London
December 1935

78: HMV DB 2807/DB 6850
78: Victor 14516/M 774
CD: Biddulph LWH 017

Geneva
November 1956

LP: Decca LXT 5308/SXL 2222
LP: Decca ECS 691
CD: Decca 433 8952/433 9032

Intermezzo in A minor op 76 no 7

London
December 1932

78: HMV DB 1897
78: Victor M 202
LP: Discocorp IGI 296
CD: Pearl GEMMCD 9385
CD: Memories HR 4442-4443
CD: Biddulph LWH 017

Capriccio in C op 76 no 8

London
December 1932

78: HMV DB 2897
78: Victor M 202
LP: Discocorp IGI 296
CD: Pearl GEMMCD 9385
CD: Memories HR 4442-4443
CD: Biddulph LWH 017

Rhapsody in B minor op 79 no 1

London
December 1932

78: HMV DB 1899
78: Victor M 202
LP: Japan MZ 2319
LP: Discocorp IGI 296
CD: Pearl GEMMCD 9385
CD: Memories HR 4442-4443
CD: Biddulph LWH 017

Geneva
November 1956

LP: Decca LXT 5308/SXL 2222
LP: Decca ECS 691
CD: Decca 433 8952/433 9032

Rhapsody in G minor op 79 no 2

London
December 1932

78: HMV DB 1900
78: Victor M 202
LP: Japan MZ 2319
LP: Discocorp IGI 296
CD: Pearl GEMMCD 9385
CD: Memories HR 4442-4443
CD: Biddulph LWH 017

HMV recordings 1932-1935 are inaccurately dated in many of the re-issues

Capriccio in D minor op 116 no 1

London
December 1935

78: HMV DB 2807/DB 6851
78: Victor 14516
CD: Biddulph LWH 019

Intermezzo in A minor op 116 no 2

London
December 1935

78: HMV DB 2807/DB 6851
78: Victor 14516
CD: Biddulph LWH 019

Intermezzo in E op 116 no 4

London
December 1935

78: HMV DB 2804/DB 6851
78: Victor M 321
LP: Discocorp IGI 296
CD: Biddulph LWH 019

Intermezzo in E op 116 no 6

Geneva
November 1956

LP: Decca LXT 5308/SXL 2222
LP: Decca ECS 691
CD: Decca 433 8952/433 9032

Intermezzo in E flat op 117 no 1

London
December 1935

78: HMV DB 2805/DB 6852
78: Victor M 321
LP: Discocorp IGI 296
CD: Pearl GEMMCD 9385
CD: Memories HR 4442-4443
CD: Biddulph LWH 019
Memories incorrectly states
that recording made in Berlin

Geneva
November 1956

LP: Decca LXT 5308/SXL 2222
LP: Decca ECS 691
CD: Decca 433 8952/433 9032

Intermezzo in B flat op 117 no 2

London
December 1935

78: HMV DB 2805/DB 6852
78: Victor M 321
LP: Discocorp IGI 296
CD: Pearl GEMMCD 9385
CD: Memories HR 4442-4443
CD: Biddulph LWH 019
Memories incorrectly states
that recording made in Berlin

Intermezzo in A minor op 118 no 1

London
December 1932

78: HMV DB 1900
78: Victor M 202
LP: Discocorp IGI 296
CD: Pearl GEMMCD 9385
CD: Memories HR 4442-4443
CD: Biddulph LWH 019

Geneva
November 1956

45: Decca CEP 656/SEC 5062
LP: Decca LXT 5308/SXL 2222
LP: Decca ECS 691
CD: Decca 433 8952/433 9032

Intermezzo in A op 118 no 2

London
December 1932

78: HMV DB 1900
78: Victor M 202
LP: Discocorp IGI 296
CD: Pearl GEMMCD 9385
CD: Memories HR 4442-4443
CD: Biddulph LWH 019

Geneva
November 1956

LP: Decca LXT 5308/SXL 2222
LP: Decca ECS 691
CD: Decca 433 8952/433 9032

HMV recordings 1932-1935 are inaccurately dated in many of the re-issues

Ballade in G minor op 118 no 3

London
December 1932

78: HMV DB 1897
78: Victor M 202
LP: Japan MZ 2319
LP: EMI QALP 10361
LP: Discocorp IGI 296
CD: Pearl GEMMCD 9385
CD: Memories HR 4442-4443
CD: Biddulph LWH 019

Geneva
November 1956

45: Decca CEP 656/SEC 5062
LP: Decca LXT 5308/SXL 2222
LP: Decca ECS 691
CD: Decca 433 8952/433 9032

Intermezzo in F minor op 118 no 4

London
December 1932

78: HMV DB 1898
78: Victor M 202
LP: Discocorp IGI 296
CD: Pearl GEMMCD 9385
CD: Memories HR 4442-4443
CD: Biddulph LWH 019

Geneva
November 1956

LP: Decca LXT 5308/SXL 2222
LP: Decca ECS 691
CD: Decca 433 8952/433 9032

Romance in F op 118 no 5

London
December 1932

78: HMV DB 1898
78: Victor M 202
LP: Japan MZ 2319
LP: Discocorp IGI 296
CD: Pearl GEMMCD 9385
CD: Memories HR 4442-4443
CD: Biddulph LWH 019

Geneva
November 1956

LP: Decca LXT 5308/SXL 2222
LP: Decca ECS 691
CD: Decca 433 8952/433 9032

HMV recordings 1932-1935 are inaccurately dated in many of the re-issues

Intermezzo in E flat op 118 no 6

London
December 1932

78: HMV DB 1900
78: Victor M 202
CD: Pearl GEMMCD 9385
CD: Memories HR 4442-4443
CD: Biddulph LWH 019

Geneva
November 1956

LP: Decca LXT 5308/SXL 2222
LP: Decca ECS 691
CD: Decca 433 8952/433 9032

Intermezzo in B minor op 119 no 1

London
December 1935

78: HMV DB 2806/DB 6853
78: Victor M 321
LP: Discocorp IGI 296
CD: Biddulph LWH 019

Intermezzo in E minor op 119 no 2

London
December 1935

78: HMV DB 2806/DB 6853
78: Victor M 321
LP: Discocorp IGI 296
CD: Biddulph LWH 019

Geneva
November 1956

LP: Decca LXT 5308/SXL 2222
LP: Decca ECS 691
CD: Decca 433 8952/433 9032

Intermezzo in C op 119 no 3

London
December 1935

78: HMV DB 2807/DB 6850
78: Victor 14516/M 774
CD: Biddulph LWH 019

New York
March 1954

LP: Decca BR 3097
LP: London (USA) LL 1109
LP: London (Japan) MZ 5099

Geneva
November 1956

LP: Decca LXT 5308/SXL 2222
LP: Decca ECS 691
CD: Decca 433 8952/433 9032

Variations on an original theme op 21

London
December 1935

78: HMV DB 2808/DB 6848
78: Victor 14227
CD: Pearl GEMMCD 9385
CD: Memories HR 4442-4443
CD: Biddulph LWH 018
Memories incorrectly state
recording was made in Berlin

HMV recordings 1932-1935 are inaccurately dated in many of the re-issues

Variations on a theme of Paganini op 35, abridged versions

1922-1923	Duo Art piano roll CD: Bellaphon 690.07.013 CD: Fonè 90 F 11CD
1923	78: Polydor 65288
London 1925-1926	78: HMV D 1019-1020
London November 1929	78: HMV DB 1388-1389 78: Victor 7419-7420 LP: Parnassus 3 LP: Discocorp IGI 296 LP: EMI EX 29 03453 CD: Biddulph LWH 018

Waltzes op 39, arranged for piano solo

London December 1935	78: HMV DB 2803-2804/ DB 6849-6850 78: Victor M 321 LP: EMI QALP 10361 CD: Biddulph LWH 019 Excerpts CD: Memories HR 4442-4443

Waltzes op 39 nos 1, 2 and 15, arranged for piano solo

London December 1932	78: HMV DB 1896 78: Victor M 202 LP: Japan MZ 2319 CD: Pearl GEMMCD 9385 CD: Biddulph LWH 017 No 15 only LP: EMI QALP 10361

HMV recordings 1932-1935 are inaccurately dated in many of the re-issues

Chabrier

Habanera

New York
1954 or 1956

LP: London (USA) LL 1404

Chopin

Piano Concerto No 2, Romance (arr. Backhaus)

1908-1920

Welte Mignon piano roll
LP: Welte Legacy 702

1925-1926

Duo Art piano roll
CD: Bellaphon 690.07.013

Piano Sonata No 2 op 35

Geneva
July 1950

LP: Decca LXT 2435

Ballade No 1 in G minor op 23

Geneva
November 1950

LP: Decca LX 3044

Berceuse in D flat op 57

London
1926-1927

78: HMV DB 1033

London
June 1928

78: HMV DB 1131
CD: Pearl GEMMCD 9902
Pearl states that recording
was made in 1927

Etude in C op 10 no 1

London
1908

G & T 05508
Victor 71045

London
1925-1926

78: HMV DB 928

London
January 1928

78: HMV DB 1132
78: Victor M 42
LP: Discocorp IGI 286
LP: EMI EX 29 03453/29 01001
CD: Pearl GEMMCD 9902
Pearl states that recording
was made in 1927

London
1934

78: HMV DB 2059

Etude in A minor op 10 no 2

1923

78: Polydor 61875

London
1925-1926

78: HMV DB 928

London
January 1928

78: HMV DB 1132
78: Victor M 42
LP: Discocorp IGI 286
LP: EMI EX 29 03453/29 01001
CD: Pearl GEMMCD 9902
Pearl states that recording
was made in 1927

Geneva
October 1952

LP: Decca LX 3091

Etude in E op 10 no 3

London
January 1928

78: HMV DB 1132
78: Victor M 42
LP: Discocorp IGI 286
LP: EMI EX 29 03453/29 01001
CD: Pearl GEMMCD 9902
Pearl states that recording
was made in 1927

Geneva
July 1950

78: Decca SX 63008
45: Decca 45-71063/CEP 602
LP: Decca LX 3044

Etude in C sharp minor op 10 no 4

London
January 1928

78: HMV DB 1133
78: Victor M 42
LP: Discocorp IGI 286
LP: EMI EX 29 03453/29 01001
CD: Pearl GEMMCD 9902
Pearl states that recording
was made in 1927

Etude in G flat op 10 no 5

London
1908

G & T 05514

London
January 1928

78: HMV DB 1133
78: Victor M 42
LP: Discocorp IGI 286
LP: EMI EX 29 03453/29 01001
CD: Pearl GEMMCD 9902
Pearl states that recording
was made in 1927

Geneva
October 1952

LP: Decca LX 3091

Lugano
June 1953

CD: Eremitage ERM 105

Etude in E flat minor op 10 no 6

London
January 1928

78: HMV DB 1133
78: Victor M 42
LP: Discocorp IGI 286
LP: EMI EX 29 03453/29 01001
CD: Pearl GEMMCD 9902
Pearl states that recording
was made in 1927

Etude in C op 10 no 7

London
1910

G & T 05553

London
1925-1926

78: HMV DB 929
78: Victor 7270

London
January 1928

78: HMV DB 1132
78: Victor M 42
LP: Discocorp IGI 286
LP: EMI EX 29 03453/29 01001
CD: Pearl GEMMCD 9902
Pearl states that recording
was made in 1927

Etude in F op 10 no 8

London
January 1928

78: HMV DB 1133
78: Victor M 42
LP: Discocorp IGI 286
LP: EMI EX 29 03453/29 01001
CD: Pearl GEMMCD 9902
Pearl states that recording
was made in 1927

Geneva
October 1952

LP: Decca LX 3091

Etude in F minor op 10 no 9

London
January 1928

78: HMV DB 1134
78: Victor M 42
LP: Discocorp IGI 286
LP: EMI EX 29 03453/29 01001
CD: Pearl GEMMCD 9902
Pearl states that recording
was made in 1927

Etude in A flat op 10 no 10

London
January 1928

78: HMV DB 1134
78: Victor M 42
LP: Discocorp IGI 286
LP: EMI EX 29 03453/29 01001
CD: Pearl GEMMCD 9902
Pearl states that recording
was made in 1927

Geneva
October 1952

LP: Decca LX 3091

Etude in E flat op 10 no 11

London
January 1928

78: HMV DB 1134
78: Victor M 42
LP: Discocorp IGI 286
LP: EMI EX 29 03453/29 01001
CD: Pearl GEMMCD 9902
Pearl states that recording
was made in 1927

Etude in C minor op 10 no 12 "Revolutionary"

London
1925-1926

78: HMV DB 928

London
January 1928

78: HMV DB 1134
78: Victor M 42
LP: Discocorp IGI 286
LP: EMI EX· 29 03453/29 01001
CD: Pearl GEMMCD 9902
Pearl states that recording
was made in 1927

Etude in A flat op 25 no 1

London
1910

G & T 24159
Victor 74159

London
January 1928

78: HMV DB 1178
78: Victor M 42
LP: Discocorp IGI 286
LP: EMI EX 29 03453/29 01001
CD: Pearl GEMMCD 9902
Pearl states that recording
was made in 1927

Geneva
October 1952

LP: Decca LX 3091

Lugano
June 1953

CD: Eremitage ERM 105

Etude in F minor op 25 no 2

1923

78: Polydor 61875

London
January 1928

78: HMV DB 1178
78: Victor M 42
LP: Discocorp IGI 286
LP: EMI EX 29 03453/29 01001
CD: Pearl GEMMCD 9902
Pearl states that recording
was made in 1927

Geneva
October 1952

LP: Decca LX 3091

Lugano
June 1953

CD: Eremitage ERM 105

New York
April 1956

LP: Decca BR 3097

Etude in F op 25 no 3

1923

London
1925-1926

London
January 1928

Geneva
October 1952

Lugano
June 1953

78: Polydor 61875

78: HMV DB 928

78: HMV DB 1179
78: Victor M 42
LP: Discocorp IGI 286
LP: EMI EX 29 03453/29 01001
CD: Pearl GEMMCD 9902
Pearl states that recording
was made in 1927

LP: Decca LX 3091

CD: Eremitage ERM 105

Etude in A minor op 25 no 4

London
January 1928

78: HMV DB 1179
78: Victor M 42
LP: Discocorp IGI 286
LP: EMI EX 29 03453/29 01001
CD: Pearl GEMMCD 9902
Pearl states that recording
was made in 1927

Etude in E minor op 25 no 5

London
June 1928

78: HMV DB 1179
78: Victor M 42
LP: Discocorp IGI 286
LP: EMI EX 29 03453/29 01001
CD: Pearl GEMMCD 9902
Pearl states that recording
was made in 1927

Etude in G sharp minor op 25 no 6

London
June 1928

78: HMV DB 1179
78: Victor M 42
LP: Discocorp IGI 286
LP: EMI EX 29 03453/29 01001
CD: Pearl GEMMCD 9902
Pearl states that recording
was made in 1927

London
1910

G & T 24159
Victor 74159

Geneva
October 1952

LP: Decca LX 3091

Lugano
June 1953

CD: Eremitage ERM 105

Etude in C sharp minor op 25 no 7

London
June 1928

78: HMV DB 1180
78: Victor M 42
LP: Discocorp IGI 286
LP: EMI EX 29 03453/29 01001
CD: Pearl GEMMCD 9902
Pearl states that recording
was made in 1927

Geneva
October 1952

LP: Decca LX 3091

Etude in D flat op 25 no 8

London
1908

G & T 05514

London
January 1928

78: HMV DB 1179
78: Victor M 42
LP: Discocorp IGI 286
LP: EMI EX 29 03453/29 01001
CD: Pearl GEMMCD 9902
Pearl states that recording
was made in 1927

Geneva
October 1952

LP: Decca LX 3091

Lugano
June 1953

CD: Eremitage ERM 105

Etude in G flat op 25 no 9

London
1908

G & T 05514

London
January 1928

78: HMV DB 1180
78: Victor M 42
LP: Discocorp IGI 286
LP: EMI EX 29 03453/29 01001
CD: Pearl GEMMCD 9902
Pearl states that recording
was made in 1927

Geneva
October 1952

LP: Decca LX 3091

Lugano
June 1953

CD: Eremitage ERM 105

Etude in B minor op 25 no 10

London
January 1928

78: HMV DB 1180
78: Victor M 42
LP: Discocorp IGI 286
LP: EMI EX 29 03453/29 01001
CD: Pearl GEMMCD 9902
Pearl states that recording
was made in 1927

Etude in A minor op 25 no 11

1923

78: Polydor 65463

London
January 1928

78: HMV DB 1178
78: Victor M 42
LP: Discocorp IGI 286
LP: EMI EX 29 03453/29 01001
CD: Pearl GEMMCD 9902
Pearl states that recording
was made in 1927

Geneva
October 1952

LP: Decca LX 3091

Etude in C minor op 25 no 12

London
January 1928

78: HMV DB 1178
78: Victor M 42
LP: Discocorp IGI 286
LP: EMI EX 29 03453/29 01001
CD: Pearl GEMMCD 9902
Pearl states that recording
was made in 1927

Impromptu No 4 in C sharp minor op 66 (Fantaisie-Impromptu)

London
1908

G & T 05511
Victor 88158
LP: Parnassus 3

London
1933

78: HMV DB 2059
CD: Pearl GEMMCD 9902

Mazurka No 17 in B flat minor op 24 no 4

Geneva
November 1950

45: Decca CEP 602
LP: Decca LX 3044/LW 5026

Mazurka No 20 in D flat op 30 no 3

Geneva
July 1950

78: Decca SX 63008
45: Decca CEP 602
LP: Decca LX 3044/LW 5026

Mazurka No 24 in C op 33 no 3

Geneva
July 1950

78: Decca SX 63008
45: Decca CEP 602
LP: Decca LX 3044/LW 5026

Nocturne No 8 in D flat op 27 no 2

Lugano
June 1953

CD: Eremitage ERM 105

Polonaise No 3 in A op 40 no 1

1923

78: Polydor 65463

Polonaise No 6 in A flat op 53 (Polonaise-Fantaisie)

London
1924

78: HMV D 888

Prélude in C op 28 no 1

London
1908

G & T 05508
Victor 71045

London
1925-1926

78: HMV DB 928

London
1933

78: HMV DB 2059

Valse No 1 in E flat op 18 (Grande valse brillante)

London
January 1928

78: HMV DB 1131
CD: Pearl GEMMCD 9902
Pearl states that recording
was made in 1927

Lugano
June 1953

CD: Eremitage ERM 105

Valse No 2 in A flat op 34 no 1

Geneva
November 1950

45: Decca 45-71063
LP: Decca LX 3044

Valse No 5 in A flat op 42

London
1910

G & T 05533

London
1924

78: HMV D 888

Valse No 6 in D flat op 64 no 1

London
1910

G & T 05533

1923

78: Polydor 61875

London
1925-1926

78: HMV DB 929
78: Victor 7270
CD: Pearl GEMMCD 9902

Valse No 11 in G flat op 70 no 1

London
1910

G & T 05543

Valse No 14 in E minor op. posth.

London
1910

G & T 05543

Daquin

Le coucou

1908   Victor 20345

Debussy

Clair de lune

Geneva   LP: London (USA) LL 1404
October 1955   LP: Decca ECS 515

Marche écossaise

Geneva   LP: London (USA) LL 1404
October 1955   LP: Decca ECS 515

Délibes

Naila, Waltz (arr. Dohnanyi)

1908-1920   Duo Art piano roll
                                      LP: Japan 25AC 245

1922-1923   Duo Art piano roll
                                      CD: Bellaphon 690.07.013
                                      CD: Fonè 90F 11 CD

London
1924   78: HMV D 788

London
November 1925   78: HMV DB 926
                                      78: Victor 6582
                                      LP: EMI EX 29 03453

Dvorak

Humoresque (number not specified)

1908   Victor 20203

Falla

Danza espanola

New York   LP: London (USA) LL 1404
1954 or 1956

Gounod

Faust, Waltz

1908-1920   DEA piano roll
                                       LP: ABACCA 001

Grieg

Piano Concerto

London   New Symphony   G & T 05523-05524
1910   Orchestra   Monarch 044520-044521
                    Ronald   Abridged version

London   New Symphony   78: HMV DB 2074-2076/
October 1933   Orchestra   DB 7560-7562 auto
                    Barbirolli   78: Victor M 204
                                       LP: EMI EX 29 03433

Handel

Harmonious Blacksmith (Air and Variations from Suite No 5)

London   G & T 05509
1908   Victor 88160
                                       LP: EMI EX 29 03453

Haydn

Fantasia in C

Geneva
April 1958

45: Decca CEP 656/SEC 5062
LP: Decca LXT 5457
LP: Decca ECS 692
CD: Decca 433 9002/433 9032

Lugano
May 1960

CD: Eremitage ERM 105

Piano Sonata No 34 in E minor

Geneva
April 1958

LP: Decca LXT 5457
LP: Decca ECS 692
CD: Decca 433 9002/433 9032

Piano Sonata No 48 in C

Geneva
April 1958

LP: Decca LXT 5457
LP: Decca ECS 692
CD: Decca 433 9002/433 9032

Piano Sonata No 52 in E flat

Geneva
April 1958

LP: Decca LXT 5457
LP: Decca ECS 692
CD: Decca 433 9002/433 9032

Lugano
May 1960

CD: Eremitiage ERM 105

Variations in F minor

Geneva
April 1958

LP: Decca LXT 5457
LP: Decca ECS 692
CD: Decca 433 9002/433 9032

Lugano
May 1960

CD: Eremitage ERM 105

Kreisler

Liebesleid, arr. Rachmaninov

1925-1926

Duo Art piano roll
CD: Bellaphon 690.07.013
CD: Foné 90F 11 CD

Liszt

Concert Study in F minor "La leggierezza"

March
1926

Duo Art piano roll
CD: Bellaphon 690.07.013

Waldesrauschen (2 Concert Studies G58/G145)

London
November 1925

78: HMV DB 929
78: Victor 7270
CD: Pearl GEMMCD 9902

Hungarian Rhapsody No 2 in C sharp minor

London
1910

G & T 05545-05546

London
1923-1924

78: HMV D 519

London
January 1927

78: HMV DB 1013
LP: EMI QALP 10361
LP: EMI EX 29 03453

Hungarian Rhapsody No 12 in C sharp minor

1923

78: Polydor 65287

Liebestraum No 3 in A flat

London
1908

G & T 05505
Victor 71044 /Polydor 65281

London
1924

78: HMV D 788

London
November 1925

78: HMV DB 926
78: Victor 6582
LP: EMI EX 29 03453

Transendental Study No 3 in A flat minor, after Paganini "La campanella"

London
1908

G & T 05507
Polydor 65281

Mendelssohn

Piano Concerto No 1 in G minor, arranged for piano solo

December 1926

Duo Art piano roll
CD: Fonè 90F 11 CD

A Midsummer Night's Dream, Wedding March arr. Liszt

1925-1926

Duo Art piano roll
CD: Bellaphon 690.07.013

A Midsummer Night's Dream, Scherzo arranged for piano solo

London
1927

78: HMV DB 1195

Lieder ohne Worte No 25 in G op 62 no 1

Geneva
November 1956

45: Decca CEP 640/SEC 5050
CD: Decca 433 9022/433 9032

Lieder ohne Worte No 30 in A op 62 no 6

Geneva
November 1956

45: Decca CEP 640/SEC 5050
LP: Decca 414 4981
CD: Decca 433 9022/433 9032

Lieder ohne Worte No 34 in C op 67 no 4

Geneva
November 1956

45: Decca CEP 640/SEC 5050
CD: Decca 433 9022/433 9032

Rondo capriccioso in E op 14

Geneva
November 1956

45: Decca CEP 640/SEC 5050
CD: Decca 433 9022/433 9032

Moskowski

Caprice espagnole

London
1926-1927

78: HMV D 995

London
January 1928

78: HMV DB 1130
78: Victor 7121
Both recordings coupled with
Smetana Caprice bohémien

Mozart

Piano Concerto No 26 "Coronation"

Berlin
1940

Städtische Oper
Orchestra
Zaun

78: Electrola DB 5674-5677
LP: EMI EX 29 03433

Piano Concerto No 27

Vienna
May 1955

VPO
Böhm

LP: Decca LXT 5123/ECS 749
LP: Decca ADD 116/SDD 116
CD: Decca 433 8982/433 9032

Salzburg
August 1960

VPO
Böhm

LP: Longanesi periodici GCL 14
LP: Seven Seas (Japan)
K22C-168

Piano Sonata No 4 K282

Geneva
November 1966

LP: Decca LXT 6301/SXL 6301
CD: Decca 433 9002/433 9032

Piano Sonata No 5 K283

Geneva
November 1966

LP: Decca LXT 6301/SXL 6301
CD: Decca 433 9002/433 9032

Piano Sonata No 10 K330

Geneva
October 1955

LP: Decca LXT 5167/ECS 749

Salzburg
January 1956

CD: Frequenz 991.009

Geneva
November 1961

LP: Decca LXT 6301/SXL 6301
CD: Decca 433 9002/433 9032

Piano Sonata No 11 K331

Zürich
March 1948

78: HMV DB 6810-6811

Vienna
May 1955

45: Decca CEP 579
LP: Decca LXT 5123

Salzburg
January 1956

CD: Frequenz 991.009
CD: AS-Disc AS 303

Vienna
January 1960

LP: Decca SXL 2214
CD: Decca 433 8982/433 9032

Ossiach
June 1969

LP: Decca SET 441-442
LP: London (USA) CS 6666-6667
LP: Telefunken 641.505
SET 441-442 not published

Piano Sonata No 11 K331, Turkish March

New York
April 1956

LP: Decca BR 3097

Piano Sonata No 12 K332

Geneva
November 1961

LP: Decca LXT 6301/SXL 6301
LP: Decca ECS 749
CD: Decca 433 9002/9032

Piano Sonata No 14 K457

Geneva
October 1955

LP: Decca LXT 5167
CD: Decca 433 8982/433 9032

Salzburg
January 1956

CD: Frequenz 991.009

Don Giovanni's Serenade, arr. Backhaus

1923

Duo Art piano roll
CD: Bellaphon 690.07.013
CD: Fonè 90F 11 CD

London
1924

78: HMV E 338

London
1928

78: HMV DA 944
78: Victor 1472
Coupled with Schumann/
Liszt Träumerei

Fantasia in C minor K475

Geneva
October 1955

LP: Decca LXT 5167

Salzburg
January 1956

CD: Frequenz 991.009

Rondo in A minor K511

Geneva
October 1955

LP: Decca LXT 5167

Salzburg
January 1956

CD: Frequenz 991.009

Vienna
January 1960

LP: Decca LXT 6301/SXL 6301
CD: Decca 433 8982/433 9032

Mussorgsky

Gopak

New York
1954 or 1956

LP: London (USA) LL 1404

Pick-Mangianelli

Danse d'Olaf

1922-1923

Duo Art piano roll
CD: Bellaphon 690.07.013
CD: Fonè 90F 11 CD

Rachmaninov

Prelude No 2 in C sharp minor op 3

London
1908

G & T 05504
Victor 71046
LP: EMI EX 29 03453

Anton Rubinstein

Polka op 82 no 7

1923

78: Polydor 61876

Romance op 44 no 1

1923

78: Polydor 61876

Domenico Scarlatti

2 Sonatas (numbers not specified)

London
1910

G & T 05535

Schubert

Horch! Horch! Die Lerch'!, arr. Liszt

London
1910

G & T 05550

Impromptu in C minor D899 no 1

Ossiach
June 1969

LP: Decca SET 441-442
LP: London (USA) CS 6666-6667
SET 441-442 not published

Impromptu in E flat D899 no 2

Zürich
March 1948

78: HMV DB 6790
Coupled with Beethoven
Sonata No 18

Ossiach
June 1969

LP: Decca SET 441-442
LP: London (USA) CS 6666-6667
SET 441-442 not published

Impromptu in G flat D899 no 3

Ossiach
June 1969

LP: Decca SET 441-442
LP: London (USA) CS 6666-6667
SET 441-442 not published

Impromptu in A flat D899 no 4

Ossiach
June 1969

LP: Decca SET 441-442
LP: London (USA) CS 6666-6667
SET 441-442 not published

Impromptu in F minor D935 no 1

Ossiach
June 1969

LP: Decca SET 441-442
LP: London (USA) CS 6666-6667
SET 441-442 not published

Impromptu in A flat D935 no 2

New York
March 1954

LP: Decca BR 3097
CD: Decca 433 9022/433 9032

Ossiach
June 1969
(26 June)

LP: Decca SET 441-442
LP: London (USA) CS 6666-6667
LP: Telefunken 641.505
SET 441-442 not published

Ossiach
June 1969
(28 June)

LP: Decca SET 441-442
LP: London (USA) CS 6666-6667
LP: Telefunken 641.505
SET 441-442 not published

Impromptu in B flat D935 no 3

London
January 1928

78: HMV DB 1126
78: Victor 7120

New York
March 1954

LP: Decca BR 3097

Geneva
November 1956

45: Decca CEP 641/SEC 5051
CD: Decca 433 9022/433 9032

Marche militaire in E flat D733 no 3, arr. Backhaus for piano solo

London
January 1928

78: HMV DB 1125

Moment musical in C D780 no 1

Geneva
October 1955

LP: Decca LXT 5413
CD: Decca 433 9022/433 9032

Moment musical in A flat D780 no 2

Geneva
October 1955

LP: Decca LXT 5413
CD: Decca 433 9022/433 9032

Moment musical in F minor D780 no 3

London
1910

G & T 05550

London
1925-1926

78: HMV DB 1033

London
June 1928

78: HMV DB 1126
78: Victor 7120

Geneva
October 1955

LP: Decca LXT 5413
CD: Decca 433 9022/433 9032

Moment musical in C sharp minor D780 no 4

Geneva
October 1955

LP: Decca LXT 5413
CD: Decca 433 9022/433 9032

Moment musical in F minor D780 no 5

Geneva
October 1955

LP: Decca LXT 5413
CD: Decca 433 9022/433 9032

Moment musical in A flat D780 no 6

London
1936

78: HMV DB 2809
Coupled with Soirées de Vienne

Geneva
October 1955

LP: Decca LXT 5413
CD: Decca 433 9022/433 9032

Piano Quintet in A "The Trout"

London   International
1928   String Quartet

78: HMV D 1484-1487
78: Electrola EJ 354-357

Piano Sonata No 18 D894, Minuetto

London
1928

78: HMV DB 1195

Soirées de Vienne No 6 in A, arr. Liszt

London
1936

78: HMV DB 2809
Coupled with Moment musical no 6

New York
March 1954

LP: Decca BR 3097

Geneva
November 1956

45: Decca SEC 5451
CD: Decca 433 9022/433 9032

12 Valses nobles D969

Geneva
November 1956

45: Decca CEP 641/SEC 5051
CD: Decca 433 9022/433 9032

Wanderer Fantasy, arranged for piano solo

1908-1920

Welte Mignon piano roll
LP: Welte Legacy 702

Schumann

Aufschwung (Fantasiestücke op 12)

London
October 1928

78: HMV DA 1018
78: Victor 1445
LP: EMI EX 29 03453

Des Abends (Fantasiestücke op 12)

Ossiach
June 1969

LP: Decca SET 441-442
LP: London (USA) CS 6666-6667
LP: Telefunken 641.505
SET 441-442 not published

Warum? (Fantasiestücke op 12)

Geneva
March 1951

LP: Decca LXT 2931
CD: Decca 433 9022/433 9032

New York
March 1954

LP: Decca BR 3097

Ossiach
June 1969

LP: Decca SET 441-442
LP: London (USA) CS 6666-6667
LP: Telefunken 641.505
SET 441-442 not published

Fantasia in C op 17

London
May 1937

78: HMV DB 3221-3224/
    DB 8431-8434 auto
78: Victor M 463
LP: Parnassus 3
LP: EMI EX 29 03453

Nachtstück in F op 23 no 4

London
May 1937

78: HMV DB 3224/DB 8431
78: Victor M 463
LP: Parnassus 3
LP: EMI EX 29 03453
78 issue coupled with
Fantasia in C

Novelette in E op 21 no 7

London
1910

G & T 05529

Piano Concerto

Vienna   VPO
January 1960   Wand

LP: Decca BR 3048/SWL 8022
LP: Decca ADD 201/SDD 201/VIV 43
CD: Decca 433 8992/433 9032

Träumerei (Kinderszenen)

London
1925-1926

78: HMV DB 1033

Waldszenen

Geneva
October 1955

LP: Decca LXT 5413
CD: Decca 433 8992/433 9032

Vogel als Prophet (Waldszenen)

New York
April 1956

LP: Decca BR 3097

Widmung, arr. Liszt

1925-1926

Duo Art piano roll
CD: Bellaphon 690.07.013
CD: Fonè 90F 11 CD

London
1928

78: HMV DA 944
78: Victor 1472
Coupled with Don Giovanni's
Serenade

Smetana

Caprice bohémien (Bohemian Dances Book 1)

1908-1920	Duo Art piano roll LP: Japan 25AC 245
London 1910	G & T 05534 Polydor 65310
1925-1926	Duo Art piano roll CD: Fonè 90F 11CD
London 1926-1927	78: HMV D 995 Coupled with Moskowski Caprice espagnole
London June 1928	78: HMV DB 1130 78: Victor 7121 Coupled with Moskowski Caprice espagnole

Richard Strauss

Ständchen, arranged Backhaus for piano solo

June 1923	Duo Art piano roll CD: Bellaphon 690.07.013 CD: Fonè 90F 11 CD

Wagner

Die Meistersinger von Nürnberg, Act 1 Prelude arr. Hutcheson

1925-1926   Duo Art piano roll
                                           CD: Bellaphon 690.07.013

Tannhäuser, Entry of the Guests arr. Liszt

1925-1926   Duo Art piano roll
                                           CD: Bellaphon 690.07.013

Weber

Rondo (Piano Sonata No 1 in C)

London   G & T 05510
1908   Victor 71043

ROYAL ALBERT HALL

(Manager—C. S. TAYLOR)

Tuesday, OCTOBER 19th, 1948, at 7.30 p.m.

35th Series of Symphony Concerts

THE

LONDON SYMPHONY

ORCHESTRA

(Leader : GEORGE STRATTON)

SOLOIST :

BACKHAUS

CONDUCTOR :

SIR MALCOLM SARGENT

Artur Schnabel
1882-1951

Discography compiled by John Hunt

GREAT RECORDINGS *of the* CENTURY

ARTUR SCHNABEL (1882–1951)

Beethoven

CONCERTO FOR PIANOFORTE
No. 1, Op. 15

played by

ARTUR SCHNABEL

RECORDED BY
THE GRAMOPHONE COMPANY, LIMITED, ENGLAND

Introduction

Artur Schnabel possesses a pretty comprehensive discography for one who is reported to have had such an abhorrence of entering the recording studio. Eye witnesses also argue that the records capture less than the essential magic of Schnabel on the recital platform. Nevertheless, one hears no less than a master thinker at work in that pioneering set of the Beethoven sonatas, which is comparable in its significance for gramophone history to the Decca Ring or to Fischer-Dieskau's traversal of the Schubert Lieder. Mention of Schubert reminds us also of Schnabel's intervention for the piano music of that composer, which took place in the concert halls of pre-war Berlin and in HMV's London studios.

Schnabel the composer is regrettably unrepresented in his own discography (Walter Legge's Philharmonia Orchestra did record one of his orchestral pieces), but Schnabel the Lied accompanist is to be heard in records made with his wife. The fact that these were not made with one of the truly great Lieder singers of the 1930s should not diminish their value in documenting Schnabel's mastery of the accompanist's role. It is also something he shares, in present company, with Edwin Fischer and Walter Gieseking.

If asked to name latter-day counterparts to Artur Schnabel, I might venture names such as Murray Perahia or Alfred Brendel, men who also think deeply, intellectually, about the music which they perform. Concern with actual tonal quality per se is for them, as it was for Schnabel, obviously less to the fore.

John Hunt

Montag, den 8. November 1926, abends 7¹/₂ Uhr

4. Philharmonisches Konzert

Dirigent: Wilhelm Furtwängler

Solist: Artur Schnabel

1. Symphonie Nr. 39 Es-dur . . . . . . W. A. Mozart
   Adagio-Allegro
   Andante con moto
   Menuett
   Finale

2. (Romanzero II:) Morgenklangspiel op. 19 .   Ph. Jarnach
   zum 1. Mal

3. Feuerwerk . . . . J. Strawinsky

— PAUSE —

4. Klavier-Konzert Nr. II B-dur op 83 . . . . J. Brahms
   Allegro non troppo
   Allegro appassionato
   Andante
   Allegretto grazioso

5. Ouvertüre zu „Euryanthe" . . . . . C. M. von Weber

Konzertflügel: Bechstein

Celesta: Schiedmayer Pianofortefabrik, Potsdamer Strasse 27 b

PHILHARMONIE, Montag, 22. November 1926, abends 7¹/₂ Uhr

5. PHILHARMONISCHES KONZERT

Dirigent: Wilhelm Furtwängler

Solist: Bronislaw Huberman

HÄNDEL: Wassermusik — BEETHOVEN: Violinkonzert
STRAUSS: Ein Heldenleben

Bach

Concerto in C for 2 pianos BWV 1061

London
October 1936

Karl-Ulrich
Schnabel
LSO
Boult

78: HMV DB 3041-3043/
     DB 8242-8244 auto
78: Victor M 357/AM 357/DM 357
LP: Victor LCT 1140
LP: Rococo 2060
CD: Pearl GEMMCD 9399

Chromatic Fantasy and Fugue in D BWV 903

London
June 1948

78: HMV DB 9511-9512/
     DB 21150-21151 auto
LP: Perennial 2001
LP: Rococo 2060

Gigue (English Suite No 5)

Freiburg
May 1905

Welte Mignon piano roll 389

Italian Concerto BWV 971

New York
1922

Ampico piano roll
62721/62733/62741
LP: Klavier KS 134

Prelude and Fugue No 5 in BWV 850 (Well-Tempered Clavier, Book 1)

London
June 1950

78: HMV DB 9511/DB 21151
LP: Perennial 2001
LP: Rococo 2060
78 edition coupled with
Chromatic Fantasy and
Fugue in D BWV 903

Toccata in C minor BWV 911

London
November 1937

78: HMV DA 1613-1614
78: Victor M 532/AM 532/DM 532
LP: Perennial 2001
LP: Rococo 2060
CD: Pearl GEMMCD 9376

Toccata in D BWV 912

London
November 1937

78: HMV DA 1615-1616
78: Victor M 532/AM 532/DM 532
LP: Perennial 2001
LP: Rococo 2060
CD: Pearl GEMMCD 9376

Toccata in G BWV 916

Freiburg
May 1905

Welte Mignon piano roll 396

Beethoven

Andante favori in F

London
November 1938

LP: World Records SHB 63
LP: Discocorp BWS 724
LP: Arabesque AR 8103
CD: Arabesque Z 6551

Bagatelle in A minor "Für Elise"

London
May 1932

78: HMV DB 1694/DB 2361/
    DB 7514
78: Victor M 158/DM 158/
    M 580/DM 580
LP: EMI RLS 769
CD: Pearl GEMMCD 9063

London
November 1938

78: HMV DB 3786/DB 8678
LP: HMV COLH 66
LP: Seraphim IC 6067
LP: Toshiba GR 2129
LP: World Records SHB 63
78 edition coupled with
Bagatelles op 33

7 Bagatelles op 33

London
November 1938

78: HMV DB 3783-3786/
     DB 8672-8678 auto
LP: HMV COLH 66
LP: Seraphim IC 6067
LP: Toshiba GR 2129
LP: EMI RLS 769

New York
November 1943

LP: Discocorp RR 502

11 Bagatelles op 119

London
May 1938

LP: EMI RLS 769

6 Bagatelles op 126

London
January 1937

78: HMV DB 3626-3628/
     DB 8579-8584 auto
LP: HMV COLH 66
LP: Seraphim IC 6067
LP: Toshiba GR 2129
LP: EMI RLS 769

Bagatelle in B minor op 126 no 4

New York
1944

V-Disc C 118
LP: Discocorp BWS 724
CD: Pearl GEMMCD 9063

Cello Sonata No 1 in F op 5 no 1

London   Fournier
June 1948

LP: EMI 1C 147 01382-01383M
LP: Seraphim IB 6075

Cello Sonata No 2 in G minor op 5 no 2

London   Piatigorsky
December 1934

78: HMV DB 2391-2393/
     DB 8181-8183 auto
78: Victor M 281/DM 281
LP: EMI 1C 053 03078M
LP: Seraphim 60300
LP: Discocorp RR 406

London   Fournier
June 1948

LP: EMI 1C 147 01382-01383M
LP: Seraphim IB 6075

Cello Sonata No 3 in A op 69

London   Fournier
June 1947

78: HMV DB 6464-6466/
    DB 9123-9125 auto
78: Victor M 1231/DM 1231
45: Victor WCT 1124
LP: Victor LCT 1124
LP: EMI 1C 147 01382-01383M
LP: Toshiba GR 2208
LP: Seraphim IB 6075

Cello Sonata No 4 in C op 102 no 1

London   Fournier
June 1947

78: HMV DB 6500-6501/
    DB 9555-9556 auto
45: Victor WDM 1370/WCT 1124
LP: Victor LCT 1124
LP: EMI 1C 147 01382-01383M
LP: Toshiba GR 2208
LP: Seraphim IB 6075

Cello Sonata No 5 in D op 102 no 2

London   Fournier
June 1948

78: HMV DB 6829-6831/
    DB 9438-9440 auto
45: Victor WCT 1124
LP: Victor LCT 1124
LP: EMI 1C 147 01382-01383M
LP: Toshiba GR 2208
LP: Seraphim IB 6075

Fantasia in G minor op 77

London
January 1937

78: HMV DB 3625/DB 8583-8584
LP: HMV COLH 66
LP: Toshiba GR 2129
LP: Seraphim IC 6067
LP: EMI RLS 769

Minuet in G WoO 10 no 2

New York
1922

Ampico piano roll
62291/71531
LP: Klavier KS 134

Minuet in E flat WoO 82

London
November 1938

78: HMV DB 3786/DB 8678
LP: HMV COLH 65
LP: Toshiba GR 2100
LP: Seraphim IC 6067
LP: EMI RLS 769
CD: Pearl GEMMCDS 9099
78 edition coupled with
Bagatelles op 33

Piano Concerto No 1

London
March 1932

LSO
Sargent

78: HMV DB 1690-1694/
    DB 7514-7518 auto
78: Victor M 158/AM 158/DM 158
LP: Victor LCT 6700
LP: HMV COLH 1
LP: Electrola E 60620
LP: Top Classic HC 658
LP: World Records SHB 63
LP: Toshiba GRE 4006
LP: EMI 2C 153 03881-03884M
LP: Arabesque AR 8103
CD: Arabesque Z 6549
CD: World Classics WC 44006
CD: Pearl GEMMCD 9063

Piano Concerto No 2

London
April 1935

LPO
Sargent

78: HMV DB 2573-2576/
    DB 7945-7948 auto
78: Victor M 295/AM 295/DM 295
LP: Victor LCT 6700
LP: Top Classic HC 658
LP: World Records SHB 63
LP: EMI 2C 153 03881-03884M
LP: Arabesque AR 8103
CD: Arabesque Z 6549
CD: World Classics WC 44007
CD: Pearl GEMMCD 9063

London
June 1946

Philharmonia
Dobrowen

78: HMV DB 6323-6326/
    DB 9099-9102 auto
LP: HMV COLH 2
LP: Electrola E 60621
LP: Toshiba GR 2091/GRE 4006
LP: Seraphim IC 6043
CD: Testament SBT 1020

Piano Concerto No 3

London February 1933	LPO Sargent	78: HMV DB 1940-1944/ DB 7377-7381 auto 78: Victor M 194/AM 194/DM 194 LP: Victor LCT 6700 LP: Top Classic HC 658 LP: World Records SHB 63 LP: EMI 2C 153 03881-03884M LP: Arabesque AR 8103 CD: Arabesque Z 6550 CD: World Classics WC 44008 CD: Pearl GEMMCD 9063
New York June 1945	NYPSO Szell	LP: Discocorp SID 721 LP: Melodram MEL 203 CD: Music and Arts CD 681
London May 1947	Philharmonia Dobrowen	LP: HMV COLH 3 LP: Electrola E 60622 LP: Toshiba GRE 4006 CD: Testament SBT 1021

Piano Concerto No 4

London February 1933	LPO Sargent	78: HMV DB 1886-1889/ DB 7340-7443 auto 78: Victor AM 156/DM 156 LP: Victor LCT 6700 LP: Top Classic HC 658 LP: World Records SHB 63 LP: EMI 2C 153 03881-03884M LP: Arabesque AR 8103 CD: Arabesque Z 6550 CD: World Classics WC 44007 CD: Pearl GEMMCD 9063
Chicago July 1942	Chicago SO Stock	78: Victor M 930/DM 930 LP: RCA VIC 1505/GM 43368 CD: RCA/BMG 09026 613932
London June 1946	Philharmonia Dobrowen	78: HMV DB 6303-6306/ DB 9032-9035 auto LP: Victor LCT 1131/LVT 1010 LP: HMV COLH 4 LP: Electrola E 60623 LP: Toshiba GR 2091/GRE 4006 CD: Testament SBT 1021
Columbus Ohio November 1947	Columbus SO I.Solomon	CD: Pearl GEMMCD 9063

Piano Concerto No 5 "Emperor"

London March 1932	LSO Sargent	78: HMV DB 1685-1689/ DB 7509-7513 auto 78: Victor M 155/AM 155/DM 155 LP: Victor LCT 6700 LP: Victor (Japan) LH 6 LP: Top Classic HC 658 LP: World Records SHB 63 LP: EMI 2C 153 03881-03884M LP: Arabesque AR 8103 CD: Arabesque Z 6551 CD: AS-Disc AS 114 CD: World Classics WC 44008 CD: Pearl GEMMCD 9063
Chicago July 1942	Chicago SO Stock	78: Victor M 939/DM 939 78: HMV DB 6184-6188/ DB 9011-9015 auto 45: Victor WCT 19 LP: Victor LCT 1015 LP: RCA VIC 1511/GM 43368/CCV 5028 CD: RCA/BMG 09026 613932
London May 1947	Philharmonia Galliera	78: HMV DB 6692-6696/ DB 9326-9330 auto LP: HMV COLH 5 LP: Electrola E 80485 LP: Toshiba GR 2001/GRE 4006 CD: Testament SBT 1021

Piano Sonata No 1 in F minor op 2 no 1

London
April 1934

78: HMV DB 2463-2464/
    DB 7850-7853 auto
LP: Victor LM 2158/LM 9500
LP: HMV COLH 51
LP: Toshiba GR 2099/GRM 4005
LP: Seraphim ID 6063
LP: EMI F 667.808-667.820
LP: EMI RLS 753
CD: EMI CHS 763 7652
CD: Pearl GEMMCD 9083
78 auto version coupled with
Sonata op 101 and op 14 no 2

Piano Sonata No 2 in A op 2 no 2

London
April 1933

78: HMV DB 2086-2089/
    DB 7575-7581 auto
LP: Victor LCT 1155/LM 9500
LP: HMV COLH 51
LP: Toshiba GR 2099/GRM 4005
LP: Seraphim ID 6063
LP: EMI F 667.808-667.820
LP: EMI RLS 753
CD: EMI CHS 763 7652
CD: Pearl GEMMCD 9083
78 auto version coupled with
Moonlight and Les Adieux

Piano Sonata No 3 in C op 2 no 3

London
April 1934

78: HMV DB 2646-2648/
    DB 7970-7975 auto
LP: Victor LM 2154/LM 9500
LP: HMV COLH 52
LP: Toshiba GR 2099/GRM 4005
LP: Seraphim ID 6063
LP: EMI F 667.808-667.820
LP: EMI RLS 753
CD: EMI CHS 763 7652
CD: Pearl GEMMCD 9083
78 auto version coupled with
Sonata op 31 no 2

Piano Sonata No 4 in E flat op 7

London
November 1935
and January 1937

78: HMV DB 3151-3154/
    DB 8266-8272 auto
LP: Victor LM 2156/LM 9500
LP: HMV COLH 52
LP: Toshiba GR 2099/GRM 4005
LP: Seraphim ID 6063
LP: EMI F 667.808-667.820
LP: EMI RLS 753
CD: EMI CHS 763 7652
CD: Pearl GEMMCD 9083
78 auto version coupled with
Sonata op 31 no 1

Piano Sonata No 5 in C minor op 10 no 1

London
November 1935
(unissued takes
April 1933)

78: HMV DB 3343-3344/
    DB 8379-8382 auto
LP: Victor LM 2151/LM 9500
LP: HMV COLH 53
LP: Toshiba GR 2099/GRM 4005
LP: Seraphim ID 6063
LP: EMI F 667.808-667.820
LP: EMI RLS 753
CD: EMI CHS 763 7652
CD: Pearl GEMMCD 9083
78 auto version coupled with
Sonata op 10 no 3

Piano Sonata No 6 in F op 10 no 2

London
April 1933

78: HMV DB 2354-2355/
    DB 7782-7783 auto
LP: Victor LM 2152/LM 9500
LP: HMV COLH 53
LP: Toshiba GR 2099/GRM 4005
LP: Seraphim ID 6063
LP: EMI F 667.808-667.820
LP: EMI RLS 753
CD: EMI CHS 763 7652
CD: Pearl GEMMCD 9083

Piano Sonata No 7 in D op 10 no 3

London
November 1935

78: HMV DB 3345-3347/
    DB 8379-8384 auto
LP: Victor LM 2151/LM 9500
LP: HMV COLH 53
LP: Toshiba GR 2099/GRM 4005
LP: Seraphim ID 6063
LP: EMI F 667.808-667.820
LP: EMI RLS 753
CD: EMI CHS 763 7652/Pearl GEMMCD 9099
78 auto version coupled with
Sonata op 10 no 1

Piano Sonata No 8 in C minor op 13 "Pathétique"

London
October 1933
and April 1934

78: HMV DB 2356-2358/
    DB 7777-7781 auto
LP: Victor LM 2152/LM 9500
LP: HMV COLH 54
LP: Toshiba GR 2099/GRM 4005
LP: Seraphim ID 6063
LP: EMI F 667.808-667.820
LP: EMI RLS 754
CD: EMI CHS 763 7652/Pearl GEMMCD 9099
78 auto version coupled with
Sonata op 31 no 3

Piano Sonata No 9 in E op 14 no 1

London
March 1932

78: HMV DB 1818-1819/7286-7289 auto
78: HMV DB 21438-21439/
    DB 9729-9730 auto
45: Victor WCT 1110
LP: Victor LCT 1110/LM 9500
LP: HMV COLH 54
LP: Toshiba GR 2099/GRM 4005
LP: Seraphim ID 6063
LP: EMI F 667.808-667.820
LP: EMI RLS 754
CD: EMI CHS 763 7652/Pearl GEMMCD 9099
DB 7286-7289 coupled with
Sonata op 109

Piano Sonata No 10 in G op 14 no 2

London
April 1934

78: HMV DB 2465-2466/
    DB 7854-7856 auto
LP: Victor LM 2158 /LM 9500
LP: HMV COLH 54
LP: Toshiba GR 2099/GRM 4005
LP: Seraphim ID 6063
LP: EMI F 667.808-667.820
LP: EMI RLS 754
CD: EMI CHS 763 7652/Pearl GEMMCD 9099
78 auto version coupled with
Sonatas op 2 no 1 and op 101

Piano Sonata No 11 in B flat op 22

London
April 1933

78: HMV DB 2211-2213/
    DB 7680-7685 auto
LP: Victor LM 2153/LM 9500
LP: HMV COLH 55
LP: Toshiba GR 2099/GRM 4005
LP: Seraphim IC 6064
LP: EMI F 667.808-667.820
LP: EMI RLS 754
CD: EMI CHS 763 7652/Pearl GEMMCD 9099
78 auto version coupled with
Appassionata

Piano Sonata No 12 in A flat op 26

London
April and
May 1934

78: HMV DB 2850-2852/
    DB 8078-8083 auto
LP: Victor LM 2157/LM 9500
LP: HMV COLH 55
LP: Toshiba GR 2099/GRM 4005
LP: Seraphim IC 6064
LP: EMI F 667.808-667.820
LP: EMI RLS 754
CD: EMI CHS 763 7652/Pearl GEMMCD 9099
78 auto version coupled with
Waldstein

Piano Sonata No 13 in E flat op 27 no 1

London
November 1932

78: HMV DB 1820-1821/7290-7291 auto
78: HMV DB 21402-21403/
    DB 9698-9699 auto
45: Victor WCT 1110
LP: Victor LCT 1110/LM 9500
LP: HMV COLH 56
LP: Toshiba GR 2099/GRM 4005
LP: Seraphim IC 6064
LP: EMI F 667.808-667.820
LP: EMI RLS 754
CD: EMI CHS 763 7652/Pearl GEMMCD 9099

Piano Sonata No 14 in C minor op 27 no 2 "Moonlight"

London
April 1933

78: HMV DB 2089-2090/
    DB 7579-7581 auto
LP: Victor LCT 1155/LM 9500
LP: HMV COLH 56
LP: Toshiba GR 2099/GRM 4005
LP: Seraphim IC 6064
LP: EMI F 667.808-667.820
LP: EMI RLS 754
CD: EMI CHS 763 7652
78 auto version coupled with
Les Adieux and op 2 no 2

London
June 1947
First movement only

HMV unpublished

Piano Sonata No 15 in D op 28 "Pastoral"

London
February 1932 and
February 1933
(additional
unissued takes
in 1932)

78: HMV DB 1953-1955/
    DB 7366-7371 auto
LP: Victor LCT 1154/LM 9500
LP: HMV COLH 56
LP: Toshiba GR 2099/GRM 4005
LP: Seraphim IC 6064
LP: EMI F 667.808-667.820
LP: EMI RLS 754
CD: EMI CHS 763 7652
78 auto version coupled with
Sonata op 110

Piano Sonata No 16 in G op 31 no 1

London
November 1935 and
January 1937

78: HMV DB 3154-3157/
    DB 8266-8272 auto
LP: Victor LM 2156/LM 9500
LP: HMV COLH 57
LP: Toshiba GR 21050/GRM 4005
LP: Seraphim IC 6064
LP: EMI F 667.808-667.820
LP: EMI RLS 755
CD: EMI CHS 763 7652
78 auto version coupled with
Sonata op 7

Piano Sonata No 17 in D minor op 31 no 2 "Tempest"

London
April 1934

78: HMV DB 2649-2651/
    DB 7970-7975 auto
LP: Victor LM 2154/LM 9500
LP: HMV COLH 57
LP: Toshiba GR 21050/GRM 4005
LP: Seraphim IC 6064
LP: EMI F 667.808-667.820
LP: EMI RLS 755
CD: EMI CHS 763 7652
78 auto version coupled with
Sonata op 2 no 3

Piano Sonata No 18 in E flat op 31 no 3

London
March 1932

78: HMV DB 2358-2360/
    DB 7777-7781 auto
LP: Victor LM 2152/LM 9500
LP: HMV COLH 58
LP: Toshiba GR 21050/GRM 4005
LP: Seraphim IC 6065
LP: EMI F 667.808-667.820
LP: EMI RLS 755
CD: EMI CHS 763 7652
78 auto version coupled with
Pathétique

Piano Sonata No 19 in G minor op 49 no 1

London
November 1932

78: HMV DB 1956/DB 7372
LP: Victor LCT 1154/LM 9500
LP: HMV COLH 58
LP: Toshiba GR 21050/GRM 4005
LP: Seraphim IC 6065
LP: EMI F 667.808-667.820
LP: EMI RLS 755
CD: EMI CHS 763 7652
CD: Pearl GEMMCD 9083

Piano Sonata No 20 in G op 49 no 2

London
April 1933

78: HMV DB 2214/DB 7686
LP: Victor LM 2153/LM 9500
LP: HMV COLH 58
LP: Toshiba GR 21050/GRM 4005
LP: Seraphim IC 6065
LP: EMI F 667.808-667.820
LP: EMI RLS 755
CD: EMI CHS 763 7652
CD: Pearl GEMMCD 9083

Piano Sonata No 21 in C op 53 "Waldstein"

London
April and
May 1934

78: HMV DB 2853-2855/
      DB 8078-8083 auto
LP: Victor LM 2157/LM 9500
LP: HMV COLH 59
LP: Toshiba GR 21050/GRM 4005
LP: Seraphim IC 6065
LP: EMI F 667.808-667.820
LP: EMI RLS 755
CD: EMI CHS 763 7652
78 auto version coupled with
Sonata op 26

Piano Sonata No 22 in F op 54

London
April 1933

78: HMV DB 2651-2652/7975-7976
LP: Victor LM 2155/LM 9500
LP: HMV COLH 59
LP: Toshiba GR 21050/GRM 4005
LP: Seraphim IC 6065
LP: EMI F 667.808-667.820
LP: EMI RLS 755
CD: EMI CHS 763 7652

Piano Sonata No 23 in F minor op 57 "Appassionata"

London
April 1933

78: HMV DB 2215-2217/
    DB 7680-7685 auto
LP: Victor LM 2153/LM 9500
LP: HMV COLH 59
LP: Toshiba GR 21050/GRM 4005
LP: Seraphim IC 6065
LP: EMI F 667.808-667.820
LP: EMI RLS 758
CD: EMI CHS 763 7652
78 auto version coupled with
Sonata op 22

Piano Sonata No 24 in F op 78

London
March 1932

78: HMV DB 1659-1660/7123-7125 auto
78: HMV DB 21476-21477/
    DB 9748-9749 auto
45: Victor WCT 1109
LP: Victor LCT 1109/LM 9500
LP: HMV COLH 60
LP: Toshiba GR 21050/GRM 4005
LP: Seraphim IC 6065
LP: EMI F 667.808-667.820
LP: EMI RLS 755
CD: EMI CHS 763 7652
DB 7123-7125 coupled
with Sonata op 90

Piano Sonata No 25 in G op 79

London
November 1935

78: HMV DB 3348/8383-8384 auto
LP: Victor LM 2151/LM 9500
LP: HMV COLH 60
LP: Toshiba GR 21050/GRM 4005
LP: Seraphim IC 6065
LP: EMI F 667.808-667.820
LP: EMI RLS 758
CD: EMI CHS 763 7652

Piano Sonata No 26 in E flat op 81a "Les adieux"

London
April 1933

78: HMV DB 2091-2092/
    DB 7575-7578 auto
LP: Victor LCT 1155/LM 9500
LP: HMV COLH 60
LP: Toshiba GR 21050/GRM 4005
LP: Seraphim IC 6065
LP: EMI F 667.808-667.820
LP: EMI RLS 758
CD: EMI CHS 763 7652
78 auto version coupled with
Moonlight and op 2 no 2

Piano Sonata No 27 in G minor op 90

London
January and
February 1932

78: HMV DB 1654-1655/7123-7126 auto
78: HMV DB 21404-21405/
    DB 8713-9714 auto
45: Victor WCT 1109
LP: Victor LCT 1109/LM 9500
LP: HMV COLH 60
LP: Toshiba GR 21050/GRM 4005
LP: Seraphim IC 6065
LP: EMI F 667.808-667.820
LP: EMI RLS 758
CD: EMI CHS 763 7652
DB 7123-7126 coupled with
Sonata op 78

Piano Sonata No 28 in A op 101

London
April 1934

78: HMV DB 2467-2469/
    DB 7850-7855 auto
LP: Victor LM 2158/LM 9500
LP: HMV COLH 62
LP: Toshiba GR 21050/GRM 4005
LP: Seraphim IC 6066
LP: EMI F 667.808-667.820
LP: EMI RLS 758
CD: EMI CHS 763 7652
78 auto version coupled with
Sonatas op 2 no 1 and op 14 no 2

Piano Sonata No 29 in B flat "Hammerklavier"

London
November 1935

78: HMV DB 2955-2960/8132-8137 auto
78: Victor M 403/DM 403
LP: Victor LM 2155/LM 9500
LP: HMV COLH 61
LP: Toshiba GR 21050/GRM 4005
LP: Seraphim IC 6066
LP: EMI F 667.808-667.820
LP: EMI RLS 758
CD: EMI CHS 763 7652

Piano Sonata No 30 in E op 109

London
March 1932

78: HMV DB 1822-1824/
     DB 7286-7291 auto
45: Victor WCT 1110
LP: Victor LCT 1110/LM 9500
LP: HMV COLH 62
LP: Toshiba GR 21050/GRM 4005
LP: Seraphim IC 6066
LP: EMI F 667.808-667.820
LP: EMI RLS 758
CD: EMI CHS 763 7652
78 auto version coupled with
Sonata op 14 no 1

New York
June 1942

LP: RCA AVM 11410/GM 43368

CD Ph 456 961

Piano Sonata No 31 in A flat op 110

London
January 1932

78: HMV DB 1957-1959/
     DB 7366-7371 auto
LP: Victor LCT 1154/LM 9500
LP: HMV COLH 63
LP: Toshiba GR 21050/GRM 4005
LP: Seraphim IC 6066
LP: EMI F 667.808-667.820
LP: EMI RLS 758
CD: EMI CHS 763 7652
78 auto version coupled with
Pastoral

Piano Sonata No 32 in C minor op 111

London
January, March
and May 1932

78: HMV DB 1656-1660/7126-7129 auto
78: HMV DB 21340-21343/
    DB 9677-9680 auto
45: Victor WCT 1109
LP: Victor LCT 1109/LM 9500
LP: HMV COLH 63
LP: Toshiba GR 21050/GRM 4005
LP: Seraphim IC 6066
LP: EMI F 667.808-667.820
LP: EMI RLS 758
CD: EMI CHS 763 7652

New York
June 1942

LP: RCA AVM 11410/GM 43368
CD PR 456 961

Polonaise in C op 89

London
November 1938

LP: World Records SHB 63
LP: Discocorp BWS 724
LP: Arabesque AR 8103
CD: Arabesque Z 6551

Rondo in C op 51 no 1

London
April 1933

78: HMV DB 1944/DB 2361/DB 7377
78: Victor M 194/AM 158/DM 194
LP: HMV COLH 65
LP: Toshiba GR 2120
LP: Seraphim IC 6067
LP: EMI RLS 769
CD: Pearl GEMMCD 9063

Rondo in G op 51 no 2

New York
1922

Ampico piano roll 60613
LP: Klavier KS 134

Rondo a capriccio in G op 129 "Wut über den verlorenen Groschen"

London
January 1937

78: HMV DB 3629/DB 8585
78: HMV DB 9748/DB 21477
LP: HMV COLH 65
LP: Toshiba GR 2120
LP: Seraphim IC 6067
LP: EMI RLS 769
CD: Pearl GEMMCD 9083

Rondo in A op 164

London
January 1937

78: HMV DB 3629/DB 8585
78: HMV DB 9677/DB 21343
LP: HMV COLH 65
LP: Toshiba GR 2120
LP: Seraphim IC 6067
LP: EMI RLS 769
CD: Pearl GEMMCD 9083

Variations in F op 34

London
January 1938

78: HMV DB 3623-3624/
     DB 8579-8582 auto
LP: HMV COLH 65
LP: Toshiba GR 2120
LP: Seraphim IC 6067
LP: World Records SHB 63

Variations in E flat op 35 "Eroica"

London
November 1938

78: HMV DB 3787-3789/
     DB 8672-8677 auto
LP: Victor LCT 6700
LP: HMV COLH 65
LP: Toshiba GR 2120
LP: Seraphim IC 6067
LP: EMI RLS 769

32 Variations on a waltz by Diabelli op 120

London
October and
November 1937

78: HMV DB 3519-3525/
     DB 8500-8506 auto
LP: HMV COLH 64/HQM 1197
LP: Toshiba GR 2130
LP: Seraphim IC 6067
LP: EMI RLS 769
CD 456 961

Violin Sonata No 5 in F op 24 "Kreutzer"

New York   Szigeti
April 1948

LP: Columbia (USA) M6X 31513
LP: MJA 1969
LP: Melodram MEL 204
CD: Pearl GEMMCD 9026

Violin Sonata No 10 in G op 96

New York   Szigeti
April 1948

LP: Columbia (USA) M6X 31513
LP: MJA 1969
LP: Melodram MEL 204
CD: Pearl GEMMCD 9026

Brahms

Piano Concerto No 1

London	l.PO	78: HMV DB 3712-3717/
January and	Szell	DB 8614-8619 auto
December 1938		78: Victor M 677/DM 677
		LP: Rococo 2022
		LP: World Records SH 223
		LP: EMI 1C 181 52348-52349M
		CD: Pearl GEMMCD 9376

Piano Concerto No 2

London	BBC SO	78: HMV DB 2696-2701/
November 1935	Boult	DB 7797-7802 auto
		78: Victor M 305/DM 305
		LP: HMV COLH 82
		LP: Toshiba GR 2050
		LP: World Records SH 109
		LP: EMI 1C 181 52348-52349M
		CD: Pearl GEMMCD 9399

Intermezzo in A minor op 116 no 2

London
June 1947

78: HMV DB 6505
LP: HMV HQM 1142
LP: Toshiba GR 2195
LP: Seraphim 60115

Intermezzo in E flat op 117 no 1

London
June 1947

78: HMV DB 6505
LP: HMV HQM 1142
LP: Toshiba GR 2195
LP: Seraphim 60115

Intermezzo in C op 119 no 3

Freiburg
May 1905

Welte Mignon piano roll 386

Liebestreu'

London   Behr-Schnabel
November 1932

78: HMV DA 1294
LP: Rococo 5370

Nicht mehr zu dir zu gehen

London   Behr-Schnabel
November 1932

78: HMV DA 1294
LP: Rococo 5370

Piano Trio No 1 in B op 8

Edinburgh August 1947	Szigeti, Fournier	Unpublished radio broadcast <u>Third movement missing</u>
London September 1947	Szigeti, Fournier	Unpublished radio broadcast

Rhapsody in B minor op 79 no 1

London June 1947	HMV unpublished

Rhapsody in G minor op 79 no 2

New York 1922	Ampico piano roll 62353
London June 1947	78: HMV DB 6504 LP: HMV HQM 1142 LP: Toshiba GR 2195 LP: Seraphim 60115

Violin Sonata No 1 in G op 78

London September 1947	Szigeti	Unpublished radio broadcast

Violin Sonata No 2 in A op 100

London September 1947	Szigeti	LP: Discocorp RR 488

Chopin

Etude in G flat op 10 no 5

Freiburg
May 1905

Welte Migon piano roll 390

Etude in F minor op 25 no 2

Freiburg
May 1905

Welte Migon piano roll 387

Etude in F op 25 no 3

Germany
after 1905

Hupfeld Animatic 55770

Nocturne in G minor op 15 no 3

Freiburg
May 1905

Welte Migon piano roll 393

Prélude No 23 in F op 28

Freiburg
May 1905

Welte Mignon piano roll 394

Dvorak

Piano Quintet in A op 81

London February 1934	Pro Arte String Quartet	78: HMV DB 2177-2180/ DB 7676-7679 auto 78: Victor M 219 LP: Discocorp BWS 718 LP: World Records SH 408

Lanner

Old Viennese Waltz

Freiburg May 1905	Welte Mignon piano roll 384

Mendelssohn

Piano Trio in D minor op 49

London September 1947	Szigeti, Fournier	Unpublished radio broadcast

Mozart

Concerto for 2 pianos K365

London	Karl-Ulrich	78: HMV DB 3033-3035/
October 1936	Schnabel	DB 8216-8218 auto
	LSO	78: Victor M 484/DM 484
	Boult	LP: Victor LCT 1140
		LP: HMV COLH 90
		LP: Toshiba GR 2157
		LP: EMI EX 29 00723
		CD: EMI CHS 763 7032
		CD: Arabesque Z 6590

Piano Concerto No 17 K453, 2nd movement bars 1-127 only

New York	New Friends	LP: Discocorp RR 502
March 1942	of Music	CD: Music and Arts CD 750
	Orchestra	
	Stiedry	

Piano Concerto No 19 K459

London	LSO	78: HMV DB 3095-3098/
January 1937	Sargent	DB 8298-8300 auto
		78: Victor M 389/DM 389
		LP: HMV COLH 90
		LP: Toshiba GR 2157
		LP: World Records SH 142
		CD: EMI CHS 763 7032
		CD: Arabesque Z 6590

Piano Concerto No 20 K466

New York December 1944	NYPSO Szell	LP: MJA 1971 LP: Discocorp BWS 723 CD: Music and Arts CD 750
London June 1948	Philharmonia Süsskind	45: Victor WHMV 1012 LP: Victor LHMV 1012 LP: Turnabout THS 65046 LP: EMI 2C 051 43166 LP: EMI EX 29 00723 CD: EMI CHS 763 7032 CD: Arabesque Z 6591

Piano Concerto No 21 K467

London January 1937	LSO Sargent	78: HMV DB 3099-3102/ DB 8355-8358 auto 78: Victor M 486/DM 486 LP: HMV COLH 67 LP: Toshiba GR 2032 LP: World Records SH 142 LP: EMI 1C 053 01341M CD: EMI CHS 763 7032 CD: Arabesque Z 6591 Also issued on LP by Franklin Mint

Piano Concerto No 22 K482

New York November 1941	NYPSO Walter	LP: MJA 1969 LP: Discocorp BWS 717 LP: Columbia (Japan) OS 7527 CD: AS-Disc AS 405 CD: Music and Arts CD 681

Piano Concerto No 23 K488

New York March 1946	NYPSO Rodzinski	LP: MKR 1004 LP: Discocorp BWS 717 CD: Music and Arts CD 632

Piano Concerto No 24 K491

Whittier California January 1946	Los Angeles PO Wallenstein	LP: MJA 1971 LP: Discocorp BWS 723 CD: Music and Arts CD 632
London June 1948	Philharmonia Süsskind	45: Victor WHMV 1012 LP: Victor LHMV 1012 LP: Turnabout THS 65045 LP: EMI 2C 051 43166 CD: EMI CHS 763 7032/EX 29 00723 CD: Arabesque Z 6592

Piano Concerto No 27 K595

London May 1934	LSO Barbirolli	78: HMV DB 2249-2252/ DB 7733-7736 auto 78: Victor M 240/DM 240 LP: HMV COLH 67 LP: Toshiba GR 2032 LP: EMI 1C 053 01341M LP: EMI EX 29 00723 CD: EMI CHS 763 7032 CD: Arabesque Z 6592
New York March 1939	National Orchestra Association Barzin	Unpublished radio broadcast

Piano Quartet No 1 K478

London January 1934	Members of Pro Arte String Quartet	78: HMV DB 2155-2148/ DB 7665-7668 auto 78: Victor M 251/DM 251 LP: Victor LM 6130 LP: HMV COLH 42 LP: Toshiba GR 2026 LP: Seraphim IC 6044 LP: EMI RLS 143 5413 CD: EMI CDH 763 0312 CD: Arabesque Z 6593

Piano Sonata No 8 in A minor K310

London
January 1939

78: HMV DB 3778-3780/
    DB 8764-8766 auto
LP: HMV COLH 305
LP: Toshiba GR 2138
CD: Arabesque Z 6593
LP editions omit first movement
exposition repeat and second
movement repeat

Piano Sonata No 12 in F K332

London
June 1946 and
June 1947

78: HMV DB 6336-6337
LP: HMV COLH 305
LP: Toshiba GR 2138
CD: EMI CHS 763 7032
CD: Arabesque Z 6591

Piano Sonata No 13 in B flat K333, 1st and 2nd movements

New York
February 1945

V-Disc C 118-119
LP: MKR 100 R
LP: Discocorp SID 721

Piano Sonata No 13 in B flat K333, 3rd movement

New York
1944

V-Disc C 119
LP: MKR 1004
LP: Discocorp SID 721

Piano Sonata No 16 in B flat K570

London
June 1948

78: HMV DB 6839-6840
LP: HMV COLH 305/HQM 1142
LP: Toshiba GR 2138
LP: Seraphim 60115
CD: EMI CHS 763 7032
CD: Arabesque Z 6590
COLH 305 and GR 2138 omit
second movement repeats

Piano Sonata No 18 in F K533/K494

New York
November 1943

LP: Discocorp RR 502
CD: Music and Arts CD 768
Third movement disfigured
by radio announcement

Rondo in A minor K511

London
June 1946

78: HMV DB 6298
LP: HMV COLH 305/HQM 1142
LP: Toshiba GR 2138/GR 2195
LP: Seraphim 60115
CD: EMI CHS 763 7032
CD: Arabesque Z 6592

Violin Sonata No 33 in E flat K481

New York   Szigeti
April 1948

LP: MJA 1969
LP: Discocorp WSA 738
CD: Pearl GEMMCD 9026

Schubert

Allegretto in C D915

London January 1939	78: HMV DB 3755/DB 8826 78: HMV DB 9700/DB 21357 LP: HMV COLH 33 LP: EMI 3C 153 01220-01222 LP: EMI EX 29 07883/RLS 7713 LP: Arabesque AR 8137

Allegro in A minor for piano duet D947 "Lebensstürme"

London October 1937	Karl-Ulrich Schnabel	78: HMV DB 1646-1647 78: Victor M 437/DM 437 LP: EMI RLS 143 5603 LP: Arabesque AR 8145

Andantino varié in B D823 no 2

London October 1937	Karl-Ulrich Schnabel	78: HMV DB 3518 78: Victor M 436/DM 436 LP: HMV COLH 308 LP: Electrola E 80872 LP: Toshiba GR 2136 LP: EMI 3C 153 01220-01222 LP: EMI RLS 143 5603 LP: Arabesque AR 8145

Divertissement à la hongroise D818

London October 1937	Karl-Ulrich Schnabel	78: HMV DB 3529-3532/ DB 8812-8815 auto 78: Victor M 436/DM 436 LP: HMV COLH 308 LP: Electrola E 80872 LP: Toshiba GR 2136 LP: EMI 3C 153 01220-01222 LP: EMI RLS 143 5603 LP: Arabesque AR 8145 GR 2136 omits repeats in first and third movements

Impromptu in C minor D899 no 1

New York
June 1942

Victor unpublished

London
June 1950

78: HMV DB 21320
45: Victor WHMV 1027
LP: Victor LHMV 1027/LCT 1019
LP: HMV BLP 1007
LP: Electrola E 80684
LP: Toshiba GR 2083
LP: EMI 1C 047 01339M
LP: EMI 2C 051 01339
LP: EMI RLS 7713
LP: Arabesque AR 8137
CD: Arabesque Z 6592

Impromptu in E D899 no 2

New York
June 1942

Victor unpublished

London
June 1950

78: HMV DB 21335
45: Victor WHMV 1027
LP: Victor LHMV 1027/LCT 1019
LP: HMV BLP 1007/HQM 1142
LP: Electrola E 80684
LP: Toshiba GR 2083
LP: Seraphim 60115
LP: EMI 1C 047 01339M
LP: EMI 2C 051 01339
LP: EMI RLS 7713
LP: Arabesque AR 8137
CD: Arabesque Z 6592

Impromptu in G flat D899 no 3

New York
June 1942

Victor unpublished

London
June 1950

78: HMV DB 21335
45: Victor WHMV 1027
LP: Victor LHMV 1027/LCT 1019
LP: HMV BLP 1007
LP: Electrola E 80684
LP: Toshiba GR 2083
LP: EMI 1C 047 01339M
LP: EMI 2C 051 01339
LP: EMI RLS 7713
LP: Arabesque AR 8137
CD: Arabesque Z 6592

Impromptu in A flat D899 no 4

Freiburg
May 1905

Welte Mignon piano roll 383

New York
June 1942

Victor unpublished

London
June 1950

78: HMV DB 21351
45: Victor WHMV 1027
LP: Victor LHMV 1027/LCT 1019
LP: HMV BLP 1007/HQM 1142
LP: Electrola E 80684
LP: Toshiba GR 2083
LP: Seraphim 60115
LP: EMI 1C 047 01339M
LP: EMI 2C 051 01339
LP: EMI RLS 7713
LP: Arabesque AR 8137
CD: Arabesque Z 6592

Impromptu in F minor D935 no 1

London
June 1950

78: HMV DB 21382
45: Victor WHMV 1027
LP: Victor LHMV 1027/LCT 1019
LP: HMV BLP 1030
LP: Electrola E 80684
LP: EMI 1C 047 01339M
LP: EMI 2C 051 01339
LP: EMI RLS 143 5603
LP: Arabesque AR 8145
CD: Arabesque Z 6572

Impromptu in A flat D935 no 2

New York
January 1942

LP: MJA 1966-4

London
June 1950

78: HMV DB 21500
45: HMV 7ER 5042
45: Victor WHMV 1027
LP: Victor LHMV 1027/LCT 1019
LP: HMV BLP 1030
LP: Electrola E 80684
LP: EMI 1C 047 01339M
LP: EMI 2C 051 01339
LP: EMI RLS 143 5603
LP: Arabesque AR 8145
CD: Arabesque Z 6572

Impromptu in B flat D935 no 3

London
June 1950

78: HMV DB 21611
45: Victor WHMV 1027
LP: Victor LHMV 1027/LCT 1019
LP: HMV BLP 1030
LP: Electrola E 80684
LP: EMI 1C 047 01339M
LP: EMI 2C 051 01339
LP: EMI RLS 143 5603
LP: Arabesque AR 8145
CD: Arabesque Z 6572

Impromptu in F minor D935 no 4

London
June 1950

78: HMV DB 21557
45: HMV 7ER 5042
45: Victor WHMV 1027
LP: Victor LHMV 1027/LCT 1019
LP: HMV BLP 1030
LP: Electrola E 80684
LP: EMI 1C 047 01339M
LP: EMI 2C 051 01339
LP: EMI RLS 143 5603
LP: Arabesque AR 8145
CD: Arabesque Z 6572

Klavierstück in E flat minor D946 no 1

New York
January 1942

LP: MJA 1966-4

Klavierstück (unspecified)

Freiburg
May 1905

Welte Mignon piano roll 395

March in E D606

London
January 1939

78: HMV DB 3760
78: Victor M 888/DM 888
LP: EMI RLS 143 5603
LP: Arabesque AR 8145
CD: Arabesque Z 6575
CD: EMI CHS 764 2592

3 Marches militaires D733

London
October 1937

Karl-Ulrich
Schnabel

78: HMV DB 3527-3528
78: Victor M 436/DM 436
LP: Electrola E 80872
LP: Toshiba GR 2136
LP: EMI RLS 7713
LP: Arabesque AR 8137

March in G D819 no 2

London
October 1937

Karl-Ulrich
Schnabel

78: HMV DB 3527
78: Victor M 436/DM 436
LP: EMI RLS 7713
LP: Arabesque AR 8137

March in B D819 no 3

London
October 1937

Karl-Ulrich
Schnabel

78: Victor M 436/DM 436

Moment musical in C D780 no 1

London
November 1937

78: HMV DB 3358/DB 8392
78: Victor M 684
LP: HMV COLH 308
LP: Seraphim IC 6045
LP: EMI RLS 7713
LP: EMI 3C 153 01220-01222
LP: EMI EX 29 07883
LP: Arabesque AR 8137
CD: Arabesque Z 6573
CD: EMI CHS 764 2592

Moment musical in A flat D780 no 2

London
November 1937

78: HMV DB 3358-3359/
    DB 8393-8394 auto
78: Victor M 684
LP: HMV COLH 308
LP: Seraphim IC 6045
LP: EMI RLS 7713
LP: EMI 3C 153 01220-01222
LP: EMI EX 29 07883
LP: Arabesque AR 8137
CD: Arabesque Z 6573
CD: EMI CHS 764 2592

Moment musical in F minor D780 no 3

London
November 1937

78: HMV DB 3359/DB 8394
78: Victor M 684
LP: HMV COLH 308
LP: Seraphim IC 6045
LP: EMI RLS 7713
LP: EMI 3C 153 01220-01222
LP: EMI EX 29 07883
LP: Arabesque AR 8137
CD: Arabesque Z 6573
CD: EMI CHS 764 2592

Moment musical in C sharp minor D780 no 4

London
November 1937

78: HMV DB 3359/DB 8394
78: Victor M 684
LP: HMV COLH 308
LP: Seraphim IC 6045
LP: EMI RLS 7713
LP: EMI 3C 153 01220-01222
LP: EMI EX 29 07883
LP: Arabesque AR 8137
CD: Arabesque Z 6573
CD: EMI CHS 764 2592

Moment musical in F minor D780 no 5

London
November 1937

78: HMV DB 3360/DB 8393
78: Victor M 684
LP: HMV COLH 308
LP: Seraphim IC 6045
LP: EMI RLS 7713
LP: EMI 3C 153 01220-01222
LP: EMI EX 29 07883
LP: Arabesque AR 8137
CD: Arabesque Z 6573
CD: EMI CHS 764 2592

Moment musical in A flat D780 no 6

London
November 1937

78: HMV DB 3360-3361/
      DB 8393-8392 auto
78: Victor M 684
LP: HMV COLH 308
LP: Seraphim IC 6045
LP: EMI RLS 7713
LP: EMI 3C 153 01220-01222
LP: EMI EX 29 07883
LP: Arabesque AR 8137
CD: Arabesque Z 6573
CD: EMI CHS 764 2592

Piano Sonata No 8 in B D575, 3rd movement bar 77 to end

New York
January 1942

LP: MJA 1966-4

Piano Sonata No 13 in A D664, incomplete (sections of all movements missing)

New York
January 1942

Unpublished radio broadcast

Piano Sonata No 16 in A minor D845, 4th movement

New York
1944

V-Disc
LP: Discocorp BWS 724

Piano Sonata No 17 in D D850

London
January 1939

78: HMV DB 3756-3760
78: Victor M 888/DM 888
LP: HMV COLH 83
LP: Toshiba GR 2052
LP: EMI 3C 153 01220-01222
LP: EMI 1C 147 01557-01558M
LP: EMI RLS 7713/EX 29 07883
LP: Arabesque AR 8137
CD: Arabesque Z 6573
CD: EMI CHS 764 2592

Piano Sonata No 20 in A D959

London
January 1937

78: HMV DB 310303107/8322-8326 auto
78: HMV DB 21418-21422/
    DB 9733-9737 auto
78: Victor M 580/DM 580
LP: HMV COLH 84
LP: EMI 1C 147 01557-01558M
LP: EMI RLS 143 5603
LP: EMI EX 29 07883
LP: Arabesque AR 8143
CD: Arabesque Z 6571
CD: EMI CHS 764 2592

Piano Sonata No 21 in B flat D960

London
January 1939

78: HMV DB 3751-3755/8826-8830 auto
78: HMV DB 21353-21357/
    DB 9700-9704 auto
LP: HMV COLH 33
LP: EMI 3C 153 01220-01222
LP: EMI 1C 147 01557-01558M
LP: EMI RLS 143 5603
LP: EMI EX 29 07883
LP: Arabesque AR 8145
CD: Arabesque Z 6575
CD: EMI CHS 764 2592

Piano Quintet in A D667 "The Trout"

London
November 1935

Hobday,
Members of
Pro Arte
String Quartet

78: HMV DB 2714-2718/
    DB 8095-8099 auto
78: Victor M 312/DM 312
LP: HMV COLH 40
LP: Toshiba GR 2020
LP: EMI 1C 137 53032-53036M
LP: EMI 2C 051 43349/RLS 7713
LP: Arabesque AR 8137
CD: Arabesque Z 6571
CD: EMI CDH 763 0312
Also issued on LP by Franklin Mint

Piano Trio No 1 in B flat D898

London
October 1947

Szigeti, Fournier

LP: Discocorp RR 488

Rondo in A D951 for piano duet

London
October 1937

Karl-Ulrich
Schnabel

78: HMV DA 1644-1645
78: Victor M 437/DM 437
LP: Electrola E 80872
LP: Toshiba GR 2136
LP: EMI RLS 7713
LP: Arabesque AR 8137

Scherzo in B flat D593

New York
1922

Ampico piano roll 62011
LP: Klavier KS 134

12 Valses nobles D969

Freiburg
May 1905

Welte Migon piano roll 385

An die Laute

London
November 1932

Behr-Schnabel

78: HMV DB 1836
LP: Rococo 5370
LP: EMI RLS 143 5603
LP: Arabesque AR 8145
78 edition coupled with
Der Erlkönig and Der Musensohn

Der Doppelgänger (Schwanengesang)

London
November 1932

Behr-Schnabel

78: HMV DB 1833
LP: Rococo 5370
LP: EMI RLS 143 5603
LP: Arabesque AR 8145
78 edition coupled with
Die Stadt

Der Erlkönig

London
November 1932

Behr-Schnabel

78: HMV DB 1836
LP: Rococo 5370
LP: EMI RLS 143 5603
LP: Arabesque AR 8145
78 edition coupled with
An die Laute and der Musensohn

Gruppe aus dem Tartarus

London
November 1932

Behr-Schnabel

78: HMV DB 1835
LP: Rococo 5370
LP: EMI RLS 143 5603
LP: Arabesque AR 8145
78 edition coupled with
Der Kreuzzug

Der Kreuzzug

London
November 1932

Behr-Schnabel

78: HMV DB 1835
LP: Rococo 5370
LP: EMI RLS 143 5603
LP: Arabesque AR 8145
78 edition coupled with
Gruppe aus dem Tartarus

Der Musensohn

London
November 1932

Behr-Schnabel

78: HMV DB 1836
LP: Rococo 5370
LP: EMI RLS 766/RLS 143 5603
LP: Arabesque AR 8145
CD: Arabesque Z 6574
78 edition coupled with An
die Laute and Der Erlkönig

Die Stadt (Schwanengesang)

London
November 1932

Behr-Schnabel

78: HMV DB 1833
LP: Rococo 5370
LP: EMI RLS 143 6593
LP: Arabesque AR 8145
78 edition coupled with
Der Doppelgänger

Schumann

Kinderszenen

London
November 1947

78: HMV DB 6502-6503
LP: HMV COLH 85
LP: Toshiba GR 2169

Piano Concerto

Glendale   Los Angeles PO
California   Wallenstein
March 1945

LP: MJA 1966-4
LP: Discocorp BWS 724

Piano Quintet in E flat

London   Pro Arte
November 1934   String Quartet

78: HMV DB 2387-2390/
    DB 7922-7925 auto
78: Victor M 267/DM 267
LP: HMV COLH 85
LP: Toshiba GR 2169
LP: Discocorp BWS 718
LP: World Records SH 408

Romance in F sharp (Romanzen op 28)

Germany
after 1905

Hupfeld Animatic 51226

Frühlingsnacht (Liederkreis op 39)

London   Behr-Schnabel
November 1932

78: HMV DB 1834
LP: Rococo 5370
Coupled with Der Soldat and
Der Schatzgräber

Der Schatzgräber

London   Behr-Schnabel
November 1932

78: HMV DB 1834
LP: Rococo 5370
LP: EMI RLS 154 7003
Coupled with Der Soldat and
Frühlingsnacht

Der Soldat

London   Behr-Schnabel
November 1932

78: HMV DB 1834
LP: Rococo 5370
LP: EMI RLS 154 7003
Coupled with Frühlingsnacht
and Der Schatzgräber

Johann Strauss

Künstlerleben, Waltz

Freiburg
May 1905

Welte Mignon piano roll
391 or 392

Josef Strauss

Dorfschwalben aus Oesterreich, Waltz

Freiburg
May 1905

Welte Mignon piano roll 382

Weber

Aufforderung zum Tanz

Freiburg
May 1905

Welte Mignon piano roll 388

Germany
after 1905

Hupfeld Animatic 50478

New York
1922

Ampico piano roll 60603
LP: Klavier KS 134
CD: Newport Classic NC 60020

London
June 1947

78: HMV DB 6491
LP: HMV HQM 1142
LP: Toshiba GR 2195
LP: Seraphim 60115

Credits

Valuable help with information for the
preparation of "Giants of the keyboard"
and "Six Wagnerian sopranos" came from :

Jonathan Brown, Paris
Dennis Brownbill, Bex
Clifford Elkin, Glasgow
Allan Evans, Flushing NY
Mathias Erhard, Berlin
Michael Gray, Alexandria VA
Syd Gray, Hove
Ken Jagger (EMI Classics), London
Gerald Kingsley, London
Roderick Krüsemann, Amsterdam
Yvonne Lakeram (Decca Records), London
Kevork Marouchian, Munich
Bruce Morrison, Gillingham
Alan Newcombe (DG), Hamburg
John Owen, London
Brian Pinder, Halifax
John Raymon, London
Seiichi Semba, Ehime
Roger Smithson, London
Neville Sumpter, Northolt
Terje Thorp, Oslo
Malcolm Walker, Harrow